MENTORING DESIGN TECHNOLOGY TEACH THE SECONDARY SCHOOL

This collection offers an evidence-based approach to mentoring and supporting design and technology teachers and educators in the secondary school and provides tried and tested strategies to support this role.

Contributors offer tasks and reflections to inspire and motivate mentors to get the best out of beginning teachers in the early stages of their career. Key topics explored include:

- Helping new D&T teachers appreciate the fundamental nature of design and technology and how this informs both why it is taught and how it is taught.
- Understanding yourself as a mentor – beliefs, values and attitudes, and how your experiences influence your approaches to teaching.
- Observing design and technology teachers' lessons and offering tools for observation and analysis.
- Risk taking in the classroom: moving teachers forward from pedestrian to innovative practice.

Filled with practical guidance on lesson planning, risk taking, and learning conversation, *Mentoring Design and Technology Teachers in the Secondary School* offers advice and guidance to support mentors in developing inspirational D&T teachers of the future. This essential guide is perfect for mentors of beginning teachers, whether trainee, newly qualified, or those who find themselves teaching the subject for the first time.

Suzanne Lawson is the PGCE secondary course leader at the University of Worcester. Previous to this she worked as a senior lecturer at Birmingham City University. She has fourteen years teaching experience working in a range of schools in the UK with a further 15 years' experience in teacher training.

Susan Wood-Griffiths was the PGCE Secondary Design and Technology subject leader at the University of Worcester until 2018. Before moving into Higher Education, she taught for 21 years in the UK and overseas. Sue has worked with many teachers and aims to develop innovative, creative teachers who share ideas and take 'intelligent' risks.

MENTORING TRAINEE AND NEWLY QUALIFIED TEACHERS

Series edited by: Susan Capel, Trevor Wright and Julia Lawrence

The **Mentoring Trainee and Newly Qualified Teachers** Series offers subject-specific, practical books designed to reinforce and develop mentors' understanding of the different aspects of their role, as well as exploring issues that mentees encounter in the course of learning to teach. The books have two main foci: First, challenging mentors to reflect critically on theory, research and evidence, on their own knowledge, their approaches to mentoring and how they work with beginning teachers in order to move their practice forward. Second, supporting mentors to effectively facilitate the development of beginning teachers. Although the basic structure of all the subject books is similar, each book is different to reflect the needs of mentors in relation to the unique nature of each subject. Elements of appropriate theory introduce each topic or issue with emphasis placed on the practical application of material. The chapter authors in the subject books have been engaged with mentoring over a long period of time and share research, evidence and their experience. We, as series editors, are pleased to extend the work in initial teacher education to the work of mentors of beginning teachers.

We hope that this series of books supports you in developing into an effective, reflective mentor as you support the development of the next generation of subject teachers.

For more information about this series, please visit: https://www.routledge.com/Mentoring-Trainee-and-Newly-Qualified-Teachers/book-series/MTNQT

Mentoring Physical Education Teachers in the Secondary School
Edited by Susan Capel and Julia Lawrence

Mentoring Design and Technology Teachers in the Secondary School
Edited by Suzanne Lawson and Susan Wood-Griffiths

MENTORING DESIGN AND TECHNOLOGY TEACHERS IN THE SECONDARY SCHOOL

A Practical Guide

Edited by Suzanne Lawson
and Susan Wood-Griffiths

Routledge
Taylor & Francis Group

LONDON AND NEW YORK

First published 2020
by Routledge
2 Park Square, Milton Park, Abingdon, Oxon OX14 4RN

and by Routledge
52 Vanderbilt Avenue, New York, NY 10017

Routledge is an imprint of the Taylor & Francis Group, an informa business

British Library Cataloguing-in-Publication Data
A catalogue record for this book is available from the British Library

Library of Congress Cataloging-in-Publication Data
A catalog record has been requested for this book

ISBN: 978-1-138-50009-9 (hbk)
ISBN: 978-1-138-54110-8 (pbk)
ISBN: 978-1-351-01197-6 (ebk)

Typeset in Interstate
by codeMantra

CONTENTS

CONTRIBUTORS

David Barlex is an acknowledged leader in design & technology education, curriculum design and curriculum materials development. He taught in comprehensive schools for 15 years before taking university positions in teacher education. He directed the Nuffield Design & Technology Project. David is well known for developing curriculum materials that support pupil learning from a constructivist perspective. He uses this approach to develop young peoples' ability to understand and critique the design decisions made by professional designers and those they make themselves. This informed the Nuffield Design & Technology publications, which have been widely used in the UK and emulated abroad - in Russia, Sweden, Canada, South Africa, Australia, and New Zealand.

Louise Beattie is the subject lead for the PGCE Secondary English course at the University of Worcester. She has twenty five years of experience working in a range of secondary schools in a variety of roles. She has worked at Head of Department level and spent ten years working as an English adviser in a local authority. This afforded her the opportunity of working in a wide array of secondary schools, special schools and primary schools. Her teaching interests include the teaching of speaking and listening and extending pupils' reading skills. Current research includes pupil transition from Key Stage 2 to 3.

Jane Burnham has taught design and technology at secondary level for fourteen years. She is head of food and nutrition in a Worcestershire secondary school where she is a food specialist with experience of teaching the subject at key stage 3, 4 and 5. As a very experienced subject mentor for teacher training, she also supports new and developing teachers to teach the subject. Jane is an associate lecturer at the University of Worcester and a qualified CIEH Level 4 trainer in the management of food safety.

Sarah Davies is the PGCE Secondary Design and Technology subject leader at Nottingham Trent University. The course prepares student teachers to teach across the material specialisms from 11-16. She has ten years teaching experience working across the East Midlands as an Advanced Skills Teacher with a further 12 years' experience working in teacher education. Sarah also teaches on the MA in Teaching and Learning and leads on the Nottingham Institute of Education IRIS Connect Project, using video-based teacher observation to support analysis and evaluation of lessons. She is currently studying for a professional doctorate in Education at Nottingham University.

Nick Givens is a Senior Lecturer in Education at the University of Exeter Graduate School of Education. He has taught in several comprehensive schools becoming head of design & technology and subsequently established a D&T department from scratch in a Sixth Form College. Since moving into university-based initial teacher education he has taught undergraduate and postgraduate trainee design & technology teachers, led an undergraduate teacher education programme and a postgraduate design & technology teacher education course. He was also an author and a field officer for the Nuffield Design & Technology Project. His research interests include curriculum development in design & technology, inclusivity within education and, most recently, approaches to teaching about Disruptive Technologies.

Gill Golder is the Director of Teacher Education and Associate Dean at the University of St Mark and St John. She has thirteen years of experience teaching the 11-18 age range in a range of comprehensive schools holding middle and senior leadership positions. Having made the move to higher education she has been recognized for excellence in teaching and learning on a range of undergraduate and postgraduate programmes. Her research interests lie in organisational structure and processes and the triumvirate relationship between policy, practice and research.

Dr Alison Hardy is a senior lecturer at the Nottingham Institute of Education, part of Nottingham Trent University (NTU), in teacher education and specialises in design and technology education. Additionally, she leads the MA Education course at NTU. Her research and teaching has centred on design and technology education since 1993, as a teacher, head of department, mentor for student teachers and teacher educator. She also worked in further education where she was responsible for curriculum development and as an overseas lecturer at the University of West Bohemia in the Czech Republic. Alison's research interest is the values we attribute to design and technology, and explores the influences and origins of these values. In 2015 she was recognised by the Association for her contribution to D&T as a teacher educator.

Dave Howard is Head of the Division of Education and Communities at the University Centre, Bradford College. Prior to this, he was variously Head of the Faculty of Education, Head of Partnerships and Head of Primary Education at the College. He taught in Primary schools for 16 years before moving to Higher Education. Dave's research interests include the inclusive practices of Teacher Education tutors in Higher Education and pupil self-assessment. He has published across a range of areas including primary science; use of IT technologies and ethics and ethical decision-making in education.

Dr Dawne Irving-Bell is a senior lecturer in Learning and Teaching Development within the Centre for Learning and Teaching at Edge Hill University and has extensive experience working across Secondary, Further and Higher Education. Previously Head of Faculty for Art, Design and Technology at a large secondary school, while working within Initial Teacher Education Dawne has led both postgraduate and undergraduate Design and Technology programmes. Her research interests focus mainly upon the formation of learner identity and pedagogical approaches to learning and teaching within STEM. Currently a senior fellow of the Higher Education Academy, Dawne is responsible for university-wide strategies to enhance student learning.

Alison Keyworth is a senior lecturer in postgraduate and professional development at the University of St Mark and St John, Plymouth.

Suzanne Lawson is the PGCE secondary course leader at the University of Worcester teaching on the postgraduate and MA programmes. Previous to this she worked as a senior lecturer at Birmingham City University where she was the PGCE design and technology programme leader and also a member of the Centre for Research in Primary Technology (CRIPT). She has fourteen years teaching experience working in a range of schools in the UK with a further 15 years' experience working in teacher training. Suzanne's main research interests are food technology and teacher education, including mentoring.

Matt McLain has been a teacher educator at Liverpool John Moores University over the past 10 years, where he currently leads the secondary programmes. Previously, he taught D&T in the Greater Merseyside area for over a decade. As a teacher, worked with teachers at a local and national level as an advanced skills teacher and lead practitioner. Matt is an active member of the Design and Technology Association and was involved with the development of the subject content for the current D&T GCSE and A Level. His wider educational research interests include signature pedagogies in D&T, particularly demonstration.

Ruth Seabrook is a principal teaching fellow, Head of Secondary Partnership and subject leader for Design and Technology (D&T) at the University of Roehampton. Before teaching for eleven years in higher education, she taught D&T for ten years before joining Roehampton to lead the PGCE course. Ruth has taught both primary and secondary D&T and now focuses on Secondary Partnership. As subject leader, she is responsible for both the undergraduate and postgraduate courses and aims to prepare teachers with excellent subject knowledge. Her main aim is to improve the quality of teaching and learning in D&T and her research interests include teaching and learning, STEM, Mentoring student teachers and improving the quality of mentoring.

Clare Shaw is a senior lecturer in primary initial teacher education at the University of St Mark and St John, Plymouth.

Torben Steeg has research and curriculum development interests that include the interactions between D&T, Computing, ICT, Science, Mathematics and Engineering and, within D&T, electronics, systems thinking, physical computing, novel technologies, disruptive technologies and the implications of the maker and hacker movements for education. He supports the PGCE in D&T at MMU and is a member of the editorial board for the D&TA's *D&T Education; An International Journal*, a founder editor of the on-line journal 'ECT Education' and a Fellow of the RSA. He has provided advice, curriculum development and CPD activity to a wide range of organisations and is the author of a range of general and academic publications.

Jacqui Vaughan is the Head of School for Initial Teacher Training at the University Centre, Bradford College. Prior to this, she was leader for the PGCE Design Technology course. The course specialised in preparing trainees to teach Food and Textiles. Prior to working in higher education Jacqui taught for 20 years in Secondary schools in West Yorkshire as subject leader and faculty leader within Design Technology. Jacqui's research interests include innovation in sharing good practice in Food teaching, ensuring that all school-aged children have access to high quality food education and how the changes to the curriculum impact standards of teaching and the quality of learning.

Alison Winson is a principal lecturer within the Institute of Education at the University Of Worcester and has been involved in teacher education for nineteen years. Alison currently heads up a team involved in training secondary and further education teachers. She has contributed to several books that have a focus on teaching and learning within the area of secondary design and technology.

Susan Wood-Griffiths is the PGCE Secondary Design and Technology subject leader at the University of Worcester. The course prepares trainees to teach food and textiles. Before working in higher education she taught for 21 years in schools across the UK, and overseas. As subject leader at the university Sue aims to develop confident, capable and creative teachers who can inspire their pupils to engage with exciting and relevant design and technology activities. Throughout the course she models good teaching practice and encourages and supports trainees to develop innovative teaching strategies; to share ideas, and to take 'intelligent' risks.

AN INTRODUCTION TO THE SERIES "A PRACTICAL GUIDE TO MENTORING BEGINNING SUBJECT TEACHERS"

Mentoring is a very important and exciting role. What could be better than supporting the development of the next generation of subject teachers? A mentor is almost certainly an effective teacher, but this doesn't automatically guarantee that he or she will be a good mentor, despite similarities in the two roles. This series of practical workbooks books covers most subjects in the secondary curriculum. They are designed specifically to reinforce mentors' understanding of different aspects of their role, for mentors to learn about and reflect on their role, to provide support for mentors in aspects of their development and enable them to analyse their success in supporting the development of beginning subject teachers (defined as trainee, newly qualified and early career teachers). This book has two main foci: first, the focus is on challenging mentors to reflect critically on theory/research/evidence, on their own knowledge, how they work with beginning teachers, how they work with more experienced teachers and on their approaches to mentoring in order to move their practice forward. Second, the focus is on supporting mentors to effectively facilitate the development of beginning teachers. Thus, some of the practical activities in the books are designed to encourage reflection, whilst others ask mentors to undertake activities with beginning teachers.

This book can be used alongside generic and subject books designed for student and newly qualified teachers. These books include *Learning to Teach in the Secondary School: A Companion to School Experience*, 8th edition (Capel, Leask and Younie, 2019) which deals with aspects of teaching and learning applicable to all subjects. This generic book also has a companion Reader: *Readings for Learning to Teach in the Secondary School* (Capel, Leask and Turner, 2010) containing articles and research papers in education suitable for master's-level study. Further, the generic book is complemented by two subject series: *Learning to Teach (subject) in the Secondary School: A Companion to School Experience*; and *A Practical Guide to Teaching (subject) in the Secondary School*. These books are designed for student teachers on different types of initial teacher education programmes (and indeed a beginning teacher you are working with may have used/currently be using them). However, these books are proving equally useful to tutors and mentors in their work with student teachers, both in relation to the knowledge, skills and understanding the student teacher is developing and some tasks which mentors might find it useful to support a beginning teacher to do.

It is also supported by a book designed for newly qualified teachers, the soon to be published *Surviving and Thriving in the Secondary School: The NQT's Essential Companion* (Capel, Lawrence, Leask and Younie, 2019), as well as *Starting to Teach in the Secondary*

School: A Companion for the Newly Qualified Teacher (Capel, Heilbronn, Leask and Turner, 2004). These titles cover material not generally needed by student teachers on an initial teacher education course, but which is needed by newly qualified teachers in their school work and early career.

The information in this book should link with the information in the generic text and relevant subject book in the two series in a number of ways. For example, mentors might want to refer a beginning teacher to read about specific knowledge, understanding and skills they are focusing on developing, or to undertake tasks in the book, either alone or with their support, then discus the tasks. It is recommended that you have copies of these books available so that you can cross-reference when needed.

In turn, the books complement a range of resources on which mentors can draw (including other mentors of beginning teachers in the same or other subjects, other teachers and a range of other resources including books, research articles and websites).

The positive feedback on *Learning to Teach* and the related books above, particularly the way they have supported the learning of student teachers in their development into effective, reflective teachers, encouraged us to retain the main features of that book in this series. Like teaching, mentoring should be research and evidence-informed. Thus, this series of books introduce theoretical, research and professional evidence-based advice and guidance to support mentors as they develop their mentoring to support beginning teachers' development. The main focus is the practical application of material. Elements of appropriate theory introduce each topic or issue, and recent research into mentoring and/or teaching and learning is integral to the presentation. Tasks are provided to help mentors identify key features of the topic or issue and reflect on and/or apply them to their own practice of mentoring beginning teachers. Although the basic structure of all the subject books is similar, each book is different to reflect the needs of mentors in relation to the unique nature of each subject.

The chapter authors in the subject books have been engaged with mentoring over a long period of time and are aiming to share research/evidence and their experience. We, as series editors, are pleased to extend the work in initial teacher education to the work of mentors of beginning teachers. We hope that this series of books supports you in developing into an effective, reflective mentor as you support the development of the next generation of subject teachers.

Susan Capel, Julia Lawrence, Trevor Wright and Sarah Younie
February 2019

References

Capel, S., Lawrence, J., Leask, M. and Younie, S. (2019) *Surviving and Thriving in the Secondary School: The NQT's Essential Companion*. London: Routledge.

Capel, S., Leask, M. and Turner, T. (2010) *Readings for Learning to Teach in the Secondary School*. London: Routledge.

Capel, S., Leask, M. and Younie, S. (2019) *Learning to teach in the secondary school. A Companion to School Experience*. 8th edn. London: Routledge.

Capel, S. Heilbronn, R., Leask, M. and Turner, T. (2004) *Starting to Teach in the Secondary School: A Companion for the Newly Qualified Teacher*. London: Routledge.

1 Models of mentoring

Gill Golder, Alison Keyworth and Clare Shaw

Introduction

Your job as a mentor is to develop a positive working relationship with a beginning teacher to enable them to grow and develop both professionally and personally. How you go about this will be influenced by a number of factors, such as your own experience of being mentored in the past and your common-sense opinions of the role. These are important starting points, but you are likely to grow as an effective mentor when you also base your approaches on evidence. This chapter is generic to all of the books in the series, but in this book we will be focusing on design and technology (D&T) teaching. The chapters focus on generic and subject-specific issues relating to teaching in a subject that is predominately practical in nature (see Chapter 10) requiring pupils to solve real and relevant problems using food (see Chapter 5) and other materials (see Chapter 6). This book is designed to support you in considering the evidence to underpin your practice and we will return to some of the main concepts covered, in the final chapter.

The chapter starts by looking at different definitions of mentoring. It then looks at the importance of the context in which you are working as a mentor, highlighting a number of documents from England and other countries, which impact on your mentoring practice. The chapter then considers three mentoring models which a mentor could adopt to inform their practice. These models underpin various roles you undertake and hence the other chapters in this book.

Objectives

At the end of this chapter, you should be able to:

- Have a greater understanding of what is meant by the term 'mentoring' for a beginning teacher.
- Have an appreciation of the key context in which you work that may influence the manner in which you act as a mentor in school.
- Have an awareness of the plethora of mentoring models that exist.
- Compare and contrast three developmental mentoring models and how these could be used to support your role as a mentor.

Before reading further, undertake Task 1.1.

Task 1.1   Mentor reflection: reflecting on your understanding of mentoring

- Reflect on what you understand by mentoring by considering the following questions
- How would you define mentoring?
- How does your definition inform your practice as a mentor?
- How do the various policy and guidance documents relevant to your context influence your mentoring practice?
- Do you base your mentoring practice on personal experience or on a model(s) of mentoring? If a model, which one(s)? Why?

Definitions of mentoring

Mentoring is widely used in many contexts for the purpose of helping people to learn and develop, both professionally and personally. There are numerous and frequently contradictory definitions of mentoring, with accompanying models of how mentoring is best approached (Haggard, Dougherty, Turban and Wilbanks, 2011). Whilst different models might utilise different terminology and vary in emphasis regarding the role of a mentor, what remains consistent is the view that mentoring is a supportive, learning relationship. The mentor, with his or her more extensive experience, is there to support the learner's development. The quality of the relationship between mentor and mentee is extremely important.

The terms mentoring and coaching are at times used interchangeably. Both aim to develop the professional or professional competencies of the client or colleague. Although mentoring and coaching have much in common, an important difference between the two is the focus of developmental activities. In mentoring the focus is on development at significant career transitions whereas in coaching the focus is on the development of a specific aspect of a professional learner's practice (CUREE, 2005).

Montgomery (2017) suggested that definitions of mentoring often involve the concept that advice and guidance to a novice, or person with limited experience, is given by an experienced person. In this way, mentoring can be seen to be hierarchical, a top-down approach largely based on a one-way flow of information.

> Mentoring involves the use of the same models and skills of questioning, listening, clarifying and reframing associated with coaching. Traditionally, however, mentoring in the workplace has tended to describe a relationship in which a more experienced colleague uses his or her greater knowledge and understanding of the work or workplace to support the development of a more junior or inexperienced member of staff.
> (Chartered Institute of Personnel and Development (CIPD), 2012, p. 1)

In contrast, other definitions of mentoring follow a less hierarchal structure. These include peer mentoring (Driscoll, Parkes, Tilley-Lubbs, Brill and Pitts Bannister, 2009) and group mentoring (Kroll, 2016). In these approaches to mentoring, the flow of information is more bidirectional. Montgomery (2017) suggested they are more personalised as mentoring is adapted to an individual mentee's goals and needs more effectively. Higgins and Thomas (2001) suggested that top-down mentoring had greater impact on short-term career outcomes and individually-driven mentoring supported long-term career development more effectively. Whether the focus is on short- or long-term tailored development of a mentee, there are common aspects to all forms of mentoring. CIPD (2012, p. 1) identified four characteristics of mentoring:

- It is essentially a supportive form of development.
- It focuses on helping a person manage their career and improve skills.
- Personal issues can be discussed productively
- Mentoring activities have both organisational and individual goals.

In education, school-based mentors play a vital role in the development of student teachers and induction of newly qualified teachers. They also support other staff at points of career development. As with mentoring in other contexts, there is a focus on learning, development and the provision of appropriate support and encouragement. The definition of a mentor outlined in the *National Standards for School-based Initial Teacher Training (ITT) Mentors* in England (Department for Education (DfE), 2016b, p. 11) is someone who 'is a suitably experienced teacher who has formal responsibility to work collaboratively within the ITT partnership to help ensure the trainee receives the highest quality training'. However, in initial teacher education in many countries, including England, assessment of the beginning teacher is integral to the mentor's role. This is supported by Pollard (2014) who suggested that the role of the mentor in ITT has developed because of three aspects, the complexity of the capabilities teachers need to meet, the focus on high professional standards in school and the transfer of knowledge from one generation to another. Before reading any further, undertake Task 1.2.

Task 1.2   Mentor reflection: understanding the term mentoring

- Research the terms 'mentoring' and 'coaching'.
- List a variety of terms that you associate with coaching and mentoring
- Make a list of common and unique characteristics for both.

The context in which you are working which underpins your mentoring practice

Mentoring is increasingly important in a range of fields, both in the UK and internationally, as a tool to support recruitment into a profession, retention in that profession, professional learning, networking and career development. In teaching, it is widely recognised that there is a strong relationship between professional learning, teaching knowledge and practices, educational leadership and pupil results (Cordingley et al., 2015). As such, there has been an increase in the development of policy and guidance documents as well as frameworks,

Table 1.1 Key external drivers influencing mentoring work

	Policy/guidance document	Author and date introduced	Key purpose
Teacher Standards Documents	Teachers' Standards (England)	DfE (2011)	Used to assess all student teachers working towards qualified teacher status (QTS) as well as newly qualified teachers completing their statutory induction period. 'Providers of ITT should assess trainees against the standards in a way that is consistent with what could reasonably be expected of a trainee teacher prior to the award of QTS' (DfE, 2011, p. 6).
	The Australian Professional Standards for teachers (Australia)	Australian Institute for Teaching and School Leadership (AITSL) (2011)	The standards are designed so that teachers know what they should be aiming to achieve at every stage of their career; to enable them to improve their practice inside and outside of the classroom. 'The Standards do this by providing a framework which makes clear the knowledge, practice and professional engagement required across teachers' careers' (AITSL, 2011, p. 2)
Core Content requirements for Initial Teacher Education	Framework of core content for Initial Teacher Training (England)	DfE (2016a)	The aim of this framework is to improve the consistency and quality of ITT courses by supporting those involved in training teachers and student teachers themselves to have a better understanding of the key elements of good ITT content.
	Differentiated Primary and Lower Secondary Teacher Education Programmes for Years 1–7 and Years 5–10 (Norway)	Ministry of Education and Research (2010)	These regulations apply to universities and university colleges that provide primary and lower secondary teacher education. They aim to ensure that teacher education institutions provide integrated, professionally oriented and research-based primary and lower secondary teacher education programmes of high academic quality.
National or Regional Standards for Educators acting as mentors	National Standards for school-based initial teacher training (ITT) mentors (England)	DfE (2016b)	The standards were developed to bring greater coherence and consistency to school-based mentoring arrangements for student teachers. They set out the minimum level of practice expected of mentors. They are used to foster consistency in the practice of mentors, raise the profile of mentoring and build a culture of mentoring in schools
	The New York State Mentoring standards Albany (USA)	The State Education Department/ The University of The State Of New York (2011)	A set of standards that guide the design and implementation of teacher mentoring programmes in New York State through teacher induction.

Table 1.1 (Cont.)

	Policy/guidance document	Author and date introduced	Key purpose
National or Regional guidelines for general coaching and mentoring practice	National framework for mentoring and coaching (England)	Centre for the Use of Resource and Evidence in Education (CUREE) (2005)	The framework was developed in order to help schools implement mentoring and coaching to assist with continuing professional development and other activities. It sets out ten principles based on evidence from research and consultation which are recommended to inform mentoring and coaching programmes in schools. The framework provides a tool for reflection on existing practice and further development and assists a mentor in self-regulation and monitoring of their own practice.
	NTC Continuum of Mentoring Practice (USA)	New Teacher Centre (NTC) (2011)	Designed to assist programme leaders as they seek to implement mentoring to support induction programmes that are capable of accelerating the development of beginning teacher effectiveness, improving teacher retention, strengthening teacher leadership and increasing pupil learning. 'It presents a holistic view of mentoring, based on six professional standards.......The continuum of mentoring practice describes three levels of development, labelled Exploring/ Emerging, Applying, Integrating/ Innovating' (NTC, 2011, p. 2).
Professional Development expectations for teachers	Standards for teachers' professional development (England)	DfE (2016c)	This is intended for 'all those working in and with, schools in order to raise expectations for professional development, to focus on achieving the best improvement in pupil outcomes and also to develop teachers as respected members of the profession' (DfE, 2016c, p. 4). There is an emphasis on using the standards to support regular reflection on existing practice and discussion between all members of the teaching community. There are five parts to the standard which, when acted upon together, ensure effective professional development.
	Ohio Standards for Professional Development (USA)	Ohio Department for Education (2015)	These define the essential elements of a strong professional learning system which is one way that school systems can support all educators and encourage improved teaching and learning.

toolkits and factsheets produced over the past few years to support educators and others in fulfilling their roles as mentors.

As a mentor, it is important to recognise and embed current policy and statutory guidance into your mentoring practice. There are a number of key documents that underpin the mentoring process in initial teacher education and beyond in England and elsewhere. These constitute the key external drivers in shaping mentoring practice in school. Being aware of these is important, but knowing how to use them to support your work with a beginning teacher can add purpose and validity to what you do (there are examples of how to do this in other chapters in this book). They also enable you to recognise the value of being a mentor in school, as 'effective professional development for teachers is a core part of securing effective teaching' (DfE, 2016c, p. 3).

Table 1.1 highlights policy and guidance documents that influence the work you do in school with a beginning teacher in England but also signposts you to examples of international equivalence documents to enable you to make comparisons internationally.

Now complete Task 1.3.

Task 1.3   The context in which you carry out your mentoring duties

Reflect on the context in which you carry out your mentoring duties. Ensure you are familiar with the relevant documents above (or, if you are working outside England, documents specific to your context). What aspects of these documents do you identify as being of most use to your work and why? Are there any implication specific to mentoring beginning D&T teachers?

Effective mentoring models

As alluded to above, there are a number of mentoring models which a mentor could adopt in order to support the growth and development of a beginning teacher. Attempts have been made to categorise different approaches to mentoring; for example, Maynard and Furlong (1995) suggested that there are three categories of mentoring: the apprentice model, the competence model and the reflective model. The apprenticeship model argues that the skills of being a teacher are best learned by supervised practice, with guidance from imitation of, experienced practitioners. The competence model suggests that learning to teach requires learning a predefined list of competences (the current Teachers Standards in England (DfE, 2011) could be described as a competence model). In this model, the mentor becomes a systematic trainer supporting a beginning teacher to meet the competences. In the reflective model, the promotion of reflective practice through mentoring is key. This requires a beginning teacher to have some mastery of the skills of teaching to be able to reflect upon their own practice and for the mentor to be a co-enquirer and facilitator rather than instructor. Task 1.4 asks you to look at three different mentoring models.

Task 1.4   Three different mentoring models

- What are the features of practice for each of these models; apprentice, compe-
  tence and reflective?
- Which features of these models do you use/want to use in our mentoring?
- When do/would you use each model of mentoring?

Maynard and Furlong (1995, p. 18) acknowledged that these three models exist but suggested that they should be taken together, in order to contribute to 'a view of mentoring that
responds to the changing needs of trainees'. It is this recognition that mentoring practices
and approaches evolve as a beginning teacher develops and the need for an examination of
different stages of development that lead us to exploring three models of mentoring in more
detail. We explore three well-known models (Clutterbuck, 2004; Daloz, 2012; Katz, 1995), all
of which focus on the need for the mentor to be flexible in their style and approach to best fit
the needs of a beginning teacher at any given stage of their development, in initial teacher
education and/or their teaching career.

Daloz's (2012) developmental model identifies two key aspects that need to be present in
order for optimal learning to take place: **challenge** and **support**. The challenge aspect refers
to your ability as a mentor to question a beginning teacher to enable them to reflect critically
on their own beliefs, behaviours and attitudes. The support aspect relies on you being able to
offer an empathetic ear, actively listen and encourage a beginning teacher to find solutions
in order to continue to develop and progress.

Daloz (2012) argues that a combination of high challenge and high support needs to be
offered by you as the mentor for a beginning teacher to learn effectively and to **'grow'** (High
challenge + high support = **growth**). At the opposite end of this spectrum is what Daloz refers
to as **'stasis'**. A beginning teacher's learning in this zone is very limited indeed as a result
of their mentor offering low levels of challenge and support (Low challenge + low support =
stasis). Where challenge is high but support is low, a beginning teacher is likely to **'retreat'**
from development (High challenge + low support = **retreat**). However, where challenge is low
but support is high, a beginning teacher is unlikely to move beyond their present situation
despite their potential for growth being on the increase. Daloz refers to this as **'confirmation'**
(Low challenge + high support = **confirmation**). You therefore need to be aware of both the
level of challenge you offer and the level of support needed by the beginning teacher.

The second model is Katz's stages of development model (1995), which describes a model
for professional growth in four stages:

1. Survival stage
2. Consolidation stage
3. Renewal stage
4. Maturity stage

During the first stage, '**Survival**', a beginning teacher is likely to show signs of being very
self-focussed and just 'getting by' or coping from day-to-day. They are likely to experience

their practice from a position of doubt and be asking questions like 'can I get to the end of the week?' or 'can I really do this day after day?'. During this initial stage, a beginning teacher may show a reluctance to take responsibility for things and, instead, look to blame others, for example, the pupils, colleagues, the school. As a mentor, observing a beginning teacher during the survival stage, you are likely to see elements of confusion and a lack of any clear rules and routines in their lessons. The beginning teacher may also demonstrate little, if any, consistency in their approach to managing behaviour. Their teaching style is often very teacher-centric and they show a reluctance to deviate from their 'script' in any way.

By the second stage, '**Consolidation**', it is likely that a beginning teacher will have begun to implement clearer rules and routines into their classrooms. There is evidence of them starting to question their own practice and being more open to alternative ways of doing things. Whilst observing a beginning teacher at this stage, you are likely to notice that their classes are generally well-managed and that the needs of the average pupil are predominantly well catered for. In addition, the beginning teacher is likely to demonstrate a greater awareness of individual pupils and their learning needs. However, they are unlikely to have gained a true grasp of how to support and cater for the needs of pupils within specific subgroups, for example, special educational needs and disability (SEND), English as an Additional Language (EAL) and Gifted and Talented (GandT).

The '**renewal**' stage is the point at which a beginning teacher becoming much more self-aware and self-critical. They have generally mastered the basics and are now striving for ways in which they can improve their practice. They are looking for strategies and ideas of how to introduce more creative and innovative activities into their lessons. As a general rule of thumb, at the 'renewal' stage beginning teachers are often at their most self-motivated and are eager to contribute to departmental discussions, offer suggestions, design additional resources and/or become involved in the running of lunch time and after-school clubs.

The final stage of Katz's model, '**maturity**', is where a beginning teacher is demonstrating signs of developing their own beliefs, teaching style and strategies. They are regularly asking themselves a number of questions which support deeper levels of reflection, both in and on practice (Schön, 1983). They are still looking to improve their practice and are still interested in new ideas and resources. However, their focus has shifted from an inwards perspective to a much broader one. They are now very much interested in the impact of their teaching on their pupils' learning and progress. Task 1.5 focuses on the responsibilities of the mentor and beginning teacher at each stage of Katz's stages of development model (1995).

Task 1.5 Responsibilities of the mentor and beginning teacher at each stage of Katz's stages of development model (1995)

In each of Katz's stages, there are responsibilities for both the mentor and beginning teacher. Identify what you would do to support a beginning teacher at each stage.

And finally, Clutterbuck's (2004) model of developmental mentoring suggests that an effective mentor wants to draw on all four of the 'helping to learn' styles (guiding, coaching, counselling and networking) (see Figure 1.1). Figure 1.1 shows that in any given

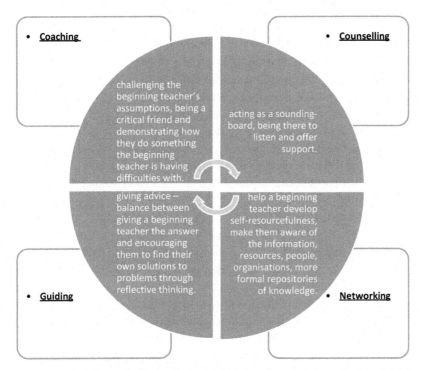

Figure 1.1 Adapted from Clutterbuck's model of developmental mentoring (2004, p. 9)

mentoring relationship, a mentor may need to adopt a different style and/or approach to challenge and support a beginning teacher at various stages of their development. In developmental mentoring, the beginning teacher sets the agenda based on their own development needs and the mentor provides insight and guidance to support the beginning teacher to achieve the desired goals. A more expert mentor will be able to select the right 'helping to learn' style for a beginning teacher's needs.

Now complete Task 1.6 which looks at Clutterbuck's model.

Task 1.6 Helping a beginning teacher to learn using Clutterbuck's (2004) model

- Consider which of the four 'helping to learn' styles you feel most comfortable with and why.
- Which do you use the least often and/or feel the least comfortable with and why?
- What could they do to overcome this?

Your ability to assess and identify the developmental stage in which a beginning teacher is operating at any given point, is a significant aspect of your role in becoming an effective mentor and ensuring growth takes places. Of equal importance, however, is your skill in adapting your own approach to fit the developmental needs of a beginning teacher. It is worth remembering that none of the three models Daloz (2012), Katz (1995) or Clutterbuck (2004) are linear in structure and, therefore, it is likely that a beginning teacher will move 'to and fro' between stages/zones, e.g. if teaching different aspects of the curriculum in which they have greater or lesser knowledge and/or confidence or starting at a new school. With each of the models considered above, it is possible to see elements of all three approaches to mentoring described by Maynard and Furlong (1995). Regardless of the mentoring model on which you prefer to base your practice, the attributes of the mentor play a crucial role in making decisions about the approach to mentoring.

There have been a number of attempts to characterise attributes of mentors. For example, Child and Merrill (2005) sought to generate an understanding of the attributes of a mentor in initial teacher education. Cho, Ramanan and Feldman (2011) described personal qualities that lie at the core of the mentor's identity and professional traits that relate to success in work-related activities. The DfE (2016b) described four separate, but related areas in the *National Standards for School-based Initial Teacher Training (ITT) mentors*, i.e. personal qualities, teaching, professionalism and self-development and working in partnership. Ragins (2016) described the attributes of a mentor as an antecedent to high quality mentoring; as something that needs to be in place before a mentor–mentee relationship begins. Task 1.7 asks you to consider the attributes of an effective mentor (see also Chapter 2).

Task 1.7   Attributes of an effective mentor

1. Considering the context and models of mentoring outlined in this chapter, reflect upon what you think the attributes of an effective mentor are. Attach a level of significance to each attribute, using three categories of significance; *essential, desirable* and *highly desirable*.
2. Having identified the attributes and the levels of significance, place five of the attributes in a prioritised list that best captures the ideal profile of a mentor of a beginning teacher.
3. Reflect on your own practice as a mentor and how you might develop the attributes that you have prioritised.

Finally, Task 1.8 asks you to reflect again on your mentoring practice after having read this chapter.

Task 1.8   Mentor reflection: reflecting on your mentoring practice

After having read this chapter, reflect how your understanding of definitions of mentoring, relevant policy and guidance documents and models of mentoring have/will impact on your practice.

Summary

Effective mentoring is a complex and demanding task, but, as with any role that enables you to have a positive impact on the development of others, it is hugely rewarding. In this chapter, we have considered the importance of:

- being aware of different definitions of mentoring
- understanding the content in which you are carrying out your role and what moral, political or theoretical drivers might influence the education system that you work in and/or your work as a mentor
- having a broad understanding of different models, or approaches to, mentoring in order to make decisions about how to carry out your role as a mentor

Further reading

It would be great to list here further reading relating to design and technology but there isn't a range to list. The ones below are useful and will support your thinking when reading the chapters of this book.

Maynard, T. and Furlong, J. (1995) 'Learning to teach and models of mentoring', in T. Kerry and A. Shelton-Mayes (eds.) *Issues in Mentoring*. London: Routledge, pp. 10–14.
    This chapter should help to deepen your knowledge of the three categories of mentoring, the apprentice model, the competence model and the reflective models.

Cordingley, P., Higgins, S., Greany, T., Buckler, N., Coles-Jordan, D., Crisp, B., Saunders, L. and Coe, R. (2015) *Developing Great Teaching: Lessons from the International Reviews into* Effective Professional Development. London: Teacher Development Trust.
    This should help you to gain an understanding of how mentoring fits into current ideas of effective continued professional development and learning.

References

Australian Institute for Teaching and School Leadership (AITSL) (2011) *The Australian Professional Standards for Teachers*. Cartlon South VIC 3053: Education Council.
Centre for the Use of Resource and Evidence in Education (CUREE) (2005) *National Framework for Mentoring and Coaching*. Coventry: CUREE.
Chartered Institute of Personnel and Development (CIPD) (2012) Coaching and mentoring fact sheet. Available at: http://CIPD.co.uk (Accessed: 15 August 2017).
Child, A. and Merrill, S. (2005) *Developing as a Secondary School Mentor: A Case Study Approach for Trainee Mentors and Their Tutors*. Exeter: Learning Matters.
Cho, C., Ramanan, R. and Feldman, M. (2011) 'Defining the ideal qualities of mentorship: A qualitative analysis of the characteristics of outstanding mentors', *The American Journal of Medicine*, 124(5), 453–458.
Clutterbuck, D. (2004) *Everyone Needs a Mentor: Fostering Talent in Your Organisation*, 4th ed. London: CIPD.
Cordingley, P., Higgins, S., Greany, T., Buckler, N., Coles-Jordan, D., Crisp, B., Saunders, L. and Coe, R. (2015) *Developing Great Teaching: Lessons from the International Reviews into Effective Professional Development*. London: Teacher Development Trust.
Daloz, L.A. (2012) *Mentor: Guiding the Journey of Adult Learners*. New York: Wiley.
Department for Education (2011) *The Teachers' Standards*. London: Crown.
Department for Education (2016a) *Framework of Core Content for Initial Teacher Training*. London: Crown.

Department for Education (2016b) *National Standards for School-Based Initial Teacher Training (ITT) Mentors.* London: Crown.

Department for Education (2016c) *Standards for Teachers' Professional Development, Implementation Guidance for School Leaders, Teachers, and Organisations That Offer Professional Development for Teacher.* London: Crown.

Driscoll, L. G., Parkes, K. A., Tilley-Lubbs, G. A., Brill, J. M. and Pitts Bannister, V. R. (2009) 'Navigating the lonely sea: Peer mentoring and collaboration among aspiring women scholars. Mentoring and Tutoring', *Partnership in Learning*, 17, 5-21.

Haggard, D. L., Dougherty, T. W., Turban, D. B. and Wilbanks, J. E. (2011) 'Who is a mentor? A review of evolving definitions and implications for research', *Journal of Management*, 37, 280-304.

Higgins, M. C. and Thomas, D. A. (2001) 'Constellations and careers: Toward understanding the effects of multiple developmental relationships', *Journal of Organizational Behavior*, 22, 223-247.

Katz, L. G. (1995) *Talks with Teachers: A Collection.* Norwood, NJ: Ablex Pub. Corp.

Kroll, J. (2016) 'What is meant by the term group mentoring?' *Mentoring and Tutoring: Partnership in Learning*, 24, 44-58.

Maynard, T. and Furlong, J. (1995) 'Learning to teach and models of mentoring', in T. Kerry and A. Shelton Mayes (eds.) *Issues in Mentoring.* London: Routledge, 10-14.

Ministry of Education and Research (2010) *Differentiated Primary and Lower Secondary Teacher Education Programmes for Years 1-7 and Years 5-10.* Olso: Ministry of Education and Research.

Montgomery, B. L. (April-June 2017) 'Mapping a mentoring roadmap and developing a supportive network for strategic career advancement', *SAGE Open*, 7, 1-13.

New Teacher Centre (2011) NTC *Continuum of Mentoring Practice.* Santa Cruz: New Teacher Centre.

Ohio Department for Education (2015) *Ohio Standards for Professional Development.* Ohio: Ohio Department for Education.

Pollard, A. (2014) *Reflective Teaching in Schools*, 4th ed. London: Bloomsbury Publishing PLC.

Ragins, B. (2016) 'From the ordinary to the extraordinary: High quality mentoring relationships at work', *Organizational Dynamics*, 45, 228-244.

Schön, D. A. (1983) *The Reflective Practitioner. How Professionals Think in Action.* New York: Basic Books.

The State Education Department/The University of the State of New York (2011) *The New York State Mentoring Standards.* Albany: The State Education Department/The University of the State of New York.

2   Understanding yourself-
beliefs, values and attitudes
how your experiences
influence your approaches
to mentoring

Alison Hardy

Introduction

This chapter focuses on how your values and beliefs about education and design and tech-nology (D&T) are formed and how they might shape your relationship with your mentee. Teachers do not always consider why they teach D&T, and so to even consider why you hold certain views and where they come from will probably be a new idea to you.

In this chapter, you will learn that your values may originate from several different places, such as your school experiences, your gender and your role. Consequently, your mentees may come with different ideas of the value of D&T and views about how pupils learn and what education is for, which may conflict with your views.

To explain and explore these theories I use my research (Hardy 2015, 2016, 2018a, 2018b) about the values different people attribute to D&T, where they come from and how they influence our approach to mentoring. The activities in the chapter are designed to help you explore your values and beliefs, as well as those your mentees.

Objectives

At the end of this chapter, you should be able to:

*   Appreciate there are a wide range of different values attributed to D&T.
*   Recognise how your D&T experiences as a pupil and teacher have shaped your beliefs and values about D&T.
*   Understand how your beliefs and values about education, learning and D&T influence your approaches to mentoring.

Your beliefs and values: origins and consequences

In this section, the terms 'beliefs' and 'values' are defined, followed by a discussion about the origins of our beliefs and values and how they influence our behaviour. The words 'value' and 'belief' are common words but difficult concepts to explain. Aiken (1980, p. 2) refers to a value as 'the importance or worth attached to activities and objects', which fits with us considering how we value D&T, the worth we give it as a subject compared to others and the contribution we think it makes to a child's education and life beyond school. Whereas Rokeach (1968) defines a value as an enduring belief, where a belief is more deeply held than an attitude and has endured over time – if this is true we should think about where our values come from.

You would probably find it difficult to explain why you hold one set of beliefs and not another. Yet, your beliefs and values originate from a multitude of sources, including your cultural and social setting – in other words the country and society you live in and more lo-cally, your family, education and community. There are different types of values, but in this chapter, the focus is on the values you attribute to D&T and education, and the values the beginning teachers you mentor also attribute to D&T.

Your beliefs and values affect your behaviour, morals, principles and attitudes (Figure 2.1). According to Rokeach (1973, p. 25), our 'beliefs are a standard that guides and determines our actions, attitudes, ideology and attempts to influence others'. Your values reveal your motivations (Hitlin and Piliavin 2004) and consequently your attitudes and behaviour; they also reveal your desires and goals (Eccles and Wigfield 2002).

By recognising where your values originate you will become a more supportive mentor. You will be able to help the mentee 'confront their own deep-seated beliefs and assumptions about learning' (Darling Hammond in Hattie 2009, p. 113) and D&T.

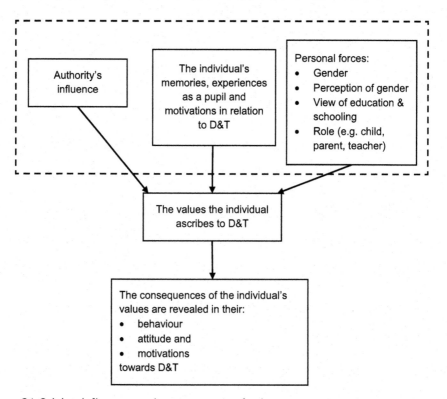

Figure 2.1 Origins, influences and consequences of values

This chapter focuses on two sources:

1.   the influence of authority and values;
2.   your personal motivations and characteristics.

First, your values and beliefs originate from your experiences and your family and personal context. When you were a child, your parents and family were the main influence; as you matured, you accepted and absorbed the beliefs and values from a wider group such as political and religious leaders, teachers, our managers and others.

Turning to your personal motivations and characteristics, of which there are many, the primary influences considered here are your childhood experiences of D&T, and the influence of your gender and perception of gender.

Your own experience in D&T as a pupil will have been shaped by what, when and how you were taught. According to Martin (2013) there have been five eras of D&T in England: making, personalising, designing, manufacturing and valuing. Although these eras partially correlate to different versions of the English National Curriculum, they do compare with aspects of the development of other countries' technology education curricula. Therefore, they are a useful framework to explore your experiences as a pupil studying D&T and as D&T teachers.

1.   If you attended school during the tripartite system (pre-1960) your experiences may have been akin to those in apprenticeships, learning 'jobs' - the era of 'making'. D&T has its origins in craft training and apprenticeships in England and other countries (e.g. Hong Kong as noted by Siu, Wong and Feng (2010) and Finland (Kananoja, 2009)), a legacy which D&T has tried to shake off.
2.   If your schooling was during the time of the School's Technology Project and the Keele Project (Penfold 1988), personalising the product began and pupils had some choices. While the processes taught in the making era pupils remained the same, pupils were given (limited) choices such as the shape of the key fob or the skirt's fabric. There were attempts in New Zealand to shift from the making era's behaviourist pedagogical practices with only partial success (Jones and Compton 2009). Likewise, in Finland pupils had some choice about 'what they want to produce for themselves' Kananoja (2009, p. 46).
3.   In England, the era of designing arrived with the National Curriculum in 1990. Practical work became design focussed, with an emphasis on user-centred design. Design also became a focus of the curricula in China and Hong Kong with an emphasis on problem-solving (Feng, Siu and Gu 2011).
4.   The 1992 version of the National Curriculum was influenced by the Engineering Council (Martin 2013; McCulloch, Jenkins and Layton 1985; Paechter 1993) and brought in the era of manufacturing. 'The curriculum not only reflected the rapidly changing practices in industry but also an increased interest by the manufacturing sector in the content of the curriculum' (Martin 2013, p. 321). Although later in Sweden (about 2010), there was pressure from technical universities in primary and secondary technical education to facilitate progression into higher education (Hallström, Hultén and Lövheim, 2014).
5.   Sustainability and the ethics of design became the focus with the 2004 version of the D&T curriculum - the era of valuing (although values had consistently featured in each version

of the National Curriculum since 1990 (Hardy 2015) and likewise in Sweden (Hallström et al. 2014)). After a period of mass consumption, D&T lessons were being used to teach pupils about the consequences of new products and to design with a more human focus.

Martin's work pre-dates the 2013 English National Curriculum which focusses on self-reliance with a shift towards the economic benefits for the individual and society (Hardy, 2016). While these eras are simplistic (Martin warns against seeing them as distinct from one another because there is overlap between the curricula), they are a useful reflective framework (Task 2.1).

Task 2.1   Personal experiences

What are your earliest memories from D&T lessons? Thinking back to when you were at school, what are your significant D&T memories? In which era were you at school? Do you agree with Martin's five and the additional 'self-reliance' era? How might your experiences compare to beginning teachers you are mentoring? Will this have implications for your mentoring role?

Over a series of interviews with pupils, D&T teachers, student teachers, senior leaders, university-based mentors and parents, I explored what they thought the value of D&T was, why it should be taught in schools – basically – what they thought the point of D&T was. The individuals were arranged into three groups of participants:

1. Group 1 were taught D&T before the National Curriculum in the personalising era
2. Group 2 went to secondary school between 1990 and 2004, during the designing and the manufacturing eras
3. Group 3 were the youngest participants and attended school after 2004 in the valuing era.

In the interviews, I explored the values they attributed to D&T (Hardy 2015, 2018a, 2018b). Comparing the values by group revealed greater similarity between the youngest (Group 3) and oldest participants' (Group 1) values. This suggests that Group 1's values, which were influenced by time as a pupil were now influencing how they taught the subject and consequently shaping Group 3's values.

The dominance of craft, design and technology (CDT) and resistant materials (Paechter 1993), and the historic purpose of D&T to prepare girls for domestic or service-industry careers (Attar in Paechter and Head, 1996; Rutland and Owen-Jackson, 2015) are potential influences on your values. Eccles and Wigfield (2002) identified that a child's gender and how they perceive gender influences motivation and values toward a subject. Perception of gender relates to the idea that we have views of how we expect different genders to behave, their desires and preferences. In D&T, this may be seen in how pupils, teachers and parents stereotype different activities and outcomes, such as textiles is for girls, robotics is for boys. While these views seem dated, values are deep-seated and may not be acknowledged externally but only seen by others who judge us by our actions and behaviour.

Research conducted by Paechter (1993) identified the dominance of resistant materials (wood, metal and plastic) in the then newly formed subject D&T; in later work, Paechter and Head (1996) explored how gender stereotypes are reinforced through 'male' and 'female' aspects of D&T. In my research, 25 years later, there was a similar pattern. For example, when a female teacher discusses the value of making and creating, she gave a textile example, and a male beginning teacher remembers making a wooden box. Older D&T teachers also give examples associated with their own gender; a male teacher discussed gears in a car and a female teacher talked about careers in the food industry. Notably, only female D&T teachers mentioned food, and male teachers did not mention textiles. However, this pattern was not replicated in the interviews with the beginning teachers. This suggests D&T is not gendered as much as it was in the early 1990s, which may be due a range of reasons such as an increase in female resistant materials-specialists and projects attempting to redress the gender imbalance in science, technology, engineering and mathematics (STEM) professions (for example, the ASPIRES project (Archer et al. 2013) and Women into Science and Engineering (WISE)). However, given the enduring nature of our values and the ongoing influence of our childhood experiences, you may be unaware that you have this perception of gender and how it influences your teaching and conversation with pupils (Murphy 2006).

D&T's origin from preparing working class girls for domestic service (Gillard 2016; Heggie 2011; Rutland and Owen-Jackson 2015) is still subtly evident, with more comments made by females than males about learning to cook in D&T. Pupils also appeared to have some gender bias but more from the boys than the girls. Only male pupils referred to traditionally stereotypical defined careers such as construction and engineering; whereas only one female pupil talked about becoming a textile designer when she left school, and other female pupils talked more generically about D&T related careers.

De Vries (2006, p. 108) reports that both genders have an 'artefact-orientated view of technology', with this being stronger for girls which results in them being less interested in technology. He refers to other research when he claims that 'girls are more interested than boys in human and social interests'. In my study, female D&T teachers appeared to strongly value pupils learning about human and social issues in D&T, with comments about sustainability, and making moral and ethical choices. Some male teachers also commented on this value, but reference points tended to be artefacts rather than systems and environments. Conversely, the male D&T teachers mention more frequently than the females the symbiotic relationship humans have with technology (see 'Technological awareness' below).

However, the number of people in my research were small and it cannot be confidently determined that this would be true across a larger group. But it may give something to reflect on (Task 2.2).

Task 2.2   Gender

Do you use gendered examples that reinforce stereotypes? Does your gender influence how you talk about the value and purpose of D&T? How might your views of gender compare to those of the beginning teachers you are mentoring?

Values attributed to D&T

In ethics, values are a standard that guide your behaviour (Feather 1975; Rokeach 1973). In D&T, values have been primarily used in relation to the subject's content. For example, pupils have learnt about values, such as technical values and moral values, to use when making judgements about a design or product (Hardy 2015; Layton 1992); or to make design decisions (Trimingham, 2008). In my research, I was curious about the range of values people attributed to D&T. Unsurprisingly, given the history of the subject as seen in Martin's five eras, there was a wide range of views about D&T's value. In fact, I identified over 25 different values. However, these could be grouped into five themes that are discussed below. While you may agree with some, others may challenge your views and beliefs about the value of D&T. Be open to this challenge.

D&T meets our economic and domestic needs

This theme focused on how D&T met both an individual's and society's economic and domestic needs. For example, many valued that pupils learnt everyday life skills to help them look after themselves and others talked about how pupils were showed possible careers and skills to use in future D&T-related careers. For some, they valued how D&T contributed to the country's international industrial and economic competitiveness. The values in this theme have been fundamental to D&T's purpose, from before it was established as a subject to the most recent version of the National Curriculum. This theme is about preparing young people to be independent and be helpful to others.

Comments revealed the utilitarian and functional purpose of D&T with many teachers referring to employment in the engineering, construction and product design sectors. For those who attributed values in this theme to D&T aim is to teach pupils skills for specific D&T-related vocations and prepare those for careers that help them prepare for future lives.

Generic and transferrable skills

Recurring features of the D&T National Curriculum have pupils learning generic skills, characteristics and abilities. These included thinking skills, learning to think creatively, problem solving and communication skills. These skills are not unique to D&T, in other words, they might also be attributed to other school subjects.

But, are these values skills or a group of behaviours, attitudes and activities useful for professional and vocational situations? It is important to explore this because the 'skills' attributed to D&T are 'catch-all' phrases. For example, 'communication skills' leads to questions such as what are the pupils learning to communicate? And to whom? And where? In D&T pupils are asked to present ideas visually and verbally, to persuade and explain, to teachers and peers. Each of these situations requires different forms of communication. So, a learning objective that states 'You will develop your communication skills' leaves many questions unanswered. So, while some people think D&T helps pupils learn communication skills, it may be unclear what the pupils would become skilful in or what skills they are learning. When discussing values about transferrable skills with your mentee you might find it helpful to use Winch's (2010) definition of a skill, which is that a skill is an ability to act in a certain way in relation to a task and involves five aspects: (1) a technique applied to a task, (2) that has been practised so becomes a habit, (3) which shows moral qualities and virtues such as persistence, (4) perceptual ability is used (5) in conjunction with propositional knowledge.

Technological awareness

A claim in the English National Curriculum (Department of Education 2013) is that D&T makes pupils aware of the impact of technology, which is an echo from the 1960s School's Technology Project, a government-funded project and a precursor to the National Curriculum. You will see that the view from 1967 is like the twenty-first century view of D&T:

> help children to get to grips with technology as a major influence in our society and, as a result, to help more of them to lead effective and satisfying lives.
>
> (Schools Council, 1967, p. 12)

> Through the evaluation of past and present design and technology, they develop a critical understanding of its impact on daily life and the wider world. [They] develop the creative, technical and practical expertise needed to perform everyday tasks confidently and to participate successfully in an increasingly technological world.
>
> (Department of Education, 2013, p. 88)

This theme of technological awareness focuses on enabling individuals to be technologically aware. First, it includes the idea that using technology is part of being human. We use technology so much that we may not even be aware where our bodies end and technology begins. Second, some thought it was important that pupils become aware of how technology determines our behaviour. For example, consider how technology has changed the way we communicate with friends and family, how technology used in a road crossing determines when and where we cross the road and so on. And finally, through D&T pupils gain a critical understanding of the impact of products on themselves and others. Issues around sustainability and the ethics of different products are often topics of discussion in D&T lessons. These ideas have always existed in the D&T National Curriculum and many teachers and beginning teachers agreed in my study that it is an important feature of the subject. But what do you and your mentee think?

Create and recognise good design

This theme centres on what many would argue is the central value of D&T: pupils designing and making products. This view is supported by the fact that the seven values within this theme relate to the D&T National Curriculum and generally have featured in every version since 1990.

In D&T, pupils are involved in the activity of making and creating. For some whom I interviewed, it was not important what the pupils were creating, or even that pupils designed the item being made, instead they focused on the value to be found in the process of using things to create something. Also, I am being deliberately ambiguous in using 'thing' and 'something' – they leave it open to interpreting making and creating in a broad sense: two or three dimension materials; virtual or tangible realities; edible, flexible, rigid or imagined materials.

Some argue that pupils need to learn about materials, processes and tools to be able to make and create. The declarative knowledge that should be taught in D&T, or the essential facts pupils should learn, is a contentious topic with some materials taking precedence over others (for example the marginalisation of food, and textiles becoming more widely associated with Art and Design than D&T). But this argument is not only about materials and making process, but also learning processes related to design. Mood boards and questionnaires as research methods appear to be out of fashion as the use of websites such as Pinterest and Core77 become the space for inspiration.

In the processes involved in designing there are several aspects to value. First, giving pupils opportunity to be creative when designing. Next the idea that pupils have freedom to make design decisions – they can decide which design to develop, how to develop it and how to make it. For the D&T teachers I interviewed, this was an important aspect to D&T, but they acknowledged that they can find it challenging to plan for pupils to have this freedom because of classroom management challenges. Hidden within this freedom is pupil's learning that ideas do not have to be right the first time, that when they first put pencil to paper, or model a first thought there is no expectation that it is a perfect solution. In D&T the premise is that we design, we analyse, we question, we alter, improve, develop, revisit, sketch and model some more, and that this leads to a resolution to the design brief not a perfect solution. In D&T, pupils are exploring 'wicked problems' (Rittel and Webber 1973) that can only be resolved not solved; this underpins the idea that when creating good design pupils need not fear the blank paper because in D&T the ideas do not have to be perfect. Finally, through designing for multiple situations and contexts pupils learn society's diversity. From the simple projects learning about anthropometrics and ergonomics through to designing for unfamiliar groups of people with disabilities, they appreciate that one size does not fit all – there is no average person.

Together these values encapsulate the uniqueness of D&T:

> Pupils are creative when designing and have no fear that designs must be right from the start because know they can analyse and evaluate designs to improve work. Using what they have learnt about people and materials, processes and tools they freely make decisions to make and create designs.
>
> (Hardy 2018b, p. 165)

Personal development and enjoyment

The values in this theme demonstrated how D&T supports a child's personal development. D&T was recognised by some as being about enjoyment, satisfaction and fulfilment. These values describe the ephemeral aspects of learning, some are specific to D&T but, like the second theme, they can link to any subject.

Some teachers held the view there are different aspects to learning in D&T. This hints at the idea that D&T requires drawing on learning from other subjects, such as mathematics, art, science and drama. Or it might suggest that pupils must balance conflicting ideas when coming to a resolution in design work, which means they balance the aesthetic with the technical aspects, cost with function, as well as the limitations of making skills and access to resources. Making these decisions involves compromise, which involves them making decisions based on values (Layton 1992); these decisions involve thinking from different perspectives.

Pupils using their hands and minds together was seen by some as a feature of D&T learning, the view that learning in D&T combines cognition with psychomotor. For example, one interviewee said: '[in D&T] that coordination between brain and hands to the extent that you're problem solving continually into what it is you that you are trying to make'.

After cognition comes affectivity, how the pupils feel in D&T lessons and afterwards. Here, you may think about how pupils enjoy the subject and why they enjoy it. There is a connection between enjoyment and satisfaction. Pupils gain resilience in persevering with ideas or making a product; consider when you have seen pupils successfully make a product using a new skill, think about how they show satisfaction. For many I interviewed this intrinsic value was central.

Hearing a child say 'I can do it!' captures the idea of developing perseverance, which in turn gives pupils confidence and resilience. It links to the previous theme where pupils are released from the inhibitions of designing the 'perfect solution', but later they face the limitations of the design ideas and work out how to improve them, thus developing perseverance as they seek a better design solution. From the first version (Department of Education and Science, 1990, p. 27) evaluating for improvement was crucial, for example 'evaluate at each stage of their work [and] make adjustments because of evaluation'. Later versions emphasised the importance of pupils to be resilient, 'test, evaluate and refine their ideas and products' (Department of Education 2013, p. 89) (Task 2.3).

Task 2.3   Values

Use these five themes to explore your values, and compare them with your mentee's values.

1.   Which theme do you most closely associate with?
2.   How do your values influence your lessons and what you teach?
3.   Ask your mentee to do the same. Compare your values and views.

Doing this task will help you frame your own values and understand how they influence your classroom practice. By comparing your values with those of your mentee it will help you understand why you both do not always agree about the purpose of a lesson, activity or unit of work. The next section discusses how differences and agreements between you may affect your mentoring relationship.

Understanding how value consensus and discrepancy affects your mentoring relationship

As you have probably seen from your responses to Task 2.3, you and your mentee agree on some values of D&T and disagree on others. This is called value consensus (agreement) and value discrepancy (disagreement) (Feather 1975). So where does this leave your working relationship? If you agreed surely your relationship would be harmonious and your beginning teacher would take on your D&T mantle, replicated in your mould? You and your department (assuming their values also aligned with yours) would not have to accommodate the beginning teacher's different views because there would be no value discrepancies to resolve (Feather 1975). Problems between you could be easily solved, it would be a congruous relationship. But how boring would that be, devoid of excitement? One of the joys (and challenges) of working with a beginning teacher is having your values questioned. Resolving differences, which may involve you shifting your values as well as challenging those of the beginning teacher, is a reward of mentoring. However, if there is significant value-discrepancy between you conflict may ensue that seems impossible to resolve. Trying to understand the values you disagree on and why there is this value-discrepancy will help with this situation. To help understand why there are discrepancies I will use examples from my research.

First, do not assume that all D&T teachers agree about the value of D&T. The D&T teachers I interviewed, whose age varied from 22 to 53 years old, only agreed on five values:

1.   Pupils learn skills to use at home (e.g. DIY, sewing and cooking).
2.   Pupils gain a critical understanding about the impact of products.
3.   In D&T lessons pupils receive careers guidance about D&T-related careers.
4.   Pupils have opportunity to make and create things.
5.   Pupils learn about materials, processes and tools.

Similarly, the beginning teachers only agreed on five values, two of which were the first two from the D&T teachers list plus these three:

1.   Pupils can be creative in design work.
2.   Pupils begin to appreciate the differences between people
3.   Pupils become more resilient because of D&T.

This congruence and disparity between the two groups suggests that at this stage in a D&T career, the beginning teachers are equally focussed on the unique contribution D&T makes to a child's education as well as the intrinsic benefit of the subject. Whereas the more established D&T teachers are in tune with examination requirements (learning about materials etc.) and life after school (careers advice). Most beginning teachers will have left school and higher education more recently than you; so, memories of how school contributed to personal development are recent enough to be a significant influence on values. At this stage in the D&T teaching career, they may be focussed not only on teaching D&T but also how D&T could benefit a child's personal development (theme 5 above). This is only speculation as the participant numbers were small but it does highlight what, and why, the value differences might be between beginning and established teachers.

Schwartz (1994, p. 21) predicted that our values can change and be acquired through 'socialisation to dominant group values'; in your relationship with a beginning teacher you are the 'dominant group' and, over time, your mentees values will become more aligned with your values rather than the other way around. As a beginning teacher becomes more embedded within a school they will acquire values from other D&T teachers. If the values they arrive with are like the department's then they will find it more straightforward to feel part of the department than beginning teachers who hold dissimilar values to you and your department. In my research, I found the D&T teachers and beginning teachers had a high degree of value concurrence from the start of the relationship, which suggests integration into a school D&T department is likely to be straightforward. The beginning teachers will find many values go unchallenged as they already match those held by school subject mentors.

This idea of smooth assimilation into a new context based on alignment of values has been researched in relation to human values by Feather (1975) but he suggests that value-discrepancies between people can be healthy. So, while the beginning teachers may settle into your department quickly because their values align closely with you, they may become dissatisfied because discrepancies arouse interest and curiosity. What a lack of disparity really means is that because there is no value disagreement within your department the beginning teachers could stagnate, because values are reinforced because no one within the D&T department is challenging the consensus.

Also, because of the power-subordinate relationship between you and the beginning teacher, if they do hold different values to you they may find it difficult to challenge or question your values because of the power-dynamic between you. Feather (1975 drawing on other sources, p. 113) suggests 'large discrepancies may be associated with fear and avoidance' and so, you may avoid acknowledging your mentee's disparate views, as it may upset your department's values and your own long-held beliefs. Therefore, you may resist challenge which questions your enduring values because to accept alternative views could threaten your department's consensus and the status quo. Avoiding conversations about your differences may lead to your mentee feeling isolated (Task 2.4).

Task 2.4   Values and the mentoring relationship

Compare your values with those of your mentee at the start and end of the placement to see if they align or change. This will help you understand each other.

Review your mentees' values to see how these match or conflict with yours and what this might mean for your relationship.

What are the consequences of working with others, or in a context, where others have different values to us? How will this influence your work as a mentor?

To move forward and allow change to happen, the challenge for you is to find the optimum discrepancy to have some influence over what happens in the classroom, without upsetting too much the congruence between yourself, your department and your mentee.

Summary

This chapter has explored how your values and beliefs about D&T are formed and how they may shape your relationship with your mentee. I hope it has given you a better understanding of:

- how your experiences, and your family and personal context have shaped your values and beliefs about education and D&T
- how your own experience in D&T as a pupil will have been shaped by what and how you were taught

- the wide range of different values attributed to D&T
- how your beliefs and values about education, learning and D&T influence your approaches to mentoring.
- why these experiences and origins will influence your classroom practice and mentoring relationships
- why the values you attribute to D&T may contrast from your mentees because of differing ages, experiences and gender

Consequently, I hope this new understanding will:

- give you an insight into your behaviour and in turn understand your mentee's values and behaviour
- have a positive effect on your relationship, where you can challenge values and you will be open to challenge from them.

Further reading

Hardy, A. (2018) Defining the value of a school subject. *Prism: Casting New Light on Learning, Theory and Practice*, 1(2), 55-82. Available at: http://bit.ly/2KZhJ6y.

Layton, D. (1992) *Values and design and technology*. Loughborough: Loughborough University.

Martin, M. (2013) Five eras of making and designing. *PATT27 technology education for the future: a play on sustainability*. Christchurch, New Zealand, pp. 318-324. Available at: www.academia.edu/5662472/Editor_of_PATT_27_Conference_Proceedings-_Technology_Education_for_the_Future_A_Play_on_Sustainability (Accessed: 21 May 2019).

Vries, d., Marc J. (2011) *Positioning technology education in the curriculum*. Rotterdam: Sense Publishers.

References

Aiken, L. R. (1980) Attitude measurement and research. *New Directions for Testing and Measurement*, 7, 1-24.

Archer, L., DeWitt, J., Osborne, J., Dillon, J., Willis, B., and Wong, B. (2013) 'Not girly, not sexy, not glamorous': Primary school girls' and parents' constructions of science aspirations. *Pedagogy, Culture & Society*, 21(1), 171-194. doi:10.1080/14681366.2012.748676.

Department of Education (2013) *The national curriculum in England framework document*. London: Department of Education.

Department of Education and Science (1990) *Technology in the national curriculum*. London: HMSO.

De Vries, M. J. (2006) Technological knowledge and artifacts: an analytical view, in Dakers, J. R. (ed.), *Defining technological literacy: towards an epistemological framework*. Gordonsville. VA, USA: Palgrave Macmillan, pp. 23-40.

Eccles, J. S. and Wigfield, A. (2002) Motivational beliefs, values, and goals. *Annual Review of Psychology*, 53(1), 109-132.

Feather, N. T. (1975) *Values in education and society*. London: Free Press (Collier Macmillan Publishers).

Feng, W., Siu, K. W. M. and Gu, J. (2011) Exploring the position of technology education in China, in De Vries, M. J. (ed.) *Positioning technology education in the curriculum*. Rotterdam: Sense Publishers, pp. 227-242.

Gillard, D. (2016). Education in England: a brief history. Available at: www.educationengland.org.uk/history/ (Accessed: 21 November 2018).

Hallström, J., Hultén, M. and Lövheim, D. (2014) The study of technology as a field of knowledge in general education: historical insights and methodological considerations from a Swedish case study, 1842-2010. *International Journal of Technology and Design Education*, 24(2), 121-139.

Hardy, A. (2018a). Defining the value of a school subject. *Prism: Casting New Light on Learning, Theory and Practice*, 1(2), 55-82. Available at: http://bit.ly/2KZhJ6y (Accessed: 21 November 2018).

Hardy, A. L. (2018b) *The value of a school subject: investigating the values attributed to design and technology by different stakeholders* (unpublished thesis).

Hardy, A. L. (2015). What's D&T for? Gathering and comparing the values of design and technology academics and trainee teachers. *Design and Technology Education: An International Journal*, 20(2), 10-21.

Hardy, A. L. (2016). What's the point of D&T? Available at: www.stem.org.uk/blog/what%E2%80%99s-point-design-and-technology (Accessed: 21 November 2018).

Hattie, J. (2009). *Visible learning: a synthesis of over 800 meta-analyses relating to achievement*. Abingdon, Oxon: Routledge.

Heggie, V. (2011). Domestic and domesticating education in the late Victorian city. *History of Education*, 40(3), 273-290.

Hitlin, S. and Piliavin, J. A. (2004) Values: reviving a dormant concept. *Annual Review of Sociology*, 30, 359-393.

Jones, A. and Compton, V. (2009) Reviewing the field of technology education in New Zealand, in Jones, A. and De Vries, M. J. (eds.) *International handbook of research and development in technology education*. Rotterdam: Sense Publisher, pp. 93-104.

Kananoja, T. (2009) Technology Education in general education in Finland, in Jones, A. and De Vries, M. J. (eds.) *International handbook of research and development in technology education*. Rotterdam: Sense Publishers, pp. 41-50.

Layton, D. (1992) *Values and design and technology*. Loughborough: Loughborough University.

Martin, M. (2013) Five eras of making and designing. *PATT27 technology education for the future: a play on sustainability*, pp. 318-324. Available at: www.academia.edu/5662472/Editor_of_PATT_27_Conference_Proceedings-_Technology_Education_for_the_Future_A_Play_on_Sustainability (Accessed: 21 May 2019).

McCulloch, G., Jenkins, E. W. and Layton, D. (1985) *Technological revolution? The politics of school science and technology in England and wales since 1945*. Oxon: Routledge.

Murphy, P. (2006) Gender and technology: gender mediation in school knowledge construction, in Dakers, J. R. (ed.) *Defining technological literacy: towards an epistemological framework*, 1st ed. Gordonsville, VA: Palgrave Macmillan, pp. 219-237.

Paechter, C. (1993) What happens when a school subject undergoes a sudden change of status? *Curriculum Studies*, 1(3), 349-363.

Paechter, C. and Head, J. (1996) Gender, identity, status and the body: life in a marginal subject. *Gender and Education*, 8(1), 21-30.

Penfold, J. (1988) *Craft design and technology: past, present and future*. Stoke on Trent: Trentham.

Rittel, H. and Webber, M. (1973) Dilemmas in a general theory of planning. *Policy Sciences; Integrating Knowledge and Practice to Advance Human Dignity*, 4(2), 155-169.

Rokeach, M. (1968) *Beliefs, attitudes and values: a theory of organization and change*. San Francisco: Jossey-Bass, Inc.

Rokeach, M. (1973) *The nature of human values*. New York: The Free Press.

Rutland, M. and Owen-Jackson, G. (2015) Food technology on the school curriculum in England: is it a curriculum for the twenty-first century? *International Journal of Technology and Design Education*, 25(4), 467–482.

Schools Council (1967). *Technology and the schools working paper 18*. London: HMSO.

Schwartz, S. H. (1994) Are there universal aspects in the structure and contents of human values? *Journal of Social Issues*, 50(4), 19–45.

Siu, Kin Wai Michael, Wong, Y. L. and Feng, W. W. (2010) Why fail? Experience of technology education in Hong Kong. *World Transactions on Engineering and Technology Education*, 8(2), 231–236.

Trimingham, R. (2008) The role of values in design decision-making. *Design and Technology Education: An International Journal*, 13(2), 37–52.

Winch, C. (2010) *Dimensions of expertise: a conceptual exploration of vocational knowledge*, 1st ed. London: Continuum.

3 What knowledge, understanding and skills do mentors of new D&T teachers need?

Ruth Seabrook

Introduction

Mentoring in design and technology (D&T), as in any subject, is a fundamental part of any teacher development programme. It plays a major role in developing the beginning teacher and, as a mentor, you can have a significant impact on outcomes and eventual success in teaching.

In this chapter, we will consider that mentoring in D&T is a specialised activity and is not suitable for all teachers to undertake. Indeed, there are ranges of characteristics that make certain teachers more appropriate for the role than others. These include a supportive, nurturing and fundamentally positive attitude, a willingness to become part of a two-way learning relationship and a reflective personality able to assist the beginning teacher with their own reflective practice. According to Williams (1993) as a mentor, you need to possess the memory of an elephant, have the patience of a saint and have an unrelenting sense of humour to achieve success.

In terms of D&T, you would also need key characteristics beyond the generic skills previously mentioned. These would include; up to date subject and curriculum knowledge, exceptional practical skills to enable modelling of your practice to the beginning teacher, a keen understanding of up-to-date health and safety processes and a strong interest in new and emerging technologies. Billett notes that 'the duality of the workplace experience is dependent on the quality of the invitation to learn from the workplace and on the extent to which the learner chooses to engage' (Billett cited in Lofthouse and Thomas 2014, p. 203). Your core knowledge and understanding therefore needs to be both modelled and shared willingly so the beginning teachers can grow and mature into confident, knowledgeable and inspiring teachers.

There are numerous benefits to working with a beginning teacher, as they will have a new, rich and varied perspective and knowledge base that can be utilised to enhance work in the department (Sayers, Morley and Barnes 2002).

Objectives

By the end of this chapter, you should be able to:

- Understand your own personal D&T subject construct and assist beginning teachers to understand their own, to subsequently audit developing subject knowledge and core skills.
- Develop good reflection on your own practice and assist beginning teachers to reflect on their own teaching experience.

- Explain the place of D&T in the curriculum and help beginning teachers to understand the changing dynamic of the local curriculum.
- Audit your skills as a mentor and understand the important role you have in educating beginning teachers.
- Recognise the value of engaging with continuing professional development (CPD) to develop your own subject pedagogy in D&T.

Subject knowledge development

Teaching is a complex and multifaceted profession. Teachers are required to be adaptable and ready for change, yet the skills and attributes traditionally associated with being a good teacher and acquired by them during teacher education do not always equip them to cope with the shifting landscape of educational and governmental change (Colucci-Gray and Fraser 2008). Few D&T beginning teachers begin training with a varied enough range of knowledge and core skills, deemed sufficient for teaching. As a mentor, you can work alongside your mentee to help build confidence and develop core knowledge and understanding (see Chapter 7 on subject knowledge auditing).

Murphy felt that 'if effectiveness of teaching is determined by the type of knowledge and how this knowledge is used then the nature of the beginning teachers' knowledge would be as important as the content' (Murphy 2005, p. 113). In order, therefore, to have professional credibility and be suitable to practice in the teaching profession, teachers need to acquire strategies and behaviours to be able to utilise knowledge and skills well to a much greater extent.

Subject knowledge is identified as one of the standards for the award of qualified teacher status (QTS) on completion of an initial teacher education (ITE) course in England (Department for Education 2012), with similar standards needing to be met in other countries. For one example, in Wales the 'Standards for Professional Learning', includes that which 'consistently extends knowledge, skills and understanding and can show how reflection and openness to challenge and support informs professional learning to progressively develop pedagogy' (Welsh Government 2013). Both Scotland and Northern Ireland have standards related to the importance of subject knowledge for teaching as well.

Appropriate subject knowledge has historically been part of any classification of the essential 'knowledge base for teaching'. Indeed Shulman (1986) in his research programme 'Knowledge Growth in Teaching' originally attempted to categorise this. Many have since developed individual classifications (Banks, Leech and Moon 1999; Owen-Jackson 2008; Turner-Bisset 1999) but all appear to agree that 'it is the active interaction of subject knowledge, school knowledge and pedagogical understanding that brings teacher professional knowledge into being' (Banks et al. 1999, p. 94).

As noted in Chapter 2, your own personal subject construct for D&T, and beliefs and values, will undoubtedly have an impact on how you teach. 'For our teachers, "knowledge" of the subject matter was as much a product of beliefs as it was an accumulation of facts and interpretation' (Wilson and Wineburg 1988 cited in Turner-Bisset 1999, p. 44). Beginning D&T teachers, on the other hand, must relate subject knowledge to those 'communities of practice' found in school. What then holds this form of knowledge together is 'personal subject construct' (Leach and Banks 1996). Lave and Wenger (1991) contend that you must allow productive access to this community of practitioners and the meaning of such activities is made transparent to the beginning teacher. At the start, the beginning teacher is almost solely dependent on your school community of practice, where there is less likely access to peer groups or outside support. It could mean they are limited in experiences and exposure to new thinking particularly if your department is not as forward looking in curriculum planning and is seated in an old-fashioned epistemology of what D&T should deliver to pupils. It is critical that the beginning teacher receives robust training whilst in school. Therefore, factoring in previous experience, core skills and subject knowledge requirements must be key when considering the mentoring and support they will receive. As a mentor, you have a responsibility to understand your own personal subject construct and go on to help your beginning teacher identify their own, and subsequent developing, core skills and subject knowledge. It is important to note here that the aim is not to 'clone' the mentor but aid the beginning teachers to develop a personal style and way of teaching. As Chapter 2 notes, it might be necessary to challenge your own values and be prepared to be challenged (Task 3.1).

Task 3.1 Personal subject construct

Understanding your own personal subject construct and how to help beginning teachers to identify their own. Refer to Figure 3.1

- Prior to your initial mentor meeting with your beginning teacher, complete the following Figure 3.1 – DEPTH 'Teacher Knowledge' Tool. This will help you to gain an understanding of your own personal subject construct and will serve as the basis for your subject knowledge for teaching.
- Explain the diagram to your mentee and get them to complete the model prior to your next meeting.
- Discuss and reflect with them on all aspects of the model to see where gaps in understanding, core skills and subject knowledge occur. Plan for these to be addressed.

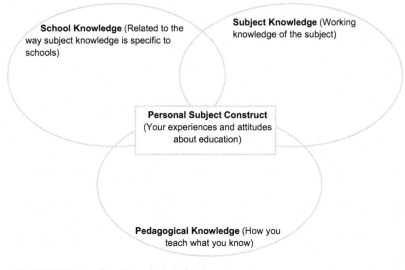

School Knowledge (Related to the way subject knowledge is specific to schools)

Subject Knowledge (Working knowledge of the subject)

Personal Subject Construct (Your experiences and attitudes about education)

Pedagogical Knowledge (How you teach what you know)

Figure 3.1 DEPTH 'Teacher Knowledge' tool

Once the teacher knowledge tool has been completed, you can then start to analyse what core skills the beginning teacher has and what needs to be included for personal professional development. Good subject knowledge input can help to validate and increase the beginning teacher's authenticity with pupils. 'Explicit teaching of key competences occurs within meaningful and authentic practice' (Snape 2015, p. 27).

Arguably, all D&T teachers must continuously address knowledge acquisition while also recognising that learning can be developed alongside that of pupils as they work together. This is often a necessity in the light of the time it takes to become familiar with the ever-increasing depth of knowledge required for teaching D&T and the regular changes to the curricular, alongside the plethora of-emerging new technologies. An important part of your role as mentor therefore is to assist your beginning teacher in this acquisistion of new knowledge and consolidation of prior knowledge into sound pedagogical teaching.

These include but not exclusively, an understanding of:

Core skills and knowledge required (Martin 2008, p. 24)

- Design and Making
- Communication
- Products and Applications
- Technological concepts
- Information Technology

Task 3.2   Audit of knowledge and skill requirements

Using your department schemes to help your beginning teacher to audit the knowledge and skills required for teaching them.

- Working with the other teachers in your department plan how best to support knowledge acquisition through observation and peer support.
- Work with the technician so that a series of workshop sessions can take place to enable them to become fully conversant with the equipment within the department.

What follows here then is the matching of what skills the beginning teacher already possesses with what they need to obtain. The expectation is that alongside you, they can acquire factual knowledge, develop mastery of the craft skills required and learn to apply this knowledge in teaching and learning contexts (Task 3.2).

According to Snape 'beginning teachers are introduced to the curriculum components, discipline content and the pedagogical implementation strategies most effective for teaching and learning in school' (Snape 2015, p. 5). These practice pedagogies should be modelled in class by you and the department staff and professional dialogue must then follow to investigate and secure the beginning teacher's understanding. An example of this could be, the beginning D&T teacher observing you demonstrating a new technique, piece of equipment or salient piece of technical knowledge and then discussion around this leading to them completing the same in a similar lesson. This form of modelling will support experimentation by the beginning teacher of new classroom strategies and teaching practices.

Utilisation of technician and support staff

The use of your D&T technician (and potentially other support staff) must not be overlooked in assisting in this learning process, as they are also a very knowledgeable and rich resource and can assist the beginning teacher with learning and capability (Tomlinson, Hobson and Malderez 2010). Beginning teachers need to learn the different types, styles and manufacturers of a multitude of D&T specialist equipment, as they move between schools. They may have received some health and safety training and technical expertise from previous schools or training providers, but with each new school will come the different nuances that go with individual D&T departments (see Chapter 9 on managing practical lessons). Technicians can be excellent at demonstrating equipment and the logistics required for safe use. Indeed, the technician is often a 'silent' observer, helping in the background but is able to give constructive feedback and help in addition to you.

Beginning D&T teachers must be supported to make all project outcomes prior to the teaching of these elements to pupils. This includes the use of all specialist equipment and computer programmes used in these projects. This will enable them to be confident in the delivery of projects with pupils and will aid knowledge acquisition.

Developing good reflective practice and assisting beginning teachers to reflect on teaching

Critical reflection and reflective practice combined with professional enquiry will undoubtedly facilitate professional learning and development for both beginning and experienced teachers, leading to improvements in teaching practice and pupil learning (McLaren 2017). Arguably, there is no question about the importance of reflection and its capacity as a driver for continuing professional development however, you should not complete this action simplistically or there will only be superficial improvements to teaching and learning.

Observation is highly valued as a tool for reflection and promoting teacher learning and development. When a beginning teacher first begins observation activity, they can find it an overwhelming experience; difficult to know what they are looking at and why, especially in the highly complex environment of the D&T classroom, where many alternate activities can be in action simultaneously. Learning how to observe an experienced teacher and understand the different skills used requires expertise and they need assistance to identify what they are seeing (Tomlinson et al. 2010).

According to O'Leary (2014), successful observation centres on five main factors: clarity of purpose, how well briefed the observers are, the opportunities to engage in substantive professional dialogue, the quality of ongoing feedback and sufficient time allocation for this to be completed.

As will be seen in Chapter 11, you need to ensure when completing observations that the focus of the lesson observations is negotiated with the beginning teacher. Both of you need to be aware of the parameters of the observation taking place. These parameters allow you to feed-forward after the lesson and provide a focus for the observation to avoid over complication.

There is a need for a shared reflective experience between yourself and the beginning teacher where you can work together to evaluate the quality of teaching and or setting targets over an extended period. They can then reflect on previous observations and identify actions from constructive criticism using suggested strategies. Lesson observation should ensure that learning is secure and that pupils are making good progress. Focused and differentiated observations solely around D&T subject knowledge or health and safety are important to assess how well they are gaining in confidence and how well they are transferring this vital information to pupils.

Fostering collaborative learning amongst yourselves is more likely to support growth and development of the beginning teacher in all aspects of teaching. Indeed, according to Lofthouse and Thomas (2017) collaborative working will consist of you working together on a challenge, piecing together ideas or creating something new through joint deliberation. For example, if a beginning teacher has a more contemporary knowledge of 3D software, they may be able to assist you and the department in knowing and understanding the potential uses of this in projects to engage pupils more fully in new or emerging technologies.

One important factor when reflecting on lesson outcomes is that of your feedback being judgemental. Lesson feedback needs to be an exercise with you initially modelling the reflection for the beginning teacher. This modelling then transfers to you assisting to develop reflection using skilful questioning, finally moving to a joint analysis of the outcomes, with them being confident to teach and reflect on teaching independently. See Chapter 11 on managing learning conversations (Task 3.3).

Task 3.3   Reflective practice exercise

- Using the O'Leary (2014) classroom observation examples in the further resources carry out a pre-agreed lesson observation with your beginning teacher on one of your own lessons, focusing them on an aspect of your teaching. (This could be D&T core knowledge related to a project you are teaching, H&S for a new piece of equipment or how you transition between activities in the classroom without chaos ensuing.)
- Discuss the lesson outcomes and reflect with them on what they saw, what strategies they witnessed and how they could embed these in planning.
- Repeat the lesson observation, this time watching them implement and utilise the strategies and pedagogical techniques used. Use this to aid reflection in your ensuing discussion.

Explain the place of D&T in your school and help beginning teachers to understand the changing dynamic of the curriculum

Reflecting briefly on the DEPTH 'Teacher Knowledge' Tool at the start of the chapter you should be able to use this to engage your beginning teacher in discussion about the position of D&T within the local curricular and its place within the school. This will depend on many factors related to the school, timetabling, how the senior management view the subject and its use for your pupils. Anyone involved in the beginning teachers training has a responsibility to provide a clear picture of the school's view on the nature of D&T and its role in providing all pupils with the knowledge and understanding to become well-reasoned adults in the made-world (Department for Education 2013).

For most beginning teachers there is a mismatch between the breadth of the curricular and the quite narrow specialism of most degree courses (Price and Reid 1993). There is also a difference in curricular in different countries and the focus in relation to education, industry and links with other subjects, which is especially pertinent for D&T.

Most beginning teachers will need a maximum breadth of understanding in their own D&T curricular at Key Stage 3 (KS3) (please refer to your own local country's identification of year groups) but also at least one full specialism at Key Stage 4 (KS4) and perhaps beyond. The beginning teacher therefore will need to become quite 'expert' in this area and you will need to build opportunities for this in timetables. You will also need to recognise the team nature of the delivery of D&T and should allow beginning teachers to become competent for teaching over a wide range of activity, whilst simultaneously acting as a consultant perhaps to colleagues over a narrower range (Price and Reid 1993). Schools and mentors are often reticent to allow beginning teachers to teach examination classes in case the quality of delivery slips and the pupils achieve less than targeted. This is understandable but if they do not get coverage across all phases, they will be unprepared in the first few years of teaching to ensure pupils make progress. What you could do then if timetabling allows, is to make provision for them to at least team-teach and be included in the planning, delivery and assessment of elements of these classes, where they can learn by being included in the lessons.

When discussing examination specifications there is often apprehension about the board chosen as although there are common elements to each, delivery and assessment can be quite different. With changes in England to the specification of GCSE courses to include more maths and science and the change of Food Technology to Food Preparation and Nutrition, beginning teachers are even less aware of the syllabuses and this causes them more apprehension when teaching it (Task 3.4).

Task 3.4   Curriculum and specification

- Go through the departments chosen syllabus, its delivery in school, and timings, regarding the Non-Examination Assessment (NEA) aspects of the course.
- Link this with how the important skills in the lower school curriculum aid the development and understanding of these new elements to pupils as they move into the examination courses.
- Explore how the latest specifications have brought changes to the curriculum.

Audit your skills as a mentor and understand the important role you have in educating beginning teachers

As part of your role as mentor you should be looking to assist your beginning teacher to identify personal training needs. This will help them with confidence in tackling new processes, materials, technologies and health and safety requirements. As Fletcher (1998) notes good mentors have many roles including being a critical friend, counsellor and personal guide and this can become a positive relationship that is as important to the development of the mentor as the mentee.

Lofthouse and Thomas (2014) concur that to ensure a productive school experience your mentoring should be positive for everyone involved. Many mentors identify part of the role as that of transitioning the beginning teacher from the role of classroom observer, through to participant, team teacher and finally teacher, where confidence has grown, and they are able to independently deliver the lesson. You should be mindful about not just 'moulding' them to your own school identity but allow them to develop a teaching style more in line with the general requirements of learning to be a teacher.

Bondyk and Searby (2013) describe different mentoring paradigms to enable categorisation of mentoring activity and terminology. They discuss three paradigms that of 'traditional', whereby mentors work within existing cultures and behaviours; 'transitional', where innovation and creativity are linked with new social-cultural conditions and lastly 'transformative', whereby new emerging ideologies are considered (Bondyk and Searby 2013 cited in Lofthouse and Thomas 2014). Viewed through the D&T curriculum; some might determine to remain with old, outdated but familiar curricular projects whilst others would engage with new programmes and embed new ideologies into teaching. Recognising this about yourself is an important aspect of your teaching ideology. Mentors who act as trailblazers, identifying emerging and new technologies to enable beginning teachers to engage in a truly updated and forward-looking curriculum, are arguably the best of mentors. Mentors are the main part of the ecology of practice that can stimulate the beginning teacher to engage fully in both workplace and learning processes (Sayers et al. 2002). For you this will therefore entail allowing the beginning teacher to engage in the same activity and enable them to apply this knowledge in the real situation of the classroom and teaching activity (Task 3.5).

Engaging with additional CPD to develop your own mentoring skills

Task 3.5   Auditing mentoring skills and knowledge

Using local government policy documentation (like those of the National Standards for School-based Initial Teacher Training Mentors (2016) for England), audit your skills and understanding of mentoring practices.

- Approach your Senior Leadership team and request any support and training available for D&T mentors to increase knowledge and mentoring skills, whether it is school based, provider, university or local authority based.
- Engage in localised training with a provider, which is generally free, out of hours or has paid cover associated.

Teachers should consider education research findings regarding all aspects of teaching, including how children learn and how to develop their knowledge and pedagogical skills. Hoyle (1980) differentiated between two types of teachers. First, those that are conscientious practitioners with a limited outlook and second those extended professionals who seek to improve practice by learning from others and through continuing professional development (Hoyle 1980 cited in Sayers et al. 2002). They are keen and continuous learners involved in research and behaviours to embed theory into practice. Historically, it was more often the practice for mentors to make a distinction between teaching and that suggested by the theorists. Many schools are now engaged in research and embedding theory into teaching strategies, through a wide range of professional developmental activities. The following case study provides an example of this.

Case study: Matt's story

Over the last 2-3 years, staff have been engaged in cycles of inquiry and reflection. As the backbone for our Continuing Professional Development & Learning (CPDL) programme, all teaching and learning support staff are required to opt-in to a small, self-regulating group, or 'Learning Community', which meets once per half-term. These meetings are made possible by the late start of the school timetable on those days, buying 50 minutes of professional learning at the fresh end of the day, without the distractions that so often impact on focus at the end of a day.

Each Learning Community has its own specific theme, drawn from a range of strategic priorities (e.g. improving classroom talk, embedding formative assessment, developing literacy, embedding positive behaviours). Teachers opt-in to a specific Learning Community based on interest or a personal development priority: although a range of inquiry, questions will be explored within each community, these questions all nest within the community's theme, allowing for individual direction but maintaining internal alignment of the group.

The focus of each Learning Community is underpinned by a piece of essential reading; in most cases, a carefully chosen book (which typically offers an accessible entry point into the 'evidence' related to an area of practice). Each member of staff is lent a copy of the book from the Learning & Development Library for use across the school year. This key reading then acts as a stimulus for the learning of the group: although the peer-coaching that takes place at each Learning Community meeting is centred on the individual's classroom experiences, the core reading provides a framework or source of inspiration with which to unpack and probe each other's experiences.

At the end of each meeting, all members commit to an action plan, consisting of a carefully constructed inquiry question (e.g. 'If I do <intervention/strategy> with <specific group of pupils>, will it achieve <desired outcome>), a consideration of the likely impact measures, and an identification of something that the individual is going to stop doing/do less of in order to find time for professional learning. Progress and development is reviewed over the course of the year. This culminates with a Celebration of Inquiry INSET day, at which all staff share professional learning in seminar sessions.

In England, the Department for Education as part of its role to develop teaching excellence has a requirement that all teachers participate in, and take responsibility for, personal professional development. This sort of practice within schools is an ideal example. Effective CPD for you is an essential part of securing effective teaching and mentoring.

Indeed, in D&T even long service teachers do not necessarily have the skills and knowledge concerning all aspects of the subject. This is especially in terms of engagement with new and emerging technologies, so it is fundamental to your ability to keep abreast with modern technology, with continuous support and in-service training (Price and Reid 1993). This should avoid the obvious pitfall that teachers will stick to comfort zones and only teach aspects of D&T and projects they are confident to deliver.

This is vital to ensure pupil engagement and uptake at examination level. At the time D&T was introduced into the curriculum in 1989 (in England), some 95% of young people studied the subject at the age of 16+. Since then this has fallen to about 8% and, with the removal of food from D&T specifications, the prediction is that it will decline further (Barlex and Steeg 2017). Mentoring beginning teachers can engage your department with new knowledge and understanding as they may have this tacit, relevant and contemporary knowledge to share with you (Task 3.6).

Task 3.6   Get involved with your own learning and CPD

- Contact your local D&T Professional Association and consider what training they have available for you to attend.
- Speak to your Senior Leadership team and have attendance at examination board meetings built into your performance management.
- Search your local area, go to your local authority contact for free 'TeachMeets' or similar local groups to join (including closed social media groups) to remain within a community of practice of other D&T teachers.
- Subscribe to D&T Blogs to keep your knowledge up to date and relevant. (See other resources for examples.)

Summary

This chapter has explored the knowledge, understanding and skills a D&T mentor needs. This includes,

- Building core skills and subject knowledge. You have an incredibly important role in the building of confidence and pedagogical excellence and must be proficient at modelling this for mentees.
- Reflection is key to beginning teachers gaining understanding and being able to work reflectively to enable learning and knowledge growth.
- Mentors should possess a range of skills and a commitment to furthering knowledge to engage in mentoring beginning teachers effectively.

- You must be able to recognise your own learning needs and have a willingness to engage with CPD not only in mentoring but also subject-related training to further your own development.

Further resources

O'Leary, M. (2014) *Classroom Observation a Guide to Effective Observation of Teaching and Learning*. New York: Routledge.

   This book is an easy-read and gives some useful pointers for carrying out successful lesson observations with a specific focus. Chapter 8 has some very useful observation proforma to use.

DfE (2016) National Standards for School-based Initial Teacher Training mentors. Available at: www.gov.uk/government/uploads/system/uploads/attachment_data/file/536891/Mentor_standards_report_Final.pdfhttps://www.data.org.uk/. (Accessed: 21 November 2018).

   This standards document is a valuable auditing tool, to help you understand your developing skills as a mentor.

Design and Technology Association website: https://www.data.org.uk/

   Excellent website with a wealth of information, resources and where you can find all the Health and Safety documentation, CPD and the Core Competences documents.

Barlex, B. and Steeg, T. https://dandtfordandt.wordpress.com/about/ (Accessed: 21 November 2018).

   This is a beneficial website that is up-to-date and has a wealth of useful thoughts and ideas for teaching modern technology.

References

Banks, F., Leech, J. and Moon, B. (1999) New Understanding of Teacher's Pedagogic Knowledge, in Leach, J. and Moon, B. (eds.) *Learners and Pedagogy*. London: Paul Chapman Publications, pp. 89–110.

Barlex, D. and Steeg, T. (2017) David and Torben for D&T. Available at: https://dandtfordandt.wordpress.com/about/ (Accessed: 21 November 2018).

Colucci-Gray, L. and Fraser, C. (2008) Contested Aspects of Becoming a Teacher: Teacher Learning and the Role of Subject Knowledge. *Europe Research Education Journal*, Vol. 7, No. 4, pp. 475–486.

Department for Education (2012) *Standard for Teachers Professional Development*. London: Department for Education.

Department for Education (2013) *The National Curriculum for England*. London: Department for Education.

Department for Education (2016) *National Standards for School-based Initial Teacher Training Mentors*. London: Department for Education.

Fletcher, S. (1998) Attaining Self-Actualisation through Mentoring European. *Journal of Teacher Education*, School of Education University of Bath. Available at: www.teacher research.net/h_attainingselfact.htm (Accessed: 5 December 2017).

Lave, J. and Wenger, E. (1991) *Situated Learning: Legitimate Peripheral Participation*. Cambridge: Cambridge University Press.

Leach, J. and Banks, F. (1996) *Investigating the Developing 'Teacher Professional Knowledge' of Student Teachers*. Lancaster: Paper at BERA Conference.

Lofthouse, R. and Thomas, U. (2014) Mentoring Student Teachers; A Vulnerable Workplace Learning Practice. *International Journal of Mentoring and Coaching in Education*, Vol. 3, No. 3, pp. 201-218.

Lofthouse, R. and Thomas, T. (2017) Concerning Collaboration: Teachers' Perspectives on Working in Partnerships to Develop Teaching Practices. *Professional Development in Education*, Vol. 43, No. 1, pp. 36-56.

Martin, M. (2008) Competence in Question: The Relevance of the Design and Technology Association Minimum Competences to Initial Teacher Education, in Norman, E. W. L. and Spendlove, D. (eds.) *The Design and Technology Association International Research Conference*. Loughborough University, 2-4 July, pp. 23-29.

McLaren, S. (2017) Critiquing Teaching: Developing Critique through Critical Reflection and Reflexive Practice, in Williams, J. and Stables, K. (eds.) *Critique in Design and Technology Education*. 1st Edition. Singapore: Springer, pp. 173-192.

Murphy, C. (2005) The Role of Subject Knowledge in Primary Trainee Teachers' Approaches to Teaching in the Topic of Area, in Hewitt, D. and Noyles, A. (eds.) *Proceedings of the Sixth British Congress on Mathematics Education*. Warwick: University of Warwick, pp. 113-119.

O'Leary, M. (2014) *Classroom Observation a Guide to Effective Observation of Teaching and Learning*. New York: Routledge.

Owen-Jackson, G. (2008) Developing Professional Knowledge in D&T Secondary Initial Teacher Education. *International Journal of Technology and Design Education*, Vol. 18, No. 3, Depth 2.

Price, G. W. and Reid, D. J. (1993) *The Delivery of Technology Content in One-Year Initial Teacher Education Partnership Schemes*. IDATER 1993 Conference, Loughborough: Loughborough University.

Sayers, S., Morley, J. and Barnes, B. (2002) *Issues in Design and Technology*. London: Routledge.

Shulman, L. S. (1986) Those Who Understand: Knowledge Growth in Teaching. *Educational Research Review*, Vol. 57, pp. 1-22.

Snape, P. (2015) Pre-service Teachers' Conclusive Principles for Teaching Technology Education. *Design and Technology Education: An International Journal*, Vol. 21, No. 2, pp. 23-31.

Tomlinson, P. D., Hobson, A. J. and Malderez, A. (2010) Mentoring in Teacher Education, in Peterson, P. Baker, E. and McGaw, B. (eds.) *International Encyclopaedia of Education*. 3rd edition, Vol. 7, pp. 749-756.

Turner-Bisset, R. (1999) The Knowledge Bases of the Expert Teacher. *British Educational Research Journal*, Vol. 25, No. 1, pp. 39-55.

Welsh Government (2013) *Professional Standards for Teaching and Leadership*. Crown http://learning.gov.wales/resources/collections/professional-standards?lang=en (Accessed: 20 October 2017).

Williams, A. (1993) Teacher Perceptions of Their Needs as Mentors in the Context of Developing School-Based Initial Teacher Education. *British Educational Research Journal*, Vol. 19, No. 4, pp. 407-420.

4 Helping new design and technology teachers get the big picture; understanding the fundamental nature of design and technology

David Barlex, Nick Givens and Torben Steeg

Introduction

Design and technology (D&T) is unlike most school subjects in that it is a construct developed especially for the National Curriculum in England. Most of those who become teachers of the subject have degrees in related areas but these do not always cover the breadth or depth of the construct as developed for the National Curriculum. Hence, many beginning teachers find themselves in a situation where they have significant gaps in their subject knowledge and understandably much time is spent in 'filling' these gaps perhaps during subject knowledge enhancement programmes before initial teacher education and the PGCE year. The result is that many D&T teachers enter the profession having acquired significant subject knowledge that is extremely useful for teaching the specific details of the subject but without having had the opportunity to consider the fundamental nature of D&T and the broad intentions for teaching it. It is essential as a beginning teacher to address this shortcoming and that discussion with subject mentors can play a key role in the endeavour of helping those starting to teach the subject to get the Big Picture with regard to both the broad intentions of teaching and the underpinning ideas that inform its fundamental nature. The rest of this chapter is in four parts. Part one considers the intentions of the subject. Part two considers the nature of the subject. Part three considers the significant ideas that underpin the nature of the subject and part four provides a summary. In each of these parts there are tasks which you can use with beginning teachers to develop their Big Picture thinking about the subject.

Objectives

At the end of this chapter, you should be able to:

- Explain why D&T is an essential component of a balanced education for all pupils.
- Describe the richness and complexity of designing as an activity and understand how to build authentic designing into your curriculum plans.

- Describe what is meant by 'technology' with reference to some of the wider debates about the nature of technology.
- Use the Big Ideas 'of' and 'about' technology to inform curriculum planning.

The intentions of the subject

It is important to step back from the detail of the teaching and consider the overall intentions of teaching young people D&T. Some argue that D&T is an essential feature of general education for ALL young people irrespective of what their career aspirations might be. Here, we identify two overarching learning intentions for the subject: **technological capability** and **technological perspective** (Task 4.1).

- We define **technological capability** as designer-maker capability, capturing the essence of technological activity as intervention in the made and natural worlds.
- We define **technological perspective** a providing insight into 'how technology works' which informs a constructively critical view of technology, pre-empting alienation from our technologically-based society and enabling consideration of how technology might be used to provide products and systems that help create the sort of society in which young people aspire to live.

Task 4.1   Technological capabilities and perspectives

Discuss with your beginning teachers what they think about the ideas of technological capability and technological perspective. Do they agree that each is an important learning intention and that teaching to just one or other of these intentions would weaken D&T as a subject?

Barlex and Steeg (2017) have put forward four arguments for teaching D&T in the schools:

An economic argument

Studying the subject enables young people, across the attainment spectrum, to understand the range of careers available in the technical, design and engineering sectors. Increasing the number of young people who study the subject enlarges and broadens the pool of young people who become interested in following a career in these sectors.

A personal argument

Studying the subject enables young people to deploy design skills and technical problem solving to address and solve practical problems at both the personal and community levels

A social argument

Studying the subject enables young people to reach informed views on questions and disputes that have matters of design and/or technology at their core

A cultural argument

Studying the subject enables young people to appreciate and understand the grand narratives of technologies and the design thinking behind them as major achievements of our culture and are able to use this understanding in responding to the technologically driven changes in the society around them

A coherent case for the place of D&T in the curriculum needs to rest on all four arguments; omitting any of them undermines the rational for keeping the subject in the curriculum for all pupils and risks leaving a hole in the taught curriculum. These arguments provide a platform for advocating the importance of the subject to senior leaders, governors, parents and pupils. For example, the economic argument might be compelling to those who wish to pursue a technical, design or engineering career, whereas the personal argument may attract those who wish to take a 'hands on' approach to their personal and community living spaces. The social argument will appeal to those who wish to be active in debating the deployment of technologies in society and the cultural argument will engage those who wish to see themselves as technologically literate. However, whatever the reasons a young person chooses to study D&T, developing both technological capability and technological perspective will be important (Task 4.2).

Task 4.2   Subject rationale

Discuss with your beginning teachers what they think about the different reasons for teaching D&T. Which if any do they think should key stakeholders consider as the main reason for teaching the subject?

Suggest to your beginner teachers that they discuss with pupils and teachers in their placement schools why they think it is important to learn/teach D&T. Ask them to compare the reasons given with the reasons given in this chapter.

The nature of the subject

In deciding what to teach in D&T, it is important to consider both the nature of design and the nature of technology. These have quite separate intellectual traditions and one of the tasks of D&T as a school subject is to bring these two traditions together in a way that is both workable and rigorous.

Design

Designing is a complex activity. Lawson (2004, p. 20) makes an intriguing analogy with playing chess:

Designing then, in terms of chess, is rather like playing with a board that has no divisions into cells, has pieces that can be invented and redefined as the game proceeds and rules that change their effects as moves are made. Even the object of the game is not defined at the outset and may change as the game wears on. Put like this it seems a ridiculous enterprise to contemplate the design process at all!

Interestingly, this mirrors to quite a large extent the requirements of the conceptual challenge that young people will tackle in the new (England) single title GCSE.

Ropohl (1997, p. 69) has further described this activity as requiring:

> [The development and design of] a novel technical system, anticipat[ing] the object to be realised through mental imagination. [The designer] has to conceive of a concrete object which does not yet exist, and he [sic] has to determine spatial and temporal details which cannot yet be observed, but will have to be created by the designing and manufacturing process.

'Conceiving ... what does not exist' (Buchanan 1996, p. 7) and 'developing and designing a novel ... system' (Ropohl 1997, p. 69) indicate that pupils will, on occasion, be required to make conceptual design decisions. 'Developing and designing a ... technical system' (Ropohl) indicates that pupils will need to make decisions about the way their design will work, that is, make technical design decisions. 'Spatial and temporal details which cannot yet be observed' (Ropohl) indicates that pupils will need to make decisions about the appearance of their designs, that is, aesthetic decisions. Finally, 'created by the ... manufacturing process' (Ropohl) indicates that students will need to consider how they will make their design, that is, constructional decisions.

Ropohl (1997) does not explicitly consider the user, yet product designers have commented on how important it is to consider the user when developing design proposals and this is now explicit in the D&T National Curriculum and the new GCSE specifications. For example, Jonathan Ive, Apple's Chief Design Officer, says, 'the design of an object defines its meaning and ultimate utility. The nature of the connection between technology and people is determined by the designer' (Department for Education and Employment 1999, p. 14). This indicates that some of the decisions made by pupils should be informed by a consideration of the user. As these considerations will be broader than any one group of users, such considerations are perhaps better described as market considerations. This indicates that pupils will need to make decisions related to the market for their product.

Decisions in these five domains (conceptual, technical, aesthetic, constructional and marketing) are not made independently of one another, for as Buchanan (1996, p. 7) states, 'a designer must attend simultaneously to many levels of detail and make numerous decisions as he or she designs'.

Hence, we have adopted a design decision making model as a useful way of describing pupils' design activity in designing and making activities. It can be represented diagrammatically as shown below (Task 4.3).

Task 4.3   Views on design

Discuss with your beginning teachers what they think about the view of design presented in this chapter. To what extent do they agree with and disagree with this view?

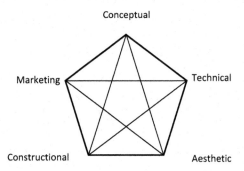

Figure 4.1 The design decision pentagon

Suggest to your beginning teachers that they use the design decision pentagon (Figure 4.1) to interrogate the design and make activities in their placement schools' D&T Key Stage 3 curriculum to identify the range of design decisions that pupils are required to make. Discuss the findings with your beginning teachers to explore whether this range is sufficient, inadequate or overly demanding and what changes might be needed to remedy any deficiencies.

Technology

Technology is not easy to define, as different philosophical positions lead to different definitions. Kelly (2010, p. 181) in his provocative book, *What Technology Wants*, discusses the idea of autonomous technology in terms of three interacting influences:

> The primary driver is pre-ordained development – what technology wants. The second driver is the influence of technological history, the gravity of the past, as in the way the size of a horse's yoke determines the size of a space rocket. The third force is society's collective free will in shaping the technium[1], or our choices.

From Kelly's perspective, it appears that the influence that mitigates against technological inevitability (society's free will) is the smallest of these influences. He entrenches this position by describing technological development in terms of a set of trends that contribute to the expression of specific technologies and how they might progress. For example, in this set he includes increasing sentience. This may give cause for concern given that deeply embedded in popular culture is the idea of machines becoming self-aware and either dominating human life, as in the film *Metropolis* (made in 1927), or deciding that humanity is antithetical to its own existence and actively waging war on humanity, as in the *Terminator* films (made in 1984, 1991, 2003 and 2009).

Nye (2006, p. 212) rejects this idea of technological autonomy:

> From the vantage point of the present, it may seem that technologies are deterministic. But this view is incorrect…. A more useful concept than determinism is technological

momentum, which acknowledges that once a system such as a railroad or an electrical grid has been designed to certain specifications and put in place it has a rigidity and direction that can seem deterministic to those who use them.

(p. 212)

Arthur (2009, p. 66) takes a different starting point in considering the nature of technology and the way it evolves. He argues that technology can be viewed as the exploitation of phenomena revealed by science. He rejects a simplistic 'technology is applied science' view but is adamant that it is from the discovery and understanding of phenomena that technologies spring. He notes that:

> It should be clear that technologies cannot exist without phenomena. But the reverse is not true. Phenomena purely in themselves have nothing to do with technology. They simply exist in our world (the physical ones at least) and we have no control over their form and existence. All we can do is use them where usable.

Naughton (in Banks 1994, p. 12) adds further weight to the rejection of a simplistic applied science view of technology when he writes that technology always involves 'ways of doing things ... a complex interaction between people and social structures on the one hand and machines on the other'. Naughton's description immediately complicates the D&T curriculum in that a consideration of machines, which many would see as a basis for a technology curriculum, becomes insufficient (Task 4.4).

Our view, informed by the preceding discussion, is that D&T as a school subject should take seriously the following aspects of technology:

- That technology is built on phenomena in the real world and pupils should develop understanding of the range of key phenomena that technology uses.
- That technology is a human activity and pupils should both experience a wide variety of technological activities and learn to consider the human and social implications of such activity.
- That our current technologies are built on previous technologies and that, in turn, the technologies being developed today will have implications for future technologies. Pupils should, therefore, develop understanding of these relationships and develop a critical mind-set about the use of technologies.

Task 4.4   Views on technology

Discuss with your beginning teachers what they think about the view of technology presented in this chapter. To what extent do they agree with and disagree with this view?

Suggest to your beginning teachers that they analyse a unit of work in their placement schools to find out if it develops a critical approach to human technological activity. If the unit of work is found to be lacking this dimension ask your beginning teachers to suggest activities that might remedy the situation.

Significant ideas that underpin the nature of the subject

The work of Harlen and colleagues (Harlen 2010) in developing statements of content for science education that were true to the nature of the subject may provide us with a useful model. They divided the content into ideas **about** science (that is, the way that science as a discipline works), and ideas **of** science (the key intellectual building blocks of science). What might be developed if the D&T community adopted such an approach? What would we list as ideas 'of' and 'about' D&T? (Task 4.5)

Ideas **about** D&T might include:

- Through D&T people develop technologies and products to intervene in the natural and made worlds;
- D&T uses knowledge, skill and understanding from a wide range of sources, especially but not exclusively science and mathematics;
- There are always many possible and valid solutions to technological and product development challenges, some of which will meet these challenges better than others;
- The worth of technologies and products developed by people is a matter of judgement;
- Technologies and products always have unintended consequences beyond intended benefit which cannot be fully predicted by those who develop them.

Task 4.5   Views about D&T

Discuss with your beginning teachers what they think about the ideas *about* D&T. To what extent do they consider them adequate? Which if any would they change? Are there any other ideas about D&T that they would add?

Ideas **of** D&T might include:

Knowledge of materials

Design and technological activity requires the use of materials; if someone is going to use materials they will need to know something about them. So, what would need to be known? Clearly, the idea of different materials having different properties is essential. Given the importance of eco-footprints then it will be useful to know something about sources of materials and how they are refined to the state where they are useful. Given the finite nature of the material world it would also be useful to know something about the estimated reserves of materials, especially those that are particularly useful and in short supply. This can be summarised as:

- Sources
- Properties
- Footprint
- Longevity

Making decisions about which materials to use are therefore complex and requires much more than a 'science' understanding of materials. De Vries (2007, p. 27) commented on this amusingly and with insight when he writes about whether an electron can be a good electron. Materials have the properties they do, intrinsically neither good nor bad, but in choosing which material to use we have to make a judgment which requires a range of knowledge and understanding. Of course, in D&T education we want young people not only to learn how to make such complex judgments for themselves, but also to analyse the judgments made by others. Hence, we believe that deliberately teaching something about materials in general is essential.

Knowledge of manufacturing

The next step, of course, is to be able to do something with these materials, and so manufacturing is an important idea of D&T. In broad sweep terms, manufacturing can be divided into four main methods (*subtraction, addition, forming and assembly*) and overlaid on each of these are methods of *finishing*. At the moment, addition is receiving considerable attention as additive manufacture is being used to produce items of both simplicity and complexity at very different scales to the point where it will almost certainly be possible, for example, to 'print' organs for transplant. So, this important area of D&T can be subdivided as:

- By subtraction
- By addition
- By forming
- By assembly
- With finishing

Deciding how a product will be made is also complex, as there will be many ways to achieve a particular 'making' outcome. This is further complicated in school in that it takes time to develop the knowledge of making processes into skilful use of those processes. So, we believe that deliberately teaching about manufacturing *in general* as well as teaching specific making skills is essential.

Knowledge of functionality

Most of the made-world has to 'work' so some knowledge of achieving functionality is required. Three categories seem useful: powering, controlling and structuring. Controlling is moving on in leaps-and-bounds with the embedding of electronic intelligence into everyday products becoming commonplace. The technology to achieve this is within the reach of schools through microcontrollers such as PICAXE, Crumble and micro:bit. Equally, providing power is developing in interesting ways in response to concerns about climate change, with a growing emphasis on the use of renewable power sources. Therefore, this important aspect of D&T can be subdivided as:

- Powering
- Controlling
- Structuring

Deciding how something is going to work involves complex decision-making. This is well exemplified by the Bayliss Wind Up radio – a radio powered by a battery isn't useful when batteries are in short supply or too expensive to buy (see https://en.wikipedia.org/wiki/Freeplay_Energy). Powering by means of human energy stored in a wound-up spring structured so it could control the release of energy slowly over time to operate a dynamo that powered the radio is an elegant application of the three 'Big' ideas concerned with function. Hence, we believe that deliberately teaching something about achieving function in general is essential.

Knowledge of design

Very little of the made-world comes into existence except through purposeful design. Knowledge of design is crucial and our conversations with teachers usually reveal that they believe many of their pupils find designing a particular challenge. In order to design four broad methods are needed: (a) identifying peoples' needs and wants, (b) identifying market opportunities, (c) generating, developing and communicating design ideas and (d) evaluating design ideas. This set of methods taken together and used sensibly enables young people to develop the abilities to envisage outcomes that do not yet exist and create them through choosing and using materials and embedding function. Hence, this important idea of D&T can be subdivided as:

- Identifying peoples' needs and wants
- Identifying market opportunities
- Generating, developing and communicating design ideas
- Evaluating design ideas

It is often argued that designing is difficult and can only be learned by tackling the activity itself (Choulerton 2015). We are convinced that identifying of a variety of design strategies and explicitly teaching pupils how to use these is important in D&T.

Knowledge of critique regarding impact

The question that immediately follows is to what extent are designed outcomes of worth?

How do they affect the lives of those who use them and those that make them? How do they affect the biosphere? Here we immediately see the need for critique. This is different from evaluation as defined in 'evaluating design ideas', in which the evaluator asks of a design idea/outcome: 'Did it do what it was supposed to?' In critique the question becomes: 'Is what it is supposed to do worth doing and what are its unintended consequences?' Two broad areas of critique are stewardship and justice. Critiquing for stewardship involves considering life cycle analysis and speculating about different economic models – the currently predominant linear economy and the circular economy as espoused by, for example, the Ellen MacArthur Foundation (2012, 2013). Regarding justice, all people should be able to live in freedom from hunger and fear and have shelter from harm. They should have opportunities to pursue happiness and make the best of their lives. The made-world, full of deliberately designed products, environments and systems, must be held to account by critique.

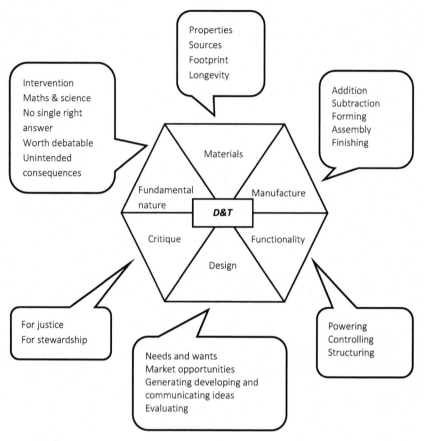

Figure 4.2 Significant ideas **of** and **about** D&T

So, critiquing the outcomes of others as well as their own is an important pupil activity for your beginning teacher to develop. This important idea of technology can be sub-divided as:

- For justice
- For stewardship

This critique should take place as a broad sweep at the level of an environment, a system or product, as well as at a more detailed level in which the decisions concerning the nature of small features within any of these can be subject to critical scrutiny.

Figure 4.2 summarises the Significant Ideas (Task 4.6).

Task 4.6   Ideas of D&T

Discuss with your beginning teachers what they think about the ideas *of* D&T. To what extent do they consider them adequate? Which if any would they change? Are there any other ideas of D&T that they would add?

Suggest to your beginning teachers that they use the significant ideas diagram (Figure 4.2) to audit the KS3 D&T National Curriculum and/or a D&T GCSE specification to identify where these ideas appear.

Note also that to gain a holistic picture of the subject, all the ideas 'of' and 'about' D&T will need to be considered together as they interact with one another when design and technological activity plays out in the hands of industrialists, politicians, the general public, designers, engineers and technologists.

Summary

- As a mentor you need to support beginning teachers of D&T, to be clear about why the subject you/they teach is in the curriculum. We have suggested four arguments that underpin D&T as an essential element of all pupils' education; the economic, the personal, the social and the cultural.
- We have also suggested that the overarching learning intentions for the subject are to develop technological capability and technological perspective.
- Developing understanding of the nature of designing and the nature of technology should be central to a D&T curriculum.
- There is a well-identified set of ideas both *about* D&T and *of* D&T that a D&T curriculum needs to encompass.
- A D&T curriculum should be designed so that the purposes, the nature and the big ideas of the subject become increasingly clear to pupils as they progress through it (Tasks 4.7 and 4.8).

Supplementary tasks

Task 4.7   Promoting the subject

Suggest to your beginning teachers that they write a flier for parents about the reasons for teaching and learning D&T. Discuss with them the extent to which the flyers reflect the different reasons for teaching the subject given in this chapter and whether the reasons are likely to convince sceptical parents as to the worth of the subject.

Task 4.8   Auditing key stage 3

Suggest to your beginning teachers that they use the significant ideas diagram (Figure 4.2) to audit their placement schools' KS3 curriculum to identify where these ideas are explicitly taught. If there appear to be significant gaps discuss with them how these might be rectified.

Summary and end note

In this chapter, we have considered the 'why' and the 'what' of teaching D&T but we have deliberately not considered the 'how' of teaching the subject. This was not because it is un-important but that lack of available space prevented us from giving it the attention it merits. In this Endnote we want to emphasise that one way to help ensure big ideas **of** and **about** D&T are all encompassed in a curriculum in a way that supports why it is important to teach the subject is to build around the 'four types of task' suggested by Barlex and Steeg (2017); designing without making, making without designing, designing and making and considering consequences.

Note

1   *What Technology Wants* focuses on human-technology relations and argues for technol-ogy as the emerging seventh kingdom of life on earth. The book invokes a giant force, the *technium*, which is 'the greater, global, massively interconnected system of technology vibrating around us'.

Further reading

Banks, F. and Barlex, D. (2014) *Teaching STEM in the secondary school Helping teachers meet the challenge.* Oxford: Routledge.

Barlex, D. and Steeg, T. (2017) *Big ideas in D & T.* Available at https://dandtfordandt.word-press.com/working-papers/big-ideas-for-dt/ (Accessed 21 November 2018).

Barlex, D. and Steeg, T. (2017) *Re-Building D & T in the secondary school curriculum Version 2.* Available at https://dandtfordandt.wordpress.com/resources/re-building-dt/ (Accessed 21 November 2018).

Barlex, D. and Williams, P., J. (eds.) (2017) *Contemporary research in technology education helping teachers develop research informed practice.* Singapore: Springer.

Williams, P. J. and Stables, K. (eds.) (2017) *Critique in design and technology education.* Singapore: Springer.

References

Arthur, W. B. (2009) *The nature of technology.* London: Allen Lane.

Barlex, D. and Steeg, T. (2017) *Re-building D&T in the secondary school curriculum Version 2.* Available at: https://dandtfordandt.wordpress.com/resources/re-building-dt/ (Accessed: 22 August 2018).

Buchanan, R. (1996) Wicked problems in design thinking, in Margolin, V. and Buchanan, R. (Eds.) *The idea of design* (pp. 3-20). Cambridge, MA: MIT.

Choulerton, D. (2015) *The current state of D&T.* Available at: www.slideshare.net/Ofstednews/design-and-technology-association-data-summer-school-keynote-2015 (Accessed 22 August 2018).

De Vries, M. (2007) Philosophical reflection on the nature of D&T, in Barlex, D. (Ed.) *Design and technology for the next generation A collection of provocative pieces, written by ex-perts in their field, to stimulate reflection and curriculum innovation* (pp. 18-31). Shropshire: CliffeCo.

Department for Education and Employment (1999) *Design and technology: the national curriculum for England.* London: Department for Education and Employment.

Ellen McArthur Foundation (2012) *Towards the circular economy Vol. 1: an economic and business rationale for an accelerated transition.* Available at: www.ellenmacarthurfoundation.org/publications/towards-the-circular-economy-vol-1-an-economic-and-business-rationale-for-an-accelerated-transition (Accessed 22 August 2018).

Ellen McArthur Foundation (2013) *Towards the circular economy Vol. 2: opportunities for the consumer goods sector.* Available at: www.ellenmacarthurfoundation.org/publications/towards-the-circular-economy-vol-2-opportunities-for-the-consumer-goods-sector (Accessed 22 August 2018).

Harlen, W. (2010) *Principles and big ideas of science education.* Hatfield: Association for Science Education.

Kelly, K. (2010) *What technology wants.* New York: Viking.

Lawson, B. (2004) *What designers know.* Oxford: Elsevier.

Naughton, J. (1994) What is 'technology'?, in F. Banks (Ed.), *Teaching technology* (pp. 7-12). London: Routledge.

Nye, D. E. (2006) *Technology matters.* Cambridge, MA: MIT.

Ropohl, G. (1997) Knowledge types in technology. *International Journal of Technology and Design Education,* 7(1), 65-72.

5 Helping beginning design and technology teachers to analyse and develop knowledge, skills and understanding of food preparation and nutrition

Jacqui Vaughan and Dave Howard

Introduction

In a new school setting, a beginning teacher will be relatively dependent on the mentor who will need to be supportive, knowledgeable and encouraging to enable the mentee to grow. Over-time the relationship will change as the mentee becomes more confident, self-assured and independent. Achieving the correct balance is a challenge itself as too much challenge and stimulation at the beginning can overawe and alienate the beginning teacher; too little later can restrict learning (McKimm et al. 2007). Being a mentor in a subject with a preponderance of practical work can be daunting. As the teacher, you have developed your own pedagogical approaches. You will be confident in how to provide a safe learning environment in which pupils can acquire knowledge and skills within a given time-frame. Enabling a beginning teacher to take on this responsibility needs careful management to ensure that you are providing a conducive, supportive environment for them to develop into effective practitioners who are also mindful of the safety and learning experience of the pupils.

This chapter will cover becoming a competent food teacher linking to the National Curriculum for Key Stage 3 and the relevant specifications for Key Stage 4 (DfE 2013a). Guidance supports the beginning teacher, with recommendations made to appropriate resources, support groups and frameworks. Links to existing theories support reflection. Advice and support throughout the chapter offer the opportunity to stimulate discussions allowing the beginning teacher to develop and establish own practice, underpinned by effective reflection.

Through the careful use of scaffolding the mentor can support the beginning teacher to gain confidence in writing suitable objectives to enable pupil progress and effective learning, utilising appropriate pedagogies.

The beginning teacher must establish confidence in the ability to use Food as a medium to develop pupils' imaginations and be creative while working safely, meeting the demands of time constraints and being prepared to challenge all abilities within groups. Tasks throughout the chapter enable the mentor to support the beginning teacher to develop self-confidence and capabilities.

The final section considers assessment and the particular subject challenges in particular, of practical work. It ends with some of the challenges a beginning teacher will face in the effective delivery of the subject.

Objectives

At the end of this chapter, you should be able to:

- Have a greater understanding of the role you will play in ensuring that beginning teachers you are mentoring gain confidence in pedagogical approaches to the subject.
- Identify the key stages in becoming a competent teacher of food and related subjects; share with beginning teachers assessment approaches to both practical and theoretical aspects of the related programmes of study.
- Recognise that the starting points of teachers of Food, Preparation and Nutrition will vary and that part of your role will be to instil a passion to deliver the subject in the most effective ways in the time available.

Becoming a competent food teacher

At Key Stage 3, food is part of the design and technology curriculum as 'cooking and nutrition'. The primary focus is 'to teach pupils how to apply the principles of nutrition and healthy eating, instil a love of cooking to open a door to one of the great expressions of human creativity' (DfE 2013, p. 3). At Key Stage 4, there is a variety of courses that a food teacher may be asked to teach including GCSE Food Preparation and Nutrition and Hospitality and Catering, offered as BTECs and GCSEs. A similar curriculum is offered across the UK although the title of the subject may be different; in Northern Ireland, it is called 'Home Economics'; in England, Design Technology (Food). It is worth looking at the Scottish Curriculum for Excellence, the Welsh School Curriculum and the Northern Ireland Curriculum to compare and contrast content. Depending on which context you are working in, the beginning teacher must use the relevant curriculum documents. Guidance from each country will contextualise the societal environment although much of the content will be generic and similar.

'Food teaching in secondary schools: knowledge and skills framework' (PHE 2015) is a guide to the knowledge and skills expected of secondary school teachers. It outlines the knowledge and skills that would be developed over time, resulting in exemplary food teaching.

The aim is to help secondary schools implement the requirements for food within the new National Curriculum for design and technology (D&T) in England, the GCSE Food Preparation and Nutrition and the Core Competences for Children and Young People aged 5-16 years. These curriculum measures, together with the other action points of the School Food Plan, seek to promote a 'pro-food' ethos in schools and heighten awareness of the integral part that food and a whole school approach plays in children's health, well-being and attainment. School food provision and how children keep themselves healthy will be monitored by the Office for Standards in Education, Children's Services and Skills (Ofsted) from September 2015 as part of the new Common Inspection Framework (PHE 2015).

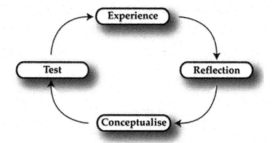

Figure 5.1 Kolb's reflective cycle (www.simplypsychology.org/learning-kolb.html)

A beginning teacher should be very reflective - of what they see in the classroom; what they see teachers and pupils doing to develop understanding of the teacher's role. Numerous reflective models that can be utilised; for example, Kolb (1984) recognises reflection as a cyclical process. Honey and Mumford (1992) identify that we are not equally skilled or comfortable at each of the four stages of the learning cycle. As a mentor, your role is to encourage and support the beginning teacher to find the most suitable method of reflection.

You may want to support the beginning teacher in identifying a suitable reflective model while considering the specific pedagogical content knowledge (PCK) (Shulman 1986) (Figure 5.1).

A typical mentor-mentee interaction would involve the following elements, within the Kolb cycle:

Using some coaching-style questions the mentor would draw out of the beginning teacher learning, including future developmental areas/targets. Such questions could include:

- What went well in the lesson today and why? Describe three positive elements of the session. (Based on concrete experience, involving first level reflections)
- What changes might you make to achieve even better outcomes? (Abstract conceptualisation)
- How does this inform your next steps? (Active experimentation including Schulman's concept of PCK)

The questions will vary depending on a range of factors but the key is that the beginning teacher is involved in personal learning, supported by a 'more knowledgeable other' (Vygotsky 1978, p. 86). As Kemmis (1985, p. 141) notes,

> we are inclined to think of reflection as something quiet and personal. My argument here is that reflection is action-oriented, social and political. Its 'product' is praxis (informed, committed action), the most eloquent and socially significant form of human action.

As the beginning teacher progresses and recognises the distinctive features of Food teaching perceptions and understanding of the reflective models may develop and change. The beginning teacher will choose the model they find most useful, most likely adopting an approach that is an amalgam or fusion of the best 'ingredients'. The same applies to mentors, no matter how experienced. We adapt our approaches over time. In addition, being a mentor allows double loop feedback to occur; this is an open-ended cycle where the teacher and the learner cooperatively examine both the learner's performance and the underlying perspectives the teacher brings to regard that performance. Thus, both the beginning teacher and the mentor reflect on learning. This emphasis on learning and the learner should be at the heart of our practice.

An initial area to explore with the beginning teacher is how to write objectives to ensure that the pupils can access the learning and understand what it is that they are learning. Working with food can provide the opportunity for pupils to unlock imaginations and be creative, to recognise their own ability using food, which they may not have previously had much experience of, and to see an instant result. No one is a 'blank slate' but beginning teachers will have different starting points in terms of knowledge, skills and experience. Having a clearly defined learning objective enables both beginning teacher and pupil to maximise this learning experience. A year seven pupil will need some initial understanding of timings, food, general hygiene and rules of working in a communal space while cooking. The early practical work planned with year seven groups tends to be a basic fruit or vegetable dish that does not require cooking. At this stage especially, it is about instilling a love for food, a desire to want to continue to have this experience and to replicate the learning on an ongoing basis.

The clear and specific objectives help the pupils focus on hygiene, timings and safety. All too often, however, the beginning teacher and the pupil, both during and at the end of the lesson rather than focusing on the objectives of the lesson, focus on the final product. In food, one cannot leave a half-finished product very easily unlike a painting or sculpture or piece of fabric. This is perhaps unique to Food teaching; in design and technology the product is extremely important, possibly more so than in other disciplines. The mentor's role is a crucial one here in supporting the beginning teacher to unpick what the specific focus of learning should be, helping establish the links to the start of the food journey and to the relevant National Curriculum or specification. As the beginning teacher gains confidence, it is also key to support them in finding ways to become advocates of this important subject. Food teaching is incredibly demanding, Successful pupil outcomes are because of the love and commitment teachers have for the subject. It is part of your role, as mentor, to encourage the beginning teacher along that journey. The joy that pupils demonstrate when they harness creativity through creating a product is often sufficient, but finding as many positives for the beginning teacher initially will be an important aspect of your early work with them.

The beginning teacher has to establish routines to ensure that the practical work is completed on time and successfully (see Chapter 9 on planning for practical activities). As a beginning teacher observes you, they may need guidance on recognising the more subtle aspects of what is happening in the classroom. You may want to ask them to complete an observation form to capture everything that happens.

The key areas of focus will be on:

- Timings
- Instructions to pupils
- The amount of support provided to pupils and how this is communicated (verbally or in written format, on a PowerPoint.)
- Effective learning (assessment)
- Managing the pupils' learning (behaviour, organisation, use of resources)

The routine to clean and tidy away after the practical is completed is also one of the most difficult aspects for a beginning teacher. Ask them to notice the key strategies that are used: How is equipment checked? How do you ensure that the room is ready for the next group? What happens if these routines are not established?

Opportunities for assessment need sharing with the pupils to prevent the focus just being on the final product. This involves the learners more and leads to greater attainment and achievement. (Such links need continually pointing out to the beginning teachers to enable them to move along the teaching–learning continuum)

Teaching ⟵ ─── ⟶ Learning

Most beginning teachers focus on teaching (the start of the line); expert teachers focus on the learning (the end of the line). The mentor role is to move the beginning teacher along the continuum. An emphasis on reflection enables the teacher to recognise and engage with the 'journey' they are on.

When organising a practical lesson there are several different approaches, mostly de-pendent on the experience, personality and practices of the department. It is helpful for the beginning teacher to experience a range of approaches but this is not always possible. However, different approaches can be discussed in mentor meetings.

If circumstances allow, the beginning teacher should be able to adopt an approach that maximises the learning opportunities for the pupils. An example of this would be:

> Pupils working independently to achieve a specific practical outcome. They would complete this by either following a written plan for the practical or following a set recipe.

Each of the aspects of the practical work should be accessible to the pupils without having to ask the beginning teacher questions at each stage; this may require: help cards, pic-tures, video clips, an appointed head chef for each group and key points demonstrated at appropriate times to support learning (mini plenary). Pupils have to be clear about the time items need to be in the oven by and expectations once they have completed the practical work. It is at these transition points that behaviour can become harder to manage. Enabling the beginning teacher to prepare for this will support the 'journey' to becoming an expert teacher. Clear guidance about moving pupils from a practical task to a written task will also be needed (Task 5.1).

Task 5.1 Classroom pedagogy

- Consider the key pedagogical approaches you would want a beginning teacher to understand prior to leading a practical food lesson.
- Work with a beginning teacher to write learning objectives that can be met by completing practical work or through alternative activity.
- How would you help establish skills in reflecting on the learning and the teaching?

As pupils gain experience in food lessons, the practical sessions should be planned to include more challenge. A mentor will enable the beginning teacher to approach these lessons with confidence; this itself is a challenge. Managing a class of inexperienced pupils cooking is daunting. A mentor needs to ensure that the beginning teacher can:

- Meet the needs of every pupil, including those identified with special and particular needs and those identified as more able.
- Differentiate the learning in different ways: by outcome; resource; support; dialogue; environment; time allocated.
- Ensure the content and approach, while meeting the requirements of the specification, are sufficiently engaging and relevant to the pupils.

Initially, pupils will also know the routines better than the beginning teacher. As we know pupils will often try to avoid clearing away and will take advantage of any signs of a lack of knowledge or experience in making this happen. The mentor needs to give the beginning teacher the necessary tools to enable them to be able to complete this effectively. Modelling of effective practice, in line with departmental and school policies, is very effective in this regard.

Expectations at the start of the lesson need to be clear: the key element is to remove ambiguity and achieve clarity and conciseness.

1. Define specific expectations
2. Communicate with no room for confusion
3. Set realistic goals
4. Review regularly
5. Offer specific and positive feedback.

As an established teacher, it can be easy to forget the level of organisation and skill that is required to carry out a successful food practical. As a mentor, you need to empower the beginning teacher with as much information as you can and then support them through the de-constructing and analysis of the lesson afterwards so they can move towards an efficient and effective model of delivery. They should not feel that they have to be clones, replicating how you do the task. Although working with a clone is a compliment to you, it will not benefit the beginning teacher. They do need to utilise your experience and expertise, however, to find effective ways and establish a professional identity. A skilled mentor will identify and nurture potential, while helping to develop understanding and insight by promoting skilful reflection. Coaching generally relates to performance improvement, in a specific skills area. Extrinsic feedback supports progress of the desired skills.

A beginning teacher should be encouraged to identify the theories that underpin learning. This is an ideal opportunity to consider the relevant theories of how pupils learn and the impact of effective teaching (Claxton 2002; Hattie 2010; Hattie and Yates 2014). The focus may well be on independent learning which accords with social constructivism whereby the teacher will provide scaffolding to support activity for the pupils to travel a distance between the actual and determined development level, otherwise known as the zone of proximal development (Vygotsky 1978). The same scaffolding analogy applies between mentor and beginning teacher; ultimately, the scaffolding should be removed (Task 5.2).

Task 5.2   Mentoring or coaching?

- Consider the requirements for a practical activity; will you be mentoring or coaching the beginning teacher to teach?
- What is your role in ensuring that the beginning teacher knows how to keep the pupils safe in a practical environment?
- Is it permissible for a mentor to intervene in the lesson?
- Is planning sufficiently focused on learning? For example, what the pupils will actually be doing and why?

The most effective method to deliver Food education is through practical experience; however, it is essential to plan for the delivery of the theoretical knowledge that underpins the practical for the learners to develop a wider knowledge of Food to include, for example, identifying nutritional value, where food grows, the function of ingredients and making wise food choices. This range of knowledge, wherever possible, is ideally interwoven within a practical lesson or linked to a practical task as this will lead to better engagement and learning from the pupils.

An experienced and successful teacher will have the expertise to move the pupils between tasks, focussing on completing the learning objectives. It is at this transition point, particularly when pupils are completing practicals at different rates, that beginning teachers find the class difficult to manage. As a mentor, you will need to examine and explore this stage of the lesson and assist the beginning teacher to recognise what is happening and managed. Often, a suitable approach is to have additional activities (interesting and short ones) planned and easily accessible. These could include websites to explore; additional facts around the objectives; support for peers; self-checklists; pupil ideas for homework.

Helping the beginning teacher to organise practical lessons in such a way that it is the expectation for pupils to complete other work once the practical is complete, will help them meet the lesson's objectives. You might want to suggest they use music for the clearing away, for example, a particular piece of music that by the end signals all clearing should be complete can work well. Alternatively, award points for groups who meet certain criteria:

- Those who are the most effective team
- Those who have the cleanest working area
- Individuals identified for excellent practice to be appointed as head chef next lesson or chef of the week this lesson

How rewards are used by the beginning teacher, consistent with departmental and school policies, can be very helpful and help establish positive relationships within the classroom.

Within the curriculum, food technology/food and nutrition is possibly the only subject in some schools where parents provide the resources on a weekly basis for the pupils. This could create an initial challenge, as parental involvement will vary according to affluence, engagement, knowledge and understanding. This does differ across authorities and schools but is still an area where, as a mentor, you will need to support the beginning teacher to enable them to find ways for the pupils to access and achieve learning outcomes through a variety of media. For example, without ingredients they could watch a YouTube demonstration on an iPad, create a relevant, written resource or create a poster or presentation to teach others.

Often beginning teachers will only plan for the pupils who provide ingredients but not planning for pupils who have not brought ingredients is not addressing the needs of all learners. This is a particular challenge and one that you will have experienced which will enable you to support your beginning teacher (Task 5.3).

Task 5.3   Resourcing the lesson

Unlike other subjects, not bringing resources can be problematic, impacting learning unless this contingency is thought about and planned for. An interesting discussion to have with the beginning teacher will be:

- Can all pupils achieve the same objective with or without ingredients?

Imagine the scenario in which 50% of the pupils have omitted some ingredients or not brought any. What advice would you give the beginning teacher?
    Things to consider:

- Frequency of this occurrence
- Technician support and budget of the department
- Group work despite a sense of 'is this fair?' from some pupils (management of expectations)
- Alternative written work that nevertheless meets the lesson's objectives
- Impact on delivering the National Curriculum or specification
- Future planning to avoid a recurrence - contingency in place.

Assessment

Assessing pupil progress at Key Stage 3 in the area of design and technology (food) may offer particular subject-specific challenges due to the nature of the subject having both practical and theoretical elements. Photographic evidence does support the assessment process, especially in Key Stage 4. Normally, in Key Stage 3, assessment is ongoing through the product-making process and, where applicable, at the final stage of the product being ready for inspection. Normal assessment strategies and practices apply, consistent with the school's own assessment policy and practices. Your role as the mentor will be to ensure that beginning teachers are familiar with, and understand the assessment policy and follow it effectively. Assessing practical work can be more of a challenge and one that is better addressed if the assessment clearly links to the learning objectives and learning outcomes. The beginning teacher will need to be able to utilise formative and summative assessment approaches appropriately. Formative assessment is very useful to gauge pupil understanding and learning *in situ*. The types of formative assessment that might be used to support a food lesson would be to evaluate a practical outcome, peer assessment, targeted questioning while delivering new information or completing a quiz or question sheet related to the topic. Summative assessment will mainly happen at the end of a series of lessons in the form of a formal assessment, e.g. marking of a completed project, a written test or a practical test. Supporting the beginning teachers to consider what it is they will be assessing and how, while planning lessons will be the most effective way to support learning and development. Most importantly, assessment must not be a 'bolt-on' but an integral part of the learning and teaching nexus (Task 5.4).

Task 5.4   Assessing practical work

- What key assessment strategies do you use during a practical lesson?
- Write three tips for undertaking effective assessment of a practical lesson.
- For theoretical underpinning of practical controlled assessments, can you provide examples to support the beginning teacher?

A passion for food: its place in the curriculum

There are problems and challenges which face beginning teachers in the early career stages and one of them is facing inadequacies in subject knowledge, skills and attributes as a teacher (Romano 2008) (see Chapter 7). Introducing the beginning teacher to the best resources and how to keep up to date with subject (knowledge and pedagogy) is an essential part of the journey. You can encourage engagement with the National Curriculum of the relevant country and utilise online fora and frameworks.

As a mentor of the subject, you need to do as much as you can to instil the ideals of teaching through the medium of food. This will involve the identification of the many cross-curricular links and opportunities for pupils to achieve success in the subject. The AKO foundation, an expert group comprising The Jamie Oliver Food Foundation, Food Teachers' Centre, British Nutrition Foundation and the University of Sheffield Food Education (AKO, 2017) identified that poor food practices are widespread in primary and secondary schools in England. This is despite the launch of the government's School Food Plan (2013). Similar groups exist across the UK, trying to influence government policy and societal practices. As the Irish Food Writers Guild has stated, 'While food education has improved, critical thinking skills and cooking experience are lacking.' (Irish Food Writers' Guild 2015).

In Chapter 7, we look at auditing of subject knowledge in design and technology. An audit of the beginner food teacher's starting point – skills and knowledge – would be extremely useful and identify any areas for development as well as current strengths. The food teacher portfolio (British Nutrition Foundation 2018) enables food teachers, at all career stages, to audit, plan, organise and record professional development. Although developed in England, this can be utilised by food teachers in Northern Ireland, Scotland and Wales, free of charge. The food teacher portfolio links to the framework of knowledge and skills (PHE 2015). The booklet also considers what makes a successful food teacher and what a teacher's professional development journey is. There is space to plan development needs and a chart on which to evidence the professional learning experiences. This portfolio would be extremely useful for a beginning teacher – to support reflection; to evidence competence in teaching the subject and to record their professional journey (Task 5.5).

Task 5.5   Professional development

Encourage your beginning teacher to register online for the audit – http://www.fooda factoflife.org.uk/section.aspx?t=0&siteId=20&sectionId=126

- Co-construct an action plan to address the areas for improvement including review points.
- Where possible, encourage the beginning teacher to network, sharing audit 'gaps' online or face to face with peers.

You also need to encourage the beginning teacher to focus on the many cross-curricular opportunities while planning lessons, encouraging them to consider cross-curricular links, areas of interest, news items and 'hot' topics. Currency in content really does engage learners and impact pupils' motivation.

Teacher workload has been under review since 2014; outcomes include a DfE-recommended poster and pamphlet directly linked to marking, planning and data management (DfE 2017). To utilise existing resources is one way to reduce the amount of hours spent planning lessons and creating resources. The Food Teachers' Centre, founded by Louse Davies in 2013, is one of the most prolific online fora and an excellent resource. Often once qualified, the beginning teacher may find they are the only food practitioner within school. Food teachers, using this online forum, are able to support each other very successfully. Ideas and resources are shared; success stories recounted and questions answered. Another resource can be a visit undertaken to a food-production factory or a food retail outlet. Additionally, visiting speakers can add currency, credibility and career aspiration; for example, a visit from a local chef or a 'Ready, Steady Cook' type event with invited guests. Involvement in food competitions, often sponsored by Local Authorities or supermarkets, are useful in raising the profile of the subject, boosting pupils' self-esteem and recruiting pupils to study the subject (Task 5.6).

Task 5.6   Subject support

- Visit http://www.foodafactoflife.org.uk/
- Review the resources available.
- Be willing to share your favourite resources, websites, subject journals etc.
- Work with your beginning teacher to plan for a visit or a visitor to enhance learning.

Summary

For a beginning teacher there are myriad opportunities to develop and hone the skills required to be an effective teacher. Observing a beginning teacher's progress can be incredibly rewarding. The role of mentor can be crucial in helping the beginning teacher establish an approach to their teaching career. Through your effective modelling and support, they can develop a professional identity. While you are raising questions with the beginning teacher, there will always be self-reflection happening, including the beginning teachers asking themselves questions. Sometimes they can be harsher self-critics than is warranted by their performance. The beginning teacher may raise questions for you about your own practice as well as theirs. This provides an opportunity for you to become the best practitioner you can be. The relationship between mentor and mentee, therefore, can be symbiotic and mutually beneficial. When we stop reflecting, we should probably stop teaching.

The list below summarises the information in the chapter.

- Although there are different curricula in the different countries, generic themes are evident. Ultimately, effective learning arises from effective teaching. Effective teaching arises from effective learning. As a mentor, you can be very influential over beginning teachers.
- Subject knowledge is as important as the associated pedagogy; beginning teachers need to observe good practice to help develop.
- The mentor as well as being a vital role model of good practice, must facilitate the beginning teacher's ability to accurately and fairly reflect
- The mentors, as advocates of this important subject, must try to sustain the motivation and commitment to Food teaching in beginning teachers
- Teaching and learning are on a continuum – the mentor is critical in helping move the beginning teacher along the continuum
- Mentors need to ensure that the practical elements of the subject are emphasised and addressed competently by the beginning teachers.

Effective assessment of practical and theoretical elements of food need to be planned, resourced and delivered with clear links to the learning outcomes and clear success criteria. A range of approaches should consider the needs of every pupil.

Be aware of the teacher workload reforms and utilise widely available resources there is no need to re-invent the wheel. With society's emphasis on obesity; healthy lifestyles and choice, the subject is particularly important. Use up to date data from reputable websites and sources.

Further resources

http://foodteacherscentre.co.uk
FOOD TEACHERS CENTRE is a UK based self-help group for secondary teachers founded by Louise Davies in 2013 and supported by experienced associates. It provides a platform to exchange best practice, give advice and support to less experienced teachers, answering practical concerns and keeping them abreast of the latest curriculum changes. It is a one-stop shop for like-minded professionals who seek help through authoritative and accurate information.

www.nutrition.org.uk/foodinschools/curriculum/the-curriculum.html
This website identifies important nutrition research, new reports, relevant policy and legislation. It captures thoughts on the facts behind the headlines, the science of nutrition and its importance to health for health professionals, academics, food industry and media. It explores why good nutrition and lifestyle choices are important for health and wellbeing across all ages.

www.jamiesfoodrevolution.org/
This website has a running count of the number of people supporting internationally the food revolution campaign. It contains up to date information about projects and groups that are working toward improving the nation's education about food and its effects on health, including the concerns around obesity, particularly in young people. It is easy to access and considers actions to become part of the food revolution.

www.foodafactoflife.org.uk/
'Food – a Fact of Life' provides a wealth of free resources about healthy eating, cooking, food and farming for children and young people aged 3–18 years. The resources are progressive, stimulate learning and support the curriculum throughout the UK. All resources aim to deliver consistent and up-to-date messages.

References

AKO Foundation (2017) *A Report on the Food Education Learning Landscape*. Available at: www.akofoundation.org (Accessed: 23 March 2018).

British Nutrition Foundation (2018) *Food in Schools*. Available at: www.nutrition.org.uk (Accessed: 14 February 2018).

Claxton, G. (2002) *Learning for Life in the 21st Century: Sociocultural*. Hoboken, NJ: Blackwell Publishing.

Department for Education (2013a) *National Curriculum Design and Technology Food*. Available at: www.gov.uk/government/publications/national-curriculum-in-england-design-and-technology-programmes-of-study (Accessed: 31 January 2018).

Department for Education (2013b) *The School Food Plan*. Available at: www.gov.uk/government/publications/the-school-food-plan (Accessed: 21 November 2018).

Department for Education (2017) *Teacher Workload: Pamphlet*. Available at: www.gov.uk/government/publications/teacher-workload-poster-and-pamphlet (Accessed: 31 January 2018).

Hattie, J. (2010) *Visible Learning*. London: Routledge.

Hattie, J. and Yates, G. (2014) *Visible Learning and the Science of How We Learn*. London: Routledge.

Honey, P. and Mumford, A. (1992) *The Manual of Learning Styles*. Maidenhead: Berkshire Peter Honey Publications.

Irish Food Writers' Guild (2015). Available at: www.irishfoodwritersguild.ie/education.html (Accessed: 31 January 2018).

Kemmis, S. (1985) 'Action Research and the Politics of Reflection', in Boud, D., Keogh, R. and Walker, D. (eds.) *Reflection: Turning Experience into Learning*. New York: Kogan Page Ltd., pp. 139–141.

Kolb, D. A. (1984) *Experiential Learning: Experience as the Source of Learning and Development*. Available at: www.learningfromexperience.com/images/uploads/process-of-experiential-learning.pdf (Accessed: 31 January 2018).

McKimm, J., Jollie, C. and Hatter, M. (2007) *Mentoring Theory and Practice Developed from 'Preparedness to Practice, Mentoring Scheme' July 1999*. London: NHSE/Imperial College School of Medicine.

PHE Public Health England (2015) *Food Teaching in Secondary Schools: Knowledge and Skills Framework*. Available at: www.gov.uk/government/publications/food-teaching-in-secondary-schools-knowledge-and-skills-framework (Accessed: 06 April 2018).

Romano, M. (2008) *Successes and Struggles during the First Year of Teaching: An Examination of Three Third-Grade Teachers*. Available at: www.google.co.uk/search?q=Romano%2C+M.+(2007)+Successes+and+struggles+during+the+first+year+of+teaching (Accessed: 05 March 2018).

Shulman, L. (1986). Those who understand: Knowledge growth in teaching. *Educational Researcher, 15*(1), pp. 4-14.

Vygotsky, L. S. (1978). *Mind in Society: The Development of Higher Psychological Processes*. Cambridge, MA: Harvard University Press.

6 Helping new D&T teachers to analyse and develop knowledge and understanding in design and technology (product design)

Matt McLain

Introduction

In other chapters we have seen, and will see, that the current professional standards for teachers in England require that beginning teachers demonstrate a high level of subject knowledge and pedagogy (DfE 2011, p. 11), including keeping up to date with developments – particularly relevant to the rapid changing nature of technology that affects the design and technology (D&T) curriculum. Similar statements are part of the professional knowledge and understanding standards for the General Teaching Councils for Scotland (GTCS) and Northern Ireland (GTCNI).

It is a commonly held view that teachers' subject knowledge is an essential component of effective teaching (DfE 2010, 2011; Shulman 1986), alongside effective pedagogical/didactic skills, and contextual knowledge of learners, schools and policy. In a recent study of D&T teachers' views about demonstration as a signature pedagogy, competence with regard to subject knowledge was ranked higher than pedagogical approaches that consolidated learning and facilitated independence (McLain 2017).

However, research indicates that subject knowledge does not appear to be the most important factor, though it may influence 'teaching effectiveness up to some level of basic competence but less so thereafter' (Hattie 2009, pp. 113-114). The teacher's **empathy** (to understanding learning and learners) and **verbal ability** (articulation of concepts and processes), combined with subject knowledge, together appear to be essential characteristics of effective teaching: 'greater than the sum of the parts and if one is missing the effectiveness is reduced by more than a third' (p. 115). The ability to deconstruct, reconstruct and communicate knowledge, engaging learners at their current level of attainment, is an essential skill for teaching, making subject competence a threshold standard, rather than a defining feature.

This chapter focuses on the tricky topic of teacher knowledge in D&T, how to help beginning teachers analyse and develop it, during initial teacher education (ITE) and early career development (Task 6.1).

Objectives

At the end of this chapter, you should be able to:

- Reflect on and recognise the complex nature of teachers' knowledge.
- Identify the key elements of D&T knowledge.
- Identify, analyse and document your areas of strength and for development.
- Plan early career subject knowledge development.

What is knowledge?

Task 6.1   Knowing knowledge

Thought experiment – What does it mean to know something? Identify an aspect of D&T knowledge that you know that a beginning teacher needs to develop, such as user-centred design. What knowledge you need to (a) explain what it means, (b) demonstrate how to do it and (c) enable learners to do it, capably and/or autonomously? How do factors such as the age of the learner affect the required knowledge? How do you know when you have sufficient knowledge?

The nature of knowledge is a complex and much debated area with its own field of study, epistemology, dating back to philosophers in ancient Greece (Scharff and Dusek 2003). Plato defined knowledge as 'justified true belief', a view much debated in the intervening years (Gettier 1963). Indeed, some of the problems with knowledge in D&T and modern assumptions about the relationship between theory and practice may stem from translations of the Greek words *epistêmê* (commonly translated as knowledge) and *technê* (translated as craft or art). The word technology stems from the Greek *technê* and epistemology from *episteme* further reinforcing an apparent division informing the knowledge verse skill debate (*cf* Scharff and Dusek 2003).

Ryle (1949) proposed a more helpful approach to knowledge, for our purposes: *knowing that* (conceptual) and *knowing how* (procedural), an idea more recently applied to technology education by McCormick (1997). This view of knowledge removes the division between mind (thinking) and body (acting), which has fuelled the debate around whether D&T is academic, practical, creative and/or vocational, since its introduction to the curriculum in the later part of the twentieth century (Kimbell, Stables and Green 1996). McCormick (1997, p. 143) describes conceptual knowledge as being actively concerned with *relationships* between '"items" of knowledge' as opposed to a passive 'collection of unrelated facts'; and procedural knowledge relates to the *application* of knowledge, such as process, problem solving and strategic thinking.

The mentor can assist the beginning D&T teacher to gain an understanding that, in addition to cultivating subject knowledge, they must also develop 'teacher knowledge' and 'knowledge for teaching'. *Teacher knowledge* encapsulates the aforementioned ability to successfully articulate knowledge taking account of prior and age-related learning. *Knowledge for teaching* focuses on the knowledge of internal and external curricular frameworks, including formal and terminal examinations, and how to develop personal capability, pedagogy and didactics. In the following sections, we will explore the nature of knowledge for the teacher and in D&T.

What is teacher knowledge?

Shulman (1986) proposed three categories of professional teacher knowledge: *subject content knowledge, pedagogical content knowledge* and *curricular knowledge*. When exploring how teachers view practice Shulman described teacher knowledge in terms of *principles, maxims* and *norms*. Principles being areas of knowledge supported by the wider body of research, maxims as the everyday practice and experience of teachers (that might be thought of as generally conscious or tacit accepted practices) and norms the values and philosophical perspectives of the individual and institutions, which influence and inform practice.

The mentor can use Shulman's principles, maxims and norms as a framework to aid reflection and challenge the beginning teacher's assumptions, to develop self-awareness and depth of knowledge. For example, research (*principle*) might indicate that collaborative design activities are effective in developing pupils' ideation (idea generation and development) skills. However, the beginning teacher's experience might be limited to pupils working on design ideas individually and build a range of assumptions, reinforced by what they observe in other classrooms (*maxim*). Furthermore, when introducing new practices into teaching they may appear to be unsuccessful, which may be because there is not yet a culture in the classroom that promotes this way of learning, or there is a lack of shared confidence (*norm*).

Beginning teachers have a limited experience to drawn on as well as limited access to what Shulman describes as 'cases' – examples of practice. Similarly, an experienced teacher can be biased by the availability of the 'cases' they have observed in their lessons, or those of colleagues. Therefore, mentor and beginning teachers' engagement with the wider D&T community of practice through research, professional updates and dialogue with teachers in other schools is essential to developing and maintaining an open mind to new ideas and a broader perspective on the effectiveness of differing pedagogical approaches to subject teaching. This in turn, facilities strategic knowledge expressed through effective lesson and curriculum design (Task 6.2).

Task 6.2 Perspectives

An effective starter to a mentoring conversation around teacher knowledge might begin with 'In 5 years' time, when you are a head of department...' Discuss the opportunities and challenges of curriculum design and teacher knowledge in D&T. What are the differences in perspective between the mentor and the beginning teacher?

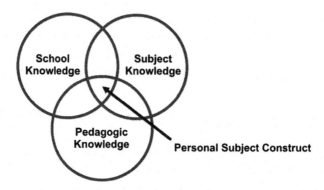

Figure 6.1 Teachers' professional knowledge (Banks, Leach and Moon 2005)

Banks, Leach and Moon (2005), building on the work of Shulman, introduced graphic model (Figure 6.1) to support the development of reflection in D&T ITE, where *school knowledge* expands curricular knowledge, focusing on the didactic transformation of knowledge (including curriculum and classroom management) and context (including cultural, historical and ideological factors).

Mentors can use these categories with beginning teachers to discuss emerging and developing knowledge, recognising that subject knowledge is not an 'entity' in its own right, unaffected by context. For example, in a D&T food lesson, the teacher might be introducing knife skills to pupils. The beginning teacher needs not only to be knowledgeable about correct and safe technique (bridge and claw methods) and tools (the correct knife and cutting board), but also mindful of the constraints of what pupils (a) know already, (b) can observe during a demonstration and (c) can access in a large classroom (pedagogical knowledge). They must also be aware of the place the demonstration has in the wider curriculum and cultural norms in the school (school knowledge). In this manner, the mentor can use these three categories as 'lenses' through which to view knowledge and experience in the classroom.

Vygotsky (1978) introduced the idea of the More Knowledgeable Other (MKO) where the teacher has a knowledge and understanding of a subject that the learner does not yet possess, and the role of the MKO is to make learning explicit in a meaningful context. The role of a mentor is to support the beginning D&T teacher, when developing an aspect of their subject knowledge, to gain an 'understanding of a process, including sequence, related knowledge and next steps' (McLain 2017, p. 2). This is more than being able to repeat a procedure competently, it is deliberate practice (Ericsson and Pool 2016), where a mentor provides feedback and the beginning teacher reflects with the aim of developing expertise. This feedback is an important means of 'holding a mirror to' a beginning teacher's practice. A skilful mentor will recognise this, framing feedback that reflects observations to prompt self-evaluation, rather than making an immediate judgement – for example 'I notice that learners..., how could you...?' rather than 'You need to develop... for the next lesson' (Task 6.3).

Task 6.3 Framing feedback

Have a mentoring conversation with a beginning teacher about their developing subject knowledge, without giving direct instructions. Focus on observations ('I noticed that...' and use questions to (a) draw out the impact that their subject knowledge had on learning and progress in the lesson and (b) identify actions for the next lesson.

Vygotsky's social constructivism focuses on how human beings learn through social interaction with peers and experts. The learner is supported by a MKO to realise personal potential, described as the 'within reach and yet to be grasped' Zone of Proximal Development (ZPD). The ZPD 'is the distance between the actual developmental level... and the level of potential development... under adult guidance or in collaboration with more capable peer' (p. 86). Therefore, the role of a teacher is to facilitate learning through approaches that are teacher-centric (e.g. modelling, explaining and questioning) and learner-centric (e.g. discovery learning, group work and designing). This is where the idea of scaffolding learning comes from, and what you must help the beginning teacher to realise is that at some point (to continue the metaphor), the scaffolding needs to come down and the structure (learning) must stand on its own (Task 6.4).

Task 6.4 Developing independence

Identify a procedure that learners use repeatedly throughout their schooling in D&T, such as using a drilling or a sewing machine. Plan a demonstration for a group of 11 year olds using the procedure for the first time. What are the key steps in the process? What are the health and safety considerations? Now plan how you would teach the same skill to the same group in three years' time. How would you adapt your approach? What are the risks of not using a scaffolded approach? (i.e. always demonstrating in the same way.)

In order to take on the role of the MKO, the beginning D&T teacher must not only model and explain concepts or procedures, they must also understand them in order to identify and address misconceptions or incorrect practice. For example, when teaching pupils to solder an electronic circuit board, the beginning D&T teacher should understand why it is important to heat both the pad on the board and the component leg in order to make a complete joint between both surfaces. This includes (a) what it looks like when it is effective and it is not and (b) how to diagnose errors (including those that cannot be observed visually). By working with a beginning D&T teacher to develop subject knowledge, the mentor is able to discuss how deeper subject knowledge helps them to assess pupils' understanding. In this way, the mentor aids the beginning teacher's deliberate practice.

Similarly, the beginning D&T teacher's knowledge of design processes and techniques will help them plan activities, for example, to avoid fixation on one or a limited range of ideas when pupils are designing (DfE, 2015a; McLellan and Nicholl, 2011).

Therefore good subject knowledge helps the beginning D&T teacher, not only to plan effective learning, by identifying the correct steps and sequences, but also to formatively and diagnostically assess pupils' progress, identify and address barriers to learning and promote progress.

What is D&T knowledge?

D&T knowledge is 'multi-dimensional' (McCormick 1997, p. 144), requiring interaction between thinking and acting. Kimbell et al. (1991) discuss the essential interaction between mind and hand, articulated in Figure 6.2, reflecting the essential role that designing and making play in D&T activity, undergirded by critiquing skills. The notion of 'task-action-capability' has been a feature of D&T, involving active and purposeful use of knowledge, often through extended design and make projects (Kimbell and Perry 2001). Knowledge in D&T is complex and extends beyond the boundaries of school subjects, as recognised in national and school curricula (Black and Harrison 1985).

In addition to knowledge about technological principles, concepts and processes (including the manipulation of materials and control of processes), designing and making is an essential component of D&T learning. This can be expressed as **design and make** (or design, make and evaluate) activities, with the associated benefits of the aforementioned mind and hand interaction through ideation and modelling, as well as the inherent limitations of the resources, facilities and knowledge available. Alternatively, focused tasks involving **mainly making** with limited or no design input (Banks and Owen-Jackson 2007) have also been popular pedagogical approaches in D&T, providing opportunity to learn and replicate craft skills and technical processes, with limited opportunity for creativity (Barlex and Trebell 2008). However, there is a risk that in teaching D&T solely through activities that involve the making of products/prototypes that these become merely making activities masquerading as design and make, with a thin veneer of aesthetic design. Similarly,

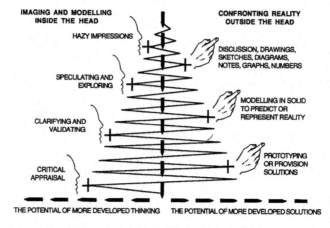

Figure 6.2 The interaction of hand and mind (Kimbell et al. 1991)

even genuine design and make activities have their limitations, as outlined above. Other approaches that encompass the wider aspects of creativity and critique include **mainly designing** activities, or designing without making (Barlex 2006; Barlex and Trebell 2008) and **exploring technology and society** (Barlex 2003). When approaching subject knowledge, it is important for the mentor and beginning teacher to be cognisant of not just the procedural knowledge (knowing how) of a technological procedure, but also of the context of how it is applied and effective pedagogical approaches. In order to do this effectively, the mentor and beginning teacher must have an understanding of the signature pedagogies in D&T, along with inherent benefits and limitations. For example, the demonstration as a signature pedagogy in D&T (McLain, 2017) is a direct teaching method well suited to mainly making activities, yet can have a limiting effect on creativity in mainly designing activities (McLellan and Nicholl, 2011; Task 6.5).

Task 6.5   Pedagogical approaches

Read and discuss the papers by McLain (2017) and McLellan and Nicholl (2011), undertaking a SWOT (strengths, weaknesses, opportunities and threats) analysis in relation to planning lessons for the following week. Discuss the benefits and limitations of 'restrictive' (e.g. direct teaching) and 'expansive' (e.g. discovery learning) pedagogical approaches in D&T. What ideas will inform lesson planning for the next week?

Challenges for D&T knowledge

Recognising the complexity of D&T knowledge, there are four key challenges that may be helpful to articulate:

The *first* is that technology is a complex word, aside from D&T as a curriculum entity. Mitcham (1994), reviewing various strands of the philosophy of technology, identifies four modes of the manifestation of technology: technology as *object* (products including clothing, utilities, tools and systems); technology as *knowledge* (skills, rules and theories); technology as *activity* (including designing and making); and technology as *volition* (including human motivation and intentionality). Viewing D&T through one of these 'modes' to the exclusion of others may limit the experience of D&T in the classroom.

The original intentions for D&T in the National Curriculum in England looked beyond school D&T "...not only to solve practical problems, to invent, optimise and realise solutions, but also so that we can acquire a sense of its enormous transformatory power".

(DES/WO 1988, p. 6)

Second, it is important to acknowledge that D&T is perceived to have a less clearly defined knowledge base than subject such as mathematics or science (DfE 2011). Bernstein (1990) explored the nature of school subjects and knowledge boundaries, developing a framework classifying subjects as having strong or weak boundaries, relating to bodies of knowledge (Bell, Morrison-Love, Wooff and McLain 2017). However, one of the great strengths of D&T,

and other subjects with so-called weaker boundaries, is the active and applied nature that draws on knowledge from other disciplines, and has a complex and changing nature, as both society and technology evolve.

Third, D&T emerged in the late twentieth century from craft education, which defined 'material areas'. These material areas have historically defined the subject emerging out of the technical crafts (de Vries 2012), which had origins in the notion of gendered technology (Bell, Hughes, and Owen-Jackson 2013). Very simply, these origins can be presented as domestic science (including cooking and needlework) for girls and woodwork and/or metalwork for boys (systems and control emerged out of science). One of the aims of the National Curriculum for D&T was to 'provide equal opportunities for boys and girls' (DES/WO 1989, p. 96). These material areas became defined in England as discrete entities with their own external examinations, such as food, graphic products, resistant materials, systems and control, and textiles. Thus leading to the misconception that these material areas were the 'subject', and teachers developing identities were bound in historical craft divisions. Paetcher (1995) described this tendency to focus on material/craft knowledge as a sub-cultural retreat. McLain (2012) describes how school and departmental culture can affect an individual teacher's vision and values, maintaining the status quo when unchallenged. Despite this intention for D&T to be one subject, the division of the subject by material area remained until 2017 in England, when the variety of General Certificate of Secondary Education (GCSE)[1] titles were subsumed under one, 'Design and Technology' (DfE, 2015a) apart from food, with a separate 'Food Preparation and Nutrition' qualification (DfE, 2015b).

Fourth, D&T education is a relatively young and largely undertheorised subject. McLain, Bell, Wooff and Morrison-Love (2018) discuss D&T as a cultural imperative, promoting children's understanding of designing and making, within a wider social and technological context. In other words, D&T must be more than training the next generation of engineers, technologists and designers. Limiting the scope of the subject to practical, vocational, technical or other equality valid purposes, potentially distracts and distorts teachers' view of the subject and its importance. An effective mentor would do well to look beyond the practical and potentially mundane concerns (de Vries, 2005) of teaching to the curriculum, to open the beginning D&T teacher's eyes to the potential of the subject to promote dispositions and alternative ways of interacting with the world. In exploring the nature of D&T pedagogy, Morrison-Love (2017) discusses transformation as a key feature of the subject, akin to the proof in mathematics and interpretation in science. The very nature of D&T is to provide children with a variety of physical and conceptual tools to view and change (or transform) the world around them to meet the needs and wants of individuals and society. In other words, D&T knowledge is knowledge for active transformation (Task 6.6).

Task 6.6   Cross curricular knowledge

Identify an aspect of D&T that draws on another discipline's body of knowledge, such as properties of materials in science or colour theory in art and design. List the similarities and differences between how this knowledge is used in the respective classrooms. What is unique about D&T, with respect to the identified knowledge? What would be the impact on the D&T curriculum if all 'shared' knowledge were omitted?

D&T knowledge in the curriculum

As outlined above, D&T knowledge is difficult to define, as it draws on many other subjects in the school curriculum, including mathematics, science, art and design, computing and the humanities as identified in the GCSE Subject Content taught from September 2017 in England (DfE 2015a). This document captured the views of stakeholders and outlines the subject content in three and a half pages, compared to one page in the previous version (QCA/WA/CEA 2007) as well as the current national curriculum programme of study (DfE 2013). This reflects attempts to address the perceived "weaker epistemological roots" for D&T, information and communication technology and citizenship (DfE, 2011, p. 24) and other contemporary threats to the subject. However, the defused nature of D&T subject knowledge can be viewed as a positive, considering the origins and intention of the subject.

Taking England as a case study in the United Kingdom, the current National Curriculum programme of study for D&T (DfE 2013) breaks the subject down into four areas for the age range 5-14 as: **design; make; evaluate**; and **technical knowledge**; with an additional category of cooking and nutrition. The specific content relating only to the teaching of food reflects the direction of policy for food education at the time, which also led to a separate GCSE Food Preparation and Nutrition (DfE 2015b) – removing food as a D&T material after the age of 14. The cooking and nutrition section expands on the technical knowledge section, which refers to structures and control systems embedded across the material areas.

Building on the National Curriculum, the GCSE D&T subject content identified two categories of knowledge:

- **technical principles** (knowing that, or conceptual knowledge), including knowledge of: technologies and their impact; materials and energy; systems and control;
- **designing and making principles** (knowing how, or procedural knowledge), including knowledge of: contextual factors, opportunities and limitations; ideation and realisation strategies;

However, curricula vary between countries and change over time, being influenced by a range of internal and external factors, such as governments' need to address issues with the health of a nation or the needs of industry, not to mention ideological leanings. Therefore, the intelligent and reflective mentor should help the beginning D&T teacher to develop the ability to evaluate and renew subject knowledge as a disposition, which will put them in good stead for a sustainable and successful career as a teacher of D&T. The Scottish Curriculum for Excellence, Welsh School Curriculum and the Northern Ireland Curriculum frame D&T learning in different manners with similarities to each other at different points in the subject's evolution from a craft to a design-oriented curriculum.

How is subject knowledge developed?

It is important for beginning teachers to review subject knowledge development and identify priority areas for development relevant to the curriculum that they are teaching – just-in-time (JIT) learning (to borrow a manufacturing idiom) rather than blindly work through a subject knowledge audit (*cf* D&TA 2017) or curriculum document without reference to what and when they will be teaching. The role of an experienced subject-specialist mentor is essential, as part of a regular dialogue around **planning**, **teaching** and **evaluating**, and the impact that it has on learning and progress. Appropriate areas for a mentor and beginning teacher to development will include:

- identifying gaps in subject content knowledge that is new (i.e. material that has not been previously studied);
- refreshing existing subject content knowledge (i.e. material that has not studied for some time);
- developing and strengthening subject content knowledge that is going to be taught in the next term;
- breaking down existing subject content knowledge into its component parts in order to introduce it to learners for the first time (i.e. addressing areas of strength, which may be at a high level, come naturally or be the result of years of practice)

The last bullet, above, is possibly the most important and may be what separates an effective mentor from an effective teacher - i.e. an effective mentor enables the beginning teacher to recognises tacit knowledge, whereas an effective teacher my not necessarily be able to articulate what they are doing and why it works. Mentors and beginning teachers can address subject knowledge issues by:

- challenging *preconceptions* and *assumptions* about what pupils know and understand, and what is appropriate to their age and prior learning;
- reflecting on *personal motivation* and *passion* for the subject, which may be transferred as an unconscious assumption that all learners feel the same way;
- identifying and exploring *common misconceptions* and *complex principles, concepts and processes*;

Figure 6.3 uses the metaphor of a pyramid for subject knowledge, with a broad *foundation* of knowledge across a range of disciplines at a relatively low level. As the beginning D&T teacher progressed through school, university, training and employment, a range of specific and narrower knowledge develops at a high level. Because of this specialisation, 'unused' knowledge is forgotten or ceases to be developed. For example, the D&T teacher with a textiles background may have studied the discipline in primary (age 5-11) or lower secondary (age 11-14) and chosen it as an option for external examination at age 16. However, they may have taken an art based route post 16 and fashion design at university. Therefore, s/he may

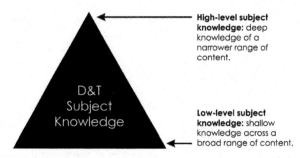

Figure 6.3 D&T subject knowledge

enter the professional with some D&T knowledge at a high level, with significant gaps in technical knowledge to teach external examination syllabi. There is also the expectation that they teach across the range of D&T disciplines in the secondary school curriculum, and the aforementioned need to break down complex knowledge.

Issues with teaching may appear to be due to limited subject knowledge, but in reality be more to do with planning appropriate sequences of learning, focused on clear learning outcomes and supported by appropriate teaching and learning methods (i.e. the ability to successfully articulate knowledge with an understanding of learning). For example, experienced D&T teachers may approach steps and procedures for processes differently in the classroom to how they would be in industry. This can be confusing for the beginning teacher, who may initially assume that the more experienced teacher is wrong or has weak/outdated knowledge; whereas the teacher may be making pragmatic and professional decisions to optimise learning in response to pedagogical/didactic and contextual factors. These factors may include:

- the age and prior experience of the learners;
- access to limited available resources in a class of 20 or more learners;
- managing risk, taking into account hazards and appropriate control measures;
- teaching wider principles beyond the specific activity, or using analogies develop conceptual understanding;

Subject knowledge is complex and beginning teachers develop it in five key ways:

1. build on prior knowledge, developed through education and experience;
2. formal training before, during and after ITE (e.g. health and safety);
3. mentoring during ITE and early career development, with experienced D&T teachers;
4. self-directed subject knowledge development to expand and deepen knowledge and skill, through reading and doing (i.e. designing and/or making);
5. learning through teaching – approaching planning, implementing and evaluating as practitioner enquiry;

Summary

This chapter has explored to help new D&T teachers to analyse and develop knowledge and understanding in design and technology noting the following:

- subject knowledge is essential, but limited without the ability to successfully articulate it with an understanding of how children learn
- teacher knowledge includes knowledge of how schools structure the curriculum and how to children learn, alongside subject knowledge
- D&T subject knowledge is complex and changing, and subject knowledge development for beginning teachers should focus on knowledge for teaching, prioritising short-, medium- and long-term needs
- potential pitfall for mentors to be aware of are gaps in knowledge, which can include areas either not studied recently (or at all) prior to teaching; and areas of seemingly strong subject knowledge where the 'building blocks' of complex knowledge may have been forgotten, leading to assumptions about what children will know or what motivates them

Further reading

Design and Technology Educational Research Hub. www.dater.org.uk
International Journal of Technology and Design Education. https://link.springer.com/journal/
    10798

Note

1   The national external and terminal assessment for 16 year olds in England, Wales and
    Northern Ireland.

References

Banks, F., Leach, J. and Moon, R. (2005). 'Extract from new understandings of teachers' ped-
    agogic knowledge', *The Curriculum Journal*, 16(3), pp. 331–340.
Banks, F. and Owen-Jackson, G. (2007). 'The role of making in design & technology', in
    Barlex, D. (ed.) *Design and Technology for the Next Generation*. Whitchurch: Cliffe and
    Company (Advertising and Marketing) Ltd. pp. 186–197.
Barlex, D. (2003). 'Considering the impact of design and technology on society – the experi-
    ence of the Young Foresight project', *The Place of Design & Technology in the Curriculum,
    PATT13 Conference Proceedings*. University of Glasgow, pp. 140–144.
Barlex, D. (2006). 'The centrality of designing – an emerging realisation from three curricu-
    lum projects', in M. J. de Vries and I. Mottier (eds.). *International Handbook of Technology
    Education*. Rotterdam: Sense Publishers, pp. 253–259
Barlex, D. and Trebell, D. (2008). 'Design-without-make: Challenging the conventional ap-
    proach to teaching and learning in a design and technology classroom', *The International
    Journal of Technology and Design Education*, 18(2), pp. 119–138.
Bell, D., Hughes, C. and Owen-Jackson, G. (2013). 'The (continuing) gender debate', in
    G. Owen-Jackson (ed.) *Debates in Design and Technology Education*. London: Routledge,
    pp.153–165.
Bell, D., Morrison-Love, D., Wooff, D. and McLain, M. (2017). 'Analysing design and technology
    as an educational construct: An investigation into its curriculum position and pedagogical
    identity', *The Curriculum Journal*, 28(4), pp. 539–558.
Bernstein, B. (1990). *The Structuring of Pedagogic Discourse: Class Codes and Control*
    (Vol.IV). London: Routledge.
Black, P. and Harrison, G. (1985). *In Place of Confusion: Technology and Science in the School
    Curriculum*. London: Nuffield Chelsea Curriculum Trust.
de Vries, M. (2012). 'Philosophy of technology', in Williams, P. J. (ed.) *Technology Education
    for Teachers*. Rotterdam: Sense Publishers, pp. 15–34.
de Vries, M. J. (2005). *Teaching about Technology: An Introduction to the Philosophy of Tech-
    nology for Non-philosophers*. Netherlands: Springer.
DES/WO (1988). *National Curriculum Design and Technology Working Group: Interim Report*.
    London: Department for Education and Science/Welsh Office.
DES/WO (1989). *Design and Technology for Ages 5 to 16: Proposal for the Secretary of State
    for Education and Science and for the Secretary of State for Wales*. London: Department
    for Education and Science/Welsh Office.
Design and Technology Assocation (2017). *Career Profile for Teachers of Design and Technol-
    ogy: Subject Competencies*. Wellesbourne: D&T Association. Available at: www.data.org.uk/
    resource-shop (Accessed: 28 July 2018).

DfE (2010). *The Importance of Teaching: The Schools White Paper 2010*. London: Department for Education. Available at: www.education.gov.uk/publications (Accessed: 28 July 2018).

DfE (2011). *The Framework for the National Curriculum. A Report by the Expert Panel for the National Curriculum Review*. London: Department for Education. Available at: www.education.gov.uk/publications (Accessed: 28 July 2018).

DfE (2013). *National Curriculum in England: Design and Technology Programmes of Study*. London: Department for Education. Available at: www.gov.uk/government/publications (Accessed: 28 July 2018).

DfE (2015a). *Design and Technology GCSE Subject Content*. London: Department for Education. Available at: www.gov.uk/government/publications (Accessed: 28 July 2018).

DfE (2015b). *Food Preparation and Nutrition GCSE Subject Content*. Available at: www.gov.uk/government/publications (Accessed: 28 July 2018).

Ericsson, A. and Pool, R. (2016). *Peak: Secrets from the New Science of Expertise*. New York: Houghton Mifflin Harcourt.

Gettier, E. L. (1963). Is justified true belief knowledge? *Analysis*, 23(6), 121-123.

Hattie, J. (2009). *Visible Learning: A Synthesis of Over 800 Meta-Analyses Relating to Achievement*. Abingdon, Oxon: Routledge.

Kimbell, R. and Perry, D. (2001). *Design and Technology in a Knowledge Economy*. London: Engineering Council.

Kimbell, R., Stables, K. and Green, R. (1996). *Understanding Practice in Design and Technology*. Buckingham: Open University Press.

Kimbell, R., Stables, K., Wheeler, T., Wosniak, A. and Kelly, V (1991). *The Assessment of Performance and Design and Technology*. London: Schools Examination and Assessment Council.

McCormick, R. (1997). 'Conceptual and procedural knowledge', *International Journal of Technology and Design Education*, 7(1-2), pp. 141-159.

McLain, M. (2012). 'An (auto) ethnographic narrative of the teaching of designing within design and technology in the English curriculum', *Procedia Social and Behavioral Sciences*, 45, pp. 318-330.

McLain, M. (2017). 'Emerging perspectives on the demonstration as a signature pedagogy in design and technology', *International Journal of Technology and Design Education*, 28(4), pp. 985-1000.

McLain, M., Bell, D., Wooff, D. and Morrison-Love, D. (2018). 'Cultural and historical roots for design and technology education: Why technology makes us human', *Research and Practice in Technology Education: Perspectives on Human Capacity and Development PATT Conference 2018*. Ireland: Athlone Institute of Technology.

McLellan, R. and Nicholl, B. (2011). '"If I was going to design a chair, the last thing I would look at is a chair": Product analysis and the causes of fixation in students' design work 11-16 years', *International Journal of Technology and Design Education*, 22(1), pp. 71-92.

Mitcham, C. (1994). *Thinking Through Technology: A Path between Engineering and Philosophy*. Chicago, IL: The University of Chicago Press.

Morrison-Love, D. (2017). 'Towards a transformative epistemology of technology education', *Journal of Philosophy of Education*, 51(1), pp. 23-37.

Paetcher, C. (1995). 'Subcultural retreat: Negotiating the design and technology curriculum', *British Educational Research Journal*, 21(1), pp. 75-87.

Qualifications and Curriculum Authority / Welsh Assembly / Council for the Curriculum, Examinations and Assessment (2007). *GCSE Subject Criteria for Design and Technology*. Available at: http://dera.ioe.ac.uk/7162/8/qca-07-3447_gcsecriteriadt.pdf (Accessed: 21 November 2018).

Ryle, G. (1949). *The Concept of Mind*. London: Penguin Books Ltd.

Scharff, R. C. and Dusek, V. (eds.) (2003). *Philosophy of Technology: The Technological Condition, An Anthology*. Oxford: Blackwell Publishing.

Shulman, L. S. (1986). 'Those who understand: Knowledge growth in teaching', *Educational Research Review*, 57(1), pp. 4-14.

Vygotsky, L. S. (1978). *Mind in Society*. Cambridge, MA: Harvard University Press.

7 A skills audit: identifying gaps in beginning design and technology (D&T) teachers' subject knowledge, skills and understanding

Suzanne Lawson and Susan Wood-Griffiths

Introduction

The aim of this chapter is to focus on skills auditing and the identification of gaps in beginning teachers' subject knowledge, skills and understanding. For beginning design and technology (D&T) teachers, the challenge is the acquisition of skills and knowledge required to teach in a multi-activity and multi-material curriculum. This often involves 'tick box' auditing procedures that for some can be empowering but for others are debilitating. This chapter will look at the mechanics of the auditing, a consideration of the effects that the deficit exposure can have on confidence and ways that mentors can support beginning teachers to develop their subject knowledge.

Objectives

At the end of this chapter you should be able to:

- Consider the nature of subject knowledge including what when and how it could be audited.
- Know how to audit subject knowledge, skills and understanding.
- Develop subject auditing tools using published guidance.
- Identify strategies to support beginning teachers to develop their subject expertise.

What is subject knowledge

Evidence suggests that a high level of subject expertise is a characteristic of good teaching (Coe et al. 2014; Sanders and Morris 2000). In 2015, a review of teacher training in England identified 'subject knowledge development' as a key priority noting the need to 'rigorously audit, track and systematically improve trainees' subject knowledge throughout the programme' (Carter 2015, p. 7). As revised more rigorous examination specifications emerge in response to Government policy, the emphasis on the importance of good subject knowledge is intensifying. The impact of changing landscapes on subject knowledge development is also discussed in Chapter 3.

So, what is subject knowledge? Grossman et al. (1989) identified the basic elements as 'content knowledge'. Grossman defines this as 'the factual information, central concepts, organising principles and ideas that exponents would recognise as making up the discipline' (Grossman et al. 1989 cited in Sanders and Morris 2000, p. 399). Many authors note that subject knowledge for trainees (beginning teachers) includes pedagogical knowledge – the knowledge of how to teach a subject effectively and how to develop effective pedagogical approaches for curriculum delivery (Glazzard and Stokoe 2011, Wright 2018). For the purposes of this chapter we are going to focus on the information/content knowledge, the subject knowledge a beginning teacher will need to have to teach pupils effectively.

Defining subject knowledge in D&T is complicated by its complex history as discussed in Chapter 2. Over time, several definitions of D&T itself have emerged as the subject has developed and these demonstrate that the nature of the subject is continually changing along with the body of knowledge needed to teach it (Owen-Jackson 2015). Acknowledging the dynamic nature of subject knowledge is important if mentors are to support early career teachers well, as is accepting that they will not know everything and may need support.

The changing models of initial teacher training will have had an impact on how beginning teachers will have acquired their subject knowledge for teaching. Most teachers now complete their training as a post graduate, and this limits the time available for developing subject knowledge. If they have completed the training within a Higher Education institute, they may have been part of a sizeable subject community and had the opportunity to work collaboratively to develop their subject knowledge and share skills with other trainees who come with differing expertise and subject strengths. If they have completed an employment-based school-led training, it is likely that they will have worked within a much smaller community if not in isolation (as the only trainee) and have not had the same opportunities for sharing. This can mean that a seemingly highly qualified beginning teacher may not have all the skills and knowledge they need to teach some aspects of the curriculum and will need some support and direction from a mentor.

In recent years, the establishment of short pre-training subject knowledge enhancement courses has sought to address this. These have provided an opportunity for participants on any D&T training route to work on developing subject knowledge and skills prior to starting their training programme, where the focus necessarily shifts towards the development of pedagogical and professional knowledge. These focussed courses provide an opportunity to start identifying where subject knowledge will need developing and to recognise that subject knowledge development is part of a lifelong learning process for teachers which will be addressed through further training, self-study and continuing professional development.

Another recent development has been the establishment of self-help forums on social media which are managed by subject experts. These have provided a useful knowledge exchange for subject communities and are particularly helpful to teachers working in isolation and to those who are new to the profession. Setting the expectation early on, that subject knowledge development is a continual process, supports a beginning teacher to recognise the need to periodically review or gauge their subject knowledge so that they can teach effectively.

Auditing subject knowledge and using published guidance

Identifying and keeping track of subject development needs can be approached in a variety of ways that are often seen and referred to as auditing. The term audit can be interchanged with examine, check or inspect, each of which are terms which imply some accountability and measurement, but this can intimidate a beginning teacher. The reality of auditing subject knowledge is that it is part of a teacher's continual reviewing of what they know now and need to know to teach their pupils in response to changing curricula. If you are an experienced teacher it will not be difficult to recall things that you no longer teach or things that you have started to teach recently that may be less familiar.

Since 1998, the Design and Technology Association (DATA) published periodically revised versions of the Minimum Competencies for Trainees to Teach Design and Technology in Secondary Schools (DATA 1998, 2003, 2010). The periodic revisions demonstrate the dynamic nature of the subject knowledge required to teach D&T well. In England and Wales, these documents were widely adopted by training providers and served to provide a definition for the subject and an audit for trainee teachers. The competencies were broken down into core skills and knowledge definitions and those that could be considered material specific. The definitive nature of these documents led to them being widely used in initial teacher training as a definitive subject knowledge audit, as well as beyond training for qualified teachers to identify what they needed to know if required to teach beyond their specialism.

The concept of an audit or competencies model has now been replaced in the current version which is presented as a Career Profile for Teachers of Design and Technology: Subject Competencies (DATA 2017). This document, presented as a spreadsheet, sets out what is required throughout a teacher's career and is intended to inform the decisions teachers make about their continued professional development. As such, it now includes a section on Leadership and Management of Design and Technology which identifies the skills, knowledge and understanding necessary for undertaking leadership roles in the subject. These documents provide a formal framework to measure progress in subject development and to plan for future support but needs to be worked with judiciously with beginning teachers so that they do not become overwhelm and can highlight progress.

It is interesting to note that this most recent version omits any mention to teaching food which is still part of the National Curriculum for Design and Technology. This might be because prior to its publication, two documents which identified the core skills and knowledge required to teach food at primary and secondary levels were published: *Food teaching in secondary schools: A framework of knowledge and skills* (Public Health England 2015b) and *Food teaching in primary schools: A framework of knowledge and skills* (Public Health England 2015a). In preparation for teaching the new Food Preparation and Nutrition GCSE, these explicit documents were supported by a *Food Teachers Professional Portfolio* programme (2015-2018) supported by the British Nutrition Foundation, the Food Teachers centre and the All Saints Educational Trust. This programme aimed to support teachers to develop and refocus their subject knowledge.

Mentors who are familiar with the DATA Career Profile and who have participated in the Food Teachers' Professional Portfolio programme will be well placed to support early career teachers to develop their subject knowledge to teach D&T and food preparation and nutrition. Furthermore, as mentors, they will be aware of the strengths and deficits in their own subject knowledge and well prepared to collaborate to support early career teachers to develop theirs. See Chapter 5 for further discussion on supporting the development of beginning D&T teachers' knowledge, skills and understanding in food preparation and nutrition.

The shift from the competency models towards the career profile models extends the remit of subject knowledge development beyond training and early career development towards continual professional development and presents a juxtaposition that will be discussed next. For early career teachers, a model that shows what they can do may be more empowering than a deficit model that indicates what they may go on to do (Task 7.1).

Task 7.1   What is knowledge?

Consider these four areas

1.   subject knowledge,
2.   professional knowledge,
3.   professional judgement.
4.   Continued professional development

- Do you know what they mean?
- How can this 'knowledge' support your personal development?
- How can you use this 'knowledge' to support an early career teacher?

The deficit model to subject knowledge – is it debilitating or empowering?

Research specific to auditing D&T subject knowledge is sparse and for that reason it is interesting to look at what researchers have said about auditing knowledge in other subject areas. Sanders and Morris (2000) identified two phenomena when considering primary PGCE mathematics knowledge. These were:

- The way in which beginning teachers react to and deal with the understanding that their subject is not of an acceptable standard.
- The impact auditing has on some beginning teachers' confidence.

As an experienced teacher, you may have looked at a new examination specification and felt totally debilitated by the breadth and depth of the content questioning your own ability. You might also have looked at some content and felt empowered by your own knowledge and understanding. It is rare for a beginning teacher to have full confidence in their knowledge. Moriarty's (1995) work notes the relationship between confidence and performance and it is this balance that you need to consider when supporting beginning teachers.

Beginning teachers can be anxious about content knowledge. It is likely that they feel they would lose some respect in the eyes of pupils should they not be able to respond appropriately to a question. Such questions are likely to revolve around skills and scientific or technical content. Hence, it would seem logical that beginning teachers are likely (particularly in the early stages of their development) to prioritise concern about content knowledge as this is where they perceive their lack of knowledge is most likely to be exposed in a teaching situation. This is supported by Capel (2007) who, although referring to physical education rather than D&T, talks about 'phases of concern' in relation to subject knowledge. Hence, beginning teachers move through self-concerns, task concerns to impact concerns. Other authors (Maynard and Furlong 1993) offer slightly different categorisations (see Chapter 1); however, the underlying premise is the 'journey' or progression focussing on self, content and pupils. Typically, a beginning teacher might move through the following phases:

- Concerns about his/her own subject knowledge.
- Understanding of the curriculum or specifications and the nuances of their subject knowledge.
- Pupils' subject knowledge and misconceptions.

Whatever the phase it is likely that any auditing will adopt a deficit model – what the beginning teacher doesn't know. Sanders and Morris (2000) categorise beginning teachers into three broad groups when considering 'behaviour' when dealing with subject knowledge deficits – ostriches, mananas and nettle graspers. 'Ostriches' refuse to believe there is a problem or because they doubt their capabilities with particular types of activity avoid such tasks. The 'Mananas', despite acknowledging that they have a problem, do little about it. These beginning teachers always have other priorities. For this group, the practical needs of the teaching influence the commitment to improve the knowledge and they defer the necessity to plug any gaps 'I am not teaching it this term'. For this group they tend to have the view that the effort to improve their mastery would outweigh the benefits that such knowledge would have on their teaching. The third group are what Saunders and Morris call the 'nettle graspers'. This group acknowledge they have a problem and are determined to do something about it.

Some beginning teachers are empowered to tackle subject knowledge deficits. Others either disbelieve or allow the intensity of the course or job to lower the priority they place on subject knowledge. Beginning teachers will give excuses – common ones are due to technical terms or non-coverage at school or in their degree (Task 7.2).

Task 7.2   Ostrich, manana or nettle grasper?

When you were a beginning teacher, were you an 'ostrich', 'manana' or 'a nettle grasper' – or indeed a combination. What did you do to address deficits in your subject knowledge? When you look at a new project, scheme of work or examination specification how do you target gaps in your own knowledge?

Wright (2018) notes that if beginning teachers see any training programme as an alternative to masters' level subject study, they are in for a shock and disappointment. The subject of most training programmes is not D&T, but education. You must not make the assumption that subject knowledge is a necessary precondition of entry into teaching (Yandell 2011). Nor can you make the assumption that subject knowledge is best acquired on the job by serving an apprenticeship working alongside more experienced colleagues. Yandell notes that such a view heralds problems as at best the beginning teacher is a clone of you and is inhibited by the boundaries of your own knowledge and second, the subject is treated as a stable, pre-existent entity. In D&T it is not. Subject knowledge may well need extensive development, but this will often depend on self-study whilst formally occupied by reading, researching and understanding about children and adolescents and how they think and learn. On an intensive training programme self-directed study inevitably has a low priority.

So, what do mentors need to do to support the beginning teacher so that any deficit model of auditing is not debilitating? You need to support beginning teachers as they come to terms with their lack of knowledge and the need to provide appropriate strategies to address deficits. You also need to challenge the deficits to provide a non-confrontational and very supportive approach to developing subject knowledge (Task 7.3).

Task 7.3   Self-assessing subject knowledge

- Consider what the beginning teacher will be required to teach and share the specification or unit of work with them. Ask them to highlight the areas where they feel their knowledge is strong and invite suggestions for where they can contribute their 'expertise' to developing a series of lessons.
- Having moved them into a position of strength, invite them to highlight the areas that they are less interested or confident in. Use this information to collaboratively plan or to make suggestions as to how they might teach these areas. Sharing ideas or signposting resources for self-study can reduce the burden of self-directed study and support the development of expertise.

Developing knowledgeable teachers

Owen-Jackson (2001) acknowledges that subject knowledge in D&T is continuously changing and developing as new scientific discoveries are made, new legislation is developed and new products are developed. New examination specifications and assessment requirements can influence what is taught, how it is assessed and can demand that even the most experienced teachers review their subject competency. This means that all teachers will need to review their knowledge to ensure that they have the latest information. It can be reassuring to a beginning teacher to recognise this and to know that their practice will necessarily evolve as they become more competent.

The concept of subject competency goes beyond subject knowledge per se to a wider discussion of knowledgeable teaching. Knowing your subject well does not always translate into being an effective teacher; it is this combined with other elements of your professional knowledge that supports you to transfer your knowledge into suitable tasks that lead to pupils' learning.

Shulman (1986) and Ball et al. (2008) discuss seven knowledge bases essential for teaching and went on to define each one. Subject content knowledge (SCK) is what has been largely discussed in this chapter and he split this into substantive (core) knowledge and syntactic knowledge which defines how the core knowledge is structured and organised within the subject. The concept of syntactic knowledge is worth considering for D&T. As a subject that is continually evolving its core content, the way that teachers respond by adapting the organisation of their teaching throughout the school is worth consideration. For example, the revised GCSE specifications may require pupils to work with a wider range of materials and technologies and for pupils to be successful the curriculum they follow further down in school may need to be reorganised in the preparation for GCSE (Task 7.4).

Task 7.4   Organising teaching

Consider how the non-examined assessment components of the GCSE have impacted on how you organise your teaching

* at Key Stage 4
* At Key Stage 3 in preparation for further study

As a mentor for a beginning teacher, it is important that you share your syntactic knowledge with a beginning teacher and are open about the challenges you face in your teaching. Knowledgeable D&T teachers will use statutory curricular frameworks, such as national curriculum programmes of study or examination specifications as frameworks but will not let them define the limits of the subject. For example, it is not a requirement to teach about climate change to children up to 14 in England, but this does not mean that it is not relevant when pupils are designing.

Effective teachers will use their syntactic knowledge to make professional judgements, with their colleagues in school and the wider subject community, about how best to educate children through practical activities involving designing and making. They will devise activities to prepare pupils to be well-rounded, sensitive, critically aware and competent individuals and citizens. Influences on these judgements will be dependent on the school situation and may be determined by local, cultural and economic factors which the beginning teacher may not be aware of, for example practical work that requires pupils to taste food may be suspended during fasting periods and the use of certain ingredients might be avoided to acknowledge pupils' cultural heritage. These decisions will also be influenced by the teacher's specialist knowledge, areas of interest and skills. For example, a teacher who has graduated in fashion may well use clothing and accessories as a focus for design. An open dialogue about these considerations will raise the awareness of beginning teachers and support the development of their syntactic subject knowledge. Inviting them to identify and share their specific subject interests and strengths with pupils can lead to an enriched curriculum (Task 7.5).

Task 7.5   Sharing your expertise

Consider the case study below.

Have you explicitly shared your subject interests with pupils or facilitated an opportunity for a trainee or beginning teacher to do this?

What do you perceive as the benefits of this

- for you?
- for the pupils?

Anya

Anya was a trainee teacher with a degree in fashion. Prior to training to teach, she had
worked for a major high street fashion chain that appeals to teenagers. She regularly shared
her undergraduate design folders with the pupils who took a real interest in her design work,
and there was an evident improvement in the presentation of their own work. In one lesson
she was teaching the pupils about production methods, she had found a case study of a
wedding dress designer which she shared as an example of one-off production. She then
passed around a garment from the high street fashion chain and asked them to identify
how they thought it was produced. The label gave away that it was a mass-produced item
manufactured overseas, and she declared that it had been one of her own designs, after the
initial disbelief, she shared the specification and her preliminary design work with the pupils.
The questions that followed led to the lesson focussing more on careers information and
guidance than manufacturing methods but her expertise as a subject specialist was clear to
her class.

Another form of professional knowledge identified by Shulman (1986) and Ball (2008)
is pedagogical content knowledge (PCK). This is defined as a combination of SKC and pedagogy that provides the specific knowledge you need for effective teaching and learning in
your subject area. All teachers have a responsibility to maintain a safe working environment
and statutory duties under The Health and Safety at Work Act (1974) and The Children Act
(1989) so it is essential to plan to teach to minimise the potential for danger and to maximise
the pupils' learning opportunities. This is discussed further in Chapter 9. For D&T teachers
this is particularly relevant as much of the learning in D&T is practical, and to be effective beginning teachers need to develop expertise in managing learning in a practical setting. This
is complex, there are no other rooms in a school that have so many potential hazards. In a
workshop there are tools, machinery, hot solder, chemicals and dust. In a food room there are
knives, electrical equipment, heat and boiling water. In textiles there are cutters, machines,
hot wax and put these factors together with a class full of pupils and a limited lesson time
and the possibilities for accidents and chaos are clear.

The school will have a policy on health and safety. A D&T teacher new to a school, whether
experienced or as a beginning teacher will need time to familiarise with the rooms they are
teaching in and the policy. As a mentor to a new colleague you will have a responsibility to
support the mentee to become familiar with the policy, and to introduce them to colleagues

and school procedures. Getting this situational knowledge is paramount to effective learning and teaching, and it is helpful to remember that this procedural information will support the beginning teacher's efficacy (Task 7.6).

Task 7.6 Knowledge to teach safely

Read the school's health and safety (H&S) policy and note things that specifically relate to your teaching. Share the annotated policy with the trainee and ask them to highlight anything further they would like to discuss. For example, do they require any further training to use specific equipment or machinery? Ask them to identify how they will address specific H&S reminders in their teaching.

Once a beginning teacher has considered how to secure a safe working environment with support from a mentor, another aspect of PCK to consider is how you adapt your SCK to the classes in a new school. All schools are different and the pupil population in one school may be very different to another. As a mentor you are best placed to advise a beginning teacher about the school population and how this might impact on what you teach. It is important that you make the mentee aware of pupils' needs and abilities as well as their cultural heritage and economic circumstances. In D&T, these factors will have a significant influence on what is taught when and how materials are procured. It is important for a mentor to highlight to a new colleague these considerations and any constraints, and specifically for a beginning teacher who may have limited awareness or relevant experience to draw upon.

They don't know what they need to know ... working with a beginning teacher

As a mentor there can be a tension between being supportive and permitting the mentee to find a way independently. Trainee teachers are recognised to be learners, but this recognition disappears once training has ceased despite the learner status continuing well into the Newly Qualified Teacher (NQT) year and beyond. Experience does not equate to subject expertise and a beginning teacher is likely to have different specialist knowledge and expertise to the mentor.

A helpful approach is to share what you do but not insist that the mentee does the same. When starting in a new school it is helpful to be given schemes of work so that a beginning teacher can see what is already in place, but it is important to remember that the beginning teacher will have acquired subject knowledge differently and as such may want to share it in different ways.

Establishing a collaborative relationship where colleagues can share their strengths can be a refreshing experience and provides opportunities for new ideas, approaches to the subject and ways of working with pupils. Further examples of this can be seen in the stakeholder comments in Chapter 13. The concept of evolving subject knowledge is important here and mentors need to remember this.

Local knowledge can be helpful in supporting the development of a beginning teacher as you will be more aware of other schools in the area and any local support networks that exist. Supporting a beginning teacher to network beyond the school with experts is one way that they can develop further expertise (Task 7.7).

Task 7.7   Engaging with experts

Use the case studies below to identify opportunities that a beginning teacher could take to develop subject knowledge from experts in your own locality to enrich the curriculum

---

Sam

Sam was a mature entrant to teaching who chose to take advantage of the opportunity to undertake a placement with a supermarket chain as part of an education and business partnership to improve his subject knowledge to teach food. Through the placement he made some contacts and was able to organise an opportunity for his GCSE pupils to visit the supermarket bakery and for a butcher to visit the school to demonstrate butchery skills.

Salma

Salma was encouraged to get involved with the local Science, Technology Engineering and Mathematics (STEM) provider. She attended a networking meeting with some other newly qualified teachers from the science department and met a representative who was demonstrating a 3D printer. The school did not have access to one at the time and she invited him to the school to demonstrate it to her class. She asked the deputy headteacher to observe the lesson to see its potential and this strengthened her case to procure one.

These examples illustrate opportunities to support the development of subject knowledge through continual professional development and take the onus away from the mentor. Recognising expertise and that subject knowledge is not fixed needs to be emphasised, it is as much why we teach something than what.

A common anxiety for a beginning teacher is the responsibility of subject knowledge when teaching examination classes and initial training can only provide limited opportunities to prepare for this. As a mentor to a beginning teacher, facilitating opportunities to assess and moderate non-examined assessments can build confidence and help develop a shared understanding of assessment criteria and standards. When new examination specifications emerge everyone is a novice assessor. The inevitable anxiety you may have had about assessing a new award is an inherent part of teaching this and supporting beginning teachers to recognise this and recommending them to seek help and opportunities work with others would be good advice. The shared concern that beginning and experienced teachers have about the responsibility of supporting pupils through examinations can be illustrated by the local collegiate networks that teachers in an area set up to work together.

Summary

The dynamic nature of D&T means that defining the subject knowledge required to teach is complex. All D&T teachers need to recognise that as new technologies develop and trends emerge subject teaching should shift. Traditional teaching approaches tended to be task orientated and focus on outcomes. Supporting a beginning teacher to teach these well was fairly straightforward. More recently, the focus has been on learning objectives and this lends the subject to respond with more contemporary approaches, using new technologies and the expertise of those that teach it. Teachers' expertise should be considered when defining subject knowledge and working with a fixed construct of defined subject knowledge can impose limits on what can be achieved. As a mentor discovering a beginning teacher's talents and strengths and supporting them to share these with pupils and colleagues will bring out the best in all. By considering the concept of auditing subject knowledge we have learnt that

- If we are not careful mentoring beginning teachers prepare them to teach in schools 'as they are' rather than 'as they might be'.
- Auditing can be debilitating and result in the enormity of the task looking too much. Build on beginning teachers' strengths and remember the curriculum should evolve with new inputs.
- Knowledgeable teachers' pay as much attention to 'why' they are teaching specific content as to 'how' they are teaching it.
- No beginning teacher, or even mentor, has a full command of the range of subject knowledge. Subject knowledge acquisition is a lifelong process.

Further resources

British Nutrition Foundation (2016) *Core competencies for children and young people aged 5-15.* Available from - www.nutrition.org.uk/foodinschools/competences/competences.html (Accessed: 23 November 2018).

Career Profile for teachers of Design and Technology: Subject Competencies (DATA 2017) *Food Teachers Professional Portfolio* programme (2015-2018) supported by the British Nutrition Foundation, the Food Teachers centre and the All Saints Educational Trust.

PHE Public Health England (2015a) *Food teaching in primary schools: knowledge and skills framework.* Available at: www.gov.uk/government/publications/food-teaching-in-primary-schools-knowledge-and-skills-framework (Accessed: 06 April 2018).

PHE Public Health England (2015b) *Food teaching in secondary schools: knowledge and skills framework.* Available at: www.gov.uk/government/publications/food-teaching-in-secondary-schools-knowledge-and-skills-framework (Accessed: 06 April 2018).

References

Ball, D. L., Thames, M. H. and Phelps, G. (2008) Content knowledge for teaching. What makes it special? *Journal of Teacher Education,* 59(5), pp. 389-407.

Capel, S. (2007) Moving beyond physical education subject knowledge to develop knowledgeable teachers, *Curriculum Journal,* 18(4), pp. 493-507.

Carter, A. (2015) *Carter review of Initial Teacher Training (ITT).* London: Department for Education.

Coe, R., Aloisi, C., Higgins, S. and Major, L. E. (2014) *What makes great teaching? Review of the underpinning research*. Millbank, London: The Sutton Trust.

Design and Technology Association (1998) *Minimum competencies for students to teach design and technology in secondary schools*. Wellesbourne: DATA.

Design and Technology Association (2003) *Minimum competencies for students to teach design and technology in secondary schools*. Wellesbourne: DATA.

Design and Technology Association (2010) *Minimum competencies for students to teach design and technology in secondary schools*. Wellesbourne: DATA.

Design and Technology Association (2017) *minimum competencies for students to teach design and technology in secondary schools*. Wellesbourne: DATA.

Food Teachers Professional Portfolio programme (2015-2018) supported by the British Nutrition Foundation, the Food Teachers centre and the All Saints Educational Trust.

Glazzard, J. and Stokoe J. (2011) *Achieving outstanding in you teaching placement*. London: Sage Publications.

Grossman, P., Wilson, S. and Shulman, L. (1989) Teachers of substance: subject matter knowledge for teaching, in Reynolds, M. (ed.) *The Knowledge base for the beginning teacher*. Oxford: Pergamon. pp. 23-36.

Maynard, T. and Furlong, J. (1995) Learning to teach and models of mentoring, in Kerry, T. and Shelton Mayes, A. (eds.) *Issues in mentoring*. London: Routledge. pp. 10-14.

Moriarty, B. (1995) Self-efficacy and mathematics: yesterday's students and tomorrow's teachers, paper presented at the *Australian Association for Research in Education*, Hobart Tasmania.

Owen-Jackson, G. (2001) *Developing subject knowledge in design and technology*. Stoke on Trent: Trentham Books.

Owen-Jackson, G. (2015) Planning to teach design and technology, in Owen Jackson, G. (ed.) *Learning to teach design and technology in the secondary school*. London: Routledge. pp.241-267.

PHE Public Health England (2015a) *Food teaching in primary schools: knowledge and skills framework*. Available at: www.gov.uk/government/publications/food-teaching-in-primary-schools-knowledge-and-skills-framework (Accessed: 06 April 2018).

PHE Public Health England (2015b) *Food teaching in secondary schools: knowledge and skills framework*. Available at: www.gov.uk/government/publications/food-teaching-in-secondary-schools-knowledge-and-skills-framework (Accessed: 06 April 2018).

Sanders, S. E and Morris, H. (2000) Exposing Student Teachers' Content knowledge: empowerment or debilitation? *Educational Studies*, 26(4), pp. 397-408.

Shulman, L. (1986) cited in Capel, S. Leask, M. and Younis, S. (2016) *Learning to teach in the secondary school*. 7th edn. London: Routledge. p. 18.

Wright, T. (2018) The pivotal importance of the mentor, in Wright, T. (ed.) *How to be a brilliant mentor*. London: Routledge. pp. 1-15.

Yandell, J. (2011) Sites of learning, in Heilbronn, R. and Yandell, J. (eds.) *Critical practice in teacher education. A study of professional learning*. London: IOE. p. 16.

8 Helping D&T teachers plan, deliver and evaluate lessons

Louise Beattie, Suzanne Lawson and Susan Wood-Griffiths

Introduction

Having considered how the mentor supports the knowledge required for the effective teaching of design and technology (D&T) for beginning teachers (Chapter 7), it is now time to think about how this can be applied to the planning of lessons and more explicitly practical sessions. Unlike other chapters in the book that focus on supporting beginning teachers in general, this chapter largely focuses specifically on supporting trainee teachers. We believe that it is during initial training that the planning process is learned so this chapter is written for mentors of trainee teachers so that they can support mentees through this learning journey.

This will cover how to support mentees with planning good solo lessons, evaluating the lessons they have taught and moving towards planning and teaching sequences. While acknowledging the experience that the mentor can bring to this collaboration, a degree of reflection upon these experiences will strengthen the mentor's approach and thereby the learning experience for the beginning teacher.

This chapter will go through the stages of planning, teaching, reflecting and developing and draw on several approaches to mentoring, including those from previous chapters, which will be applicable at different points. You will be encouraged to draw on your own pedagogical understanding as well as considering differing beliefs.

Objectives

At the end of this chapter, you should be able to:

- To reflect on the process that underpins effective lesson planning in a practical environment.
- To consider how the mentor supports the beginning teacher with adopting planning approaches and internalising the processes.
- To understand how to develop evaluative reflections over time (Task 8.1).

Task 8.1   Medium-term planning

- How do you plan for a half term or for a unit of work? Is this planning outcomes driven or skill focused?

- How do you use shared units of work and personalise them for specific ability groups?
- What are your key considerations when planning a new unit of work?

Thinking objectively about these processes will enable you to start considering your rationale and how a pedagogical understanding of planning, teaching and learning is paramount. At this stage, the process for us as experienced teachers will be internalised and we need to bring this to the foreground in order to crystallise these methods with the beginning teacher.

Supporting the planning process starting out

Owen-Jackson (2007) notes that when first thinking about lesson planning it is easy. You simply decide what to do, write it down, list resources and add timings – done. Despite the excitement of the first school experience and anticipation of using their knowledge in the classroom, the mammoth task of tailoring this for a particular class for one hour of learning can seem an unrealistic goal. Equally, there may be some beginning teachers who have the additional anxiety of teaching a material area or topic that they are not confident with or certainly less familiar.

Whether following a university-led PGCE or school-based route, the trainee teacher will have had some input on planning. This might have included the differences between a long-term plan, medium-term plan or a lesson plan (short-term plan). It will almost certainly have included some 'versions' of lesson plans or perhaps a template that they are expected to use while on school placement. Before the planning begins, a great deal of knowledge is required and it is this dawning realisation that sometimes makes the process feel overwhelming. Even with effective discussions with peers and tutors about how to plan and the rationale behind each stage, they are likely to feel some trepidation as they poise behind their laptop with many creative ideas to hone into an acceptable and useful professional document for the first time. It is not unusual for a beginning teacher to spend multiple hours planning a one-hour lesson. Owen-Jackson (2007) equates the process to a jigsaw. Small pieces interlock to make a coherent picture but like a jigsaw, you sometimes need to focus on the main pieces before you can begin to see the bigger picture.

The problem with early solo lesson planning is the default into a linear and rational sequence, based on Tyler's model of planning (Tyler 1949) and its veracity depends on its use by the beginning teacher. If used ineffectively, such plans can become segmented and compartmentalised opportunities to learn where there is little overview or real understanding of the learning by either pupil or teacher. As a starting point however, the sense of structure offered by this model allows for a rational way of approaching planning. Thus we begin with a tension within the topic of 'planning'. What comes first?

The experienced teacher may describe planning as more spontaneous, juggling aspects of subject knowledge, awareness of pedagogy, knowledge of pupils and a myriad of other considerations (John 2006, Owen-Jackson 2015), which for D&T must include health and safety. Bearing all of this in mind, a mentor needs to have stepped away from an almost nat-ural and now intuitive approach to planning and have reflected on how *personal approaches* to planning are achieved in a methodical way. As will be discussed in Chapter 11, the com-mentary, or 'thinking out loud', that ascribes to these stages and the rationale behind them will be helpful in the initial discussions with the beginning teacher and contribute to the mentoring conversations. John (2006) notes that at this point, the dialogical model can act as a powerful descriptive tool to familiarise beginning teachers with the various modes of planning and the complexities therein.

Thinking back to Maynard and Furlong's (1995) approach to mentoring (Chapter 1), this dialogue will include sharing and modelling how the mentor would plan (the apprentice model), looking at the requirements and key skills behind the planning perhaps as cited in the Teachers' Standards and the National Curriculum requirements (the competence model), and discussing how the mentor's plan worked in the classroom (the reflective model). It will also mirror the belief that interactive teaching requires planning that is flexible and practical from the start and that a dialogical model, which includes the mentee in this process, will give them a better insight into lesson planning (John 2000).

Early discussions with mentees will be based on observations during any induction period and a review of the timetable as a whole. Honing in on particular classes will afford the men-tor the opportunity of guiding the mentee towards some specific areas to think about as they approach the first planning experience. McCann comments;

> A mentor can help beginners to interrogate what they see, labelling the elements in an instructional sequence and recognizing the purpose for each instructional move. This can lead to attempts at similar practice and reflection on its efficacy.
>
> (McCann 2013, p. 90)

Mentee observations and collaborative teaching as a lesson on planning

Working together with a beginning teacher and providing an opportunity for them to deliver part of your lesson alongside observing your practice can provide a real opportunity for col-laborative learning with the mentor leading on the lesson design.

Pre-requisites/things for the mentor to plan for

The beginning teacher should have had access to your plan for the lesson to be observed (this need not be a formal plan but might be reference to the medium-term plan or an over-view of the intended learning).

As will be noted in Chapter 10, the mentee should have something specific to focus on – did the teacher thread the learning objective through the lesson and how? Did the pupils achieve the teacher's expectations and how can this be seen? What level of subject knowl-edge was required for this lesson and did it enhance the mentee's knowledge? The school or training provider might offer induction booklets or key questions. Alternatively, a quick chat at the start with a specific question will guide the mentee accordingly.

Time – this can often be difficult to find. However, even five minutes while walking to the staff room or at the end of the day can allow the mentor to elicit some initial views and thereby assess the mentee's current understanding of planning linked to learning.

Ready, steady, teach

Having been introduced to timetables, colleagues, classes and departmental schemes, the beginning teacher will be ready to lead part of a lesson. For this to be a meaningful activity, it is important that the mentee has been part of the planning process for this particular lesson or at least had a conversation with the teacher about rationale and intended learning. At this point, it is highly probable that the beginning teacher will be both nervous and excited; an aptitude for reflection afterwards will sometimes be thwarted by the fusion of many emotions and elation at having survived (Clutterbuck and Lane 2004). It is therefore the responsibility of the mentor to ensure that there is some level of focused reflection afterwards both to set precedence for good habits and to ensure that the exercise returns maximum results for the mentee. It is also worth remembering that you are modelling good practice for the explicit reflection on action (Brockbank and McGill 2007). Encouraging the beginning teacher to reflect on the 'what went well', or even 'enjoyed' as well as the areas which could be developed will enhance an overall positive mindset (Task 8.2).

Task 8.2   Mentor reflection

- From your previous reflections, what key 'jigsaw pieces' does the mentee need when beginning the planning process?
- What questions would you offer to support them with understanding the structure?
- What are the limitations in terms of time, resources and prior knowledge?
- How do you help your mentee to manage 'in-house' schemes of work?

The planning process – the bigger picture

Expert-novice studies have shown that whereas the experienced teacher can see the 'bigger picture' and use this to help them plan, the beginning teacher engages with the short-term (John 2006, Owen-Jackson 2015). While experienced teachers start with the long-term (perhaps planning for a year or two) before moving to medium term (a unit of work or short block) before focusing on individual lessons, the beginning teacher out of necessity operates in reverse by starting with the short-term plan. Owen-Jackson (2015) explains the need for knowledge and understanding of subject and process content along with an understanding of the school, how pupils learn and, specifically for D&T, the resources available needed for long-term planning. Beginning teachers do not have the experience to be skilful at long-term planning in the early stages.

The beginning teacher has so many things to learn, filter and undertake during the induction period before they start teaching. Occasionally, as a mentor, we might worry about overloading them with 'paperwork'. However, it is worth noting the value of different docu-ments and deciding which ones are imperative to the initial understanding. Knowing what pupils have to make is inevitably at the forefront of minds, particularly if this requires per-sonal skill development working with you or the departmental technician. Sometimes a lack of knowledge allows the mentee to consider the component parts of the making skill. If they are confident in using a skill or item of equipment, they do not always consider the miscon-ceptions and skill deficits of the pupils they are working with. Beginning D&T teachers are sometimes astounded when they assume that a secondary-aged school pupil has the fine motor skills to cut in a straight line. They often have not and therefore cannot advance to making the planned artefact.

There is also a danger in talking to mentee about outcomes. By focusing on the outcome, the beginning teacher can omit to focus on the learning. It is worth noting at this point the unique nature of planning for learning in D&T. Talk to the mentee about writing learning objectives (the what do you want them to learn) in terms of what pupils will 'know' and what they will 'do'. While in other subjects the 'doing' is often the vehicle to the learning in D&T, the practical ability is as important as the 'knowing' or the theory. To this end mentors can help mentees by framing objectives using the sentence stems, 'by the end of the lesson

- Pupils will know...
- Pupils will understand how
- Pupils will be able to (do) ...'

Fautley and Savage (2013) refer to this as the contextual (know) and procedural (do) outcomes.

How the D&T mentor manages this dichotomy can often depend upon the particular department and what schemes of work, equipment and resources are available. While both the mentor and the beginning teacher will have the lesson plan template at hand, it will be important to have the conversation about why, for example, experiments to show the dena-turation properties of eggs are in the scheme of work. Ideally, a medium-term plan or unit of work will show the direction of learning or intended learning outcomes and will give the beginning teacher an idea of what they are aiming for.

Owen-Jackson (2015) describes the process as a skill in articulating learning. Develop-ing understanding and skill in lesson planning helps to develop understanding and skill in teaching. Similarly, the idea of planning backwards (Griffith and Burns 2014) can allow the beginning teacher to have some overview of the learning and the time, allocated to it. Setting these ideas as foundations will help both the mentor and the mentee to hone in on individual weeks and lessons as they move towards planning the first lesson.

The planning process – individual lessons

It is important that beginning teachers have specific questions to consider when they start the planning process. This will enable them to manage thoughts and understanding while attempting to 'fill in' the lesson plan template. This is particularly important as the mentor is not only guiding them through this part of the training but also leading them towards a way of thinking about planning and, in time, internalising the process.

A lesson plan template will vary, but some of the key questions will not.

- Who am I teaching? *What is the year group, class size and ability of the pupils? What are the varying learning needs? Are there any pupils I need to focus on today?*
- What they will know and what they will do? *What is the objective of the learning? How does it follow on from the last lesson's learning?*
- How am I teaching it? *Are there specific teaching strategies or learning activities which will lend themselves to this lesson and the learning objective?*
- How will I assess learning during the lesson? *How will I monitor the pupils' access to the learning and progress with it? How will I know when to intervene to move the learning on or develop key points? Can I plan for this transition (movement) through learning?*
- How do I measure the learning after the lesson and how does this inform my next lesson plan? *How can I use today's learning and experiences to help me to plan ahead? Does the marking of written or practical work affect this process and how? Is the learning taking place over time?*

As a mentor, thinking about these questions as you model a plan or collaboratively plan, will allow you to articulate a thoughtful commentary for the mentee. The speed at which you would ordinarily plan in your head needs to be slowed down for the beginning teacher so that they can see and hear the process. This is a powerful learning experience for your mentee and validates the thinking that you undertake even if your planner cites, 'health and safety - year 9'. Owen-Jackson (2007, p. 113) talks about experienced teachers having 'plans-in-memory' and hence the experienced teacher needs to almost press the reset button. It is at this point that joint planning, with the dialogical element layered on top of the practical plan, will enable the mentee to understand your planning process, and how you have become adept at internalising the methodology (John 2006).

At this stage, the mentor is *supporting* the beginning teacher in the process before moving into the *challenge stage* (Daloz, 2012) when the mentor will guide them through a post lesson reflection. They are also using collaborative experiences in order to gain an insight into D&T teaching and how experienced teachers plan. McCann (2013) argues that regularly using collaboration as a learning experience for the mentee will not only avoid them struggling in isolation which will give them confidence and the opportunity to thrive but also introduce them to a community of teachers (Task 8.3).

Task 8.3   Reflecting on our own teaching

- Think about how you graduate your questions when working with pupils in the D&T classroom. This will no doubt be an integral part of how you manage questions in everyday lessons. Remember that your mentee will be working toward clear time-specific assessment points but will be working at different rates. Phasing your questions during post lesson discussion will scaffold the learning process for your mentee. Think back to Chapter 1 and Katz's (1995) stages of development whereby the beginning teacher moves from survival, to consolidation, to renewal and then maturity.

- Teach a lesson today and think about what questions you might ask a beginning teacher at the end of it. How would you unpick with your mentee what the pupils have actually learned in terms of 'knowing' and 'doing' rather than just focusing on the outcome? How do you measure this progress either within the lesson or overtime?

At this point, it is helpful to think about how beginning teachers will develop over the year and how we can support the rate of progression. Each person will adapt at different rates so layering the mentor commentary, the questioning and the increasingly specific questions about inclusion, differentiation and pupil progress will be one of the ways that the mentor can guide them toward supporting pupils' learning. The mentor will be constantly assessing the beginning teacher and prioritising next steps *with* them. Sometimes too many questions and targets can be debilitating to the inexperienced teacher so the mentor must carefully select question and targets that will have the biggest impact on progress. Secondly, we must focus on ensuring that the mentoring cycle is not broken. By this, we must consider how a feedback loop ensures that focused discussion and actions from one mentoring conversation are acted upon and evaluated before moving to the next.

The following table shows a suggested structure for lesson planning and some key ideas and questions for the beginning teacher and the mentor to use when they are discussing and evaluating lesson plans (Table 8.1).

Table 8.1 Thinking about the process behind the plan

Lesson stage	Objective	Activity (indicate differentiation)	Evaluation methods/ Assessment opportunities	Health and safety/ equipment/ resources
Starter It is wise to use timings in this column. Plan for extra time.	Each part of your lesson should have a clear learning purpose focusing on the 'know' and 'do' outcomes. Ideally these will connect vertically through the lesson stages, building toward the overall learning objectives.	Note here what you and the pupils will be doing when they arrive in the lesson. You may want to script your introduction to the lesson here. You should show how you are varying your teaching to suit the range of pupils including working with other adults in the classroom as applicable.	How will you know that the starter has achieved its learning objective? Is there time for a starter? What are the key messages to ensure successful learning? Will there be key questions to record here or a list of pupils you would like to focus on?	Consider here possible hazards and risk assessment. List all equipment and resources

(continued)

Table 8.1 (Cont.)

Lesson stage	Objective	Activity (indicate differentiation)	Evaluation methods/ Assessment opportunities	Health and safety/ equipment/ resources
Transition	Indicate here how you will move the lesson from the previous activity to the next one. This might be physical movement from being at the front of the lesson to work stations. **Consider how you are making the learning explicit to the pupils. This will be an important part of the teacher commentary.**			
Main activity	Each part of your lesson should have a clear learning purpose. Ideally these will connect vertically (in chunks) through the lesson stages, building toward the overall learning objectives.	How does this activity move the pupils toward achieving the learning objective? Is there a need for spot demonstrations? How will this be managed? Think about transitions and pupil movement. Is it focused, relevant and meaningful for this particular lesson? What are the key time checks?	How will you know that the activity has achieved its learning objective? Is there an opportunity for you to reflect and review before you move into the next transition? Are the pupils ready and able to move on?	Consider in advance equipment and resources. If some equipment needs sharing this needs to be factored into your planning.
Transition	Indicate here how you will move the lesson from the previous activity to the next one. **Consider how you are making the learning explicit to the pupils. This will be an important part of the teacher commentary.**			
Developmental Activity	Each part of your lesson should have a clear learning purpose. Ideally these will connect vertically through the lesson stage, building toward the overall learning objectives.	How does this activity develop the learning so far? Is there opportunity for the pupils to showcase what they have learned and apply it independently or in pairs/groups? Be explicit about how you will organise tidying up and putting away.	How might your observations or key questions elicit the pupils' progress here? How are you using your knowledge and information about pupils to inform this part of the assessment of learning?	Consider health and safety and resource implications as well as the logistics of organising the room for the next lesson.

Table 8.1 (Cont.)

Lesson stage	Objective	Activity (indicate differentiation)	Evaluation methods/ Assessment opportunities	Health and safety/ equipment/ resources
Transition	Indicate here how you will move the lesson from the previous activity to the final reflection. **Consider how you encouraging your learners to elicit learning from the lesson overall. This will be an important part of the teacher commentary as you move into an effective plenary.** **There should be a clear sense of the 'shape' of today's learning in both your mind and the learners'.**			
Plenary	*Evaluation of lesson objectives*	*Activity: Show how you will create opportunities from which you can judge the pupils' learning and thus the achievement of the lesson objectives. Are there opportunities for the pupils to measure their learning and reflect upon the 'know' and 'do' objectives and not just the outcome.* *Consider dismissal – you might want to include a script.*	*Planning for storage of practical work and careful labelling of pupils' work. Think about the logistics of organising storage.*

Teaching and evaluating lessons

The challenge here will be to ask how the plan worked in the lesson and how the beginning teacher knows this. If the mentee focused on facilitating learning at the planning stage, this will inevitably be an easier thought process. Rather than honing in on what the beginning teacher did or did not complete in the plan, the discussion should centre on the pupils' learning – most notably the 'know' and 'do' objectives. At the early stages of school experience, this will necessarily link to the activities that featured in the lesson plan but will at least begin to promote the pupil centred approach to planning and teaching. This will encourage some evaluative reflection of *how* the plan was implemented and whether or not this *facilitated* the intended learning.

It will be important for the mentor to ensure that the beginning teacher understands the difference between the planned lesson and the delivered lesson (Fautley and Savage 2013). A number of hours may have gone into the lesson plan with well-intentioned objectives but circumstances in the lesson itself might have thwarted this plan. The mentee might have encountered behaviour or timing issues which affected the planned timeline. How they reacted to this in the lesson will obviously be worthy of exploration. In many instances, post lesson observations might default to the aspects of the lesson which went 'wrong'. As will be noted in Chapter 11, from an early stage how the mentor manages this perspective will affect how the beginning teacher views the practice. Therefore the mentor should model an open and reflective approach to post lesson thinking and a positive outlook on the next lesson.

Wallace and Gravells (2007) and McCann (2013) noted that the mentor can be alert to the times when things may go wrong and that in being proactive they do not need to provide a solution. Rather, the mentor's role here is in facilitating the problem solving process to develop the mentee's ongoing understanding of teaching and overall teacher resilience (Task 8.4).

Task 8.4   Managing feedback

- How will you plan questions to begin the post lesson discussion from a positive perspective?
- How can you help beginning teachers manage emotional responses to a lesson while drilling down the subject specialist's view?

The mentor might have planned some key questions for the post lesson discussion in order to focus the beginning teacher's mind on the learning and pupil progress. **Perhaps the beginning teacher identified four able pupils and had planned two higher order thinking questions** - *how did these questions work and how was the mentee able to measure the pupils' understanding?* **Perhaps there was an creative approach to managing lesson times using music or a timer so that the maximum amount of lesson time was devoted to the learning rather than the clearing away** - *how did this strategy promote efficiency to maximise time? How did the mentee manage the movement around the room and did it enhance pupils' comprehension of the task in hand or hinder it?* As a subject specialist mentor, you are best placed to plan an effective post lesson discussion which will naturally lead into the next planning phase for the beginning teacher and ensure that they are making clear and purposeful steps toward developing practice. This also models the cyclical process behind planning that is commonly cited as assess, plan, do, review.

As a mentor, it is worth remembering that a planned or semi-structured discussion will enable greater depth of reflective thought and therefore be a more meaningful evaluation experience for the beginning teacher. Therefore, as we are observing lessons, we are also engaging with the plan and formulating ways of structuring the discussion afterwards. Are there key questions that you want to note down as they occur to you during the observation?

Different routes into teaching will have varying methods for the beginning teacher to capture evaluations of lessons. If the mentor has modelled good practice during these post lesson discussions, it will enable the mentee to begin to undertake such reflections on their own. They may have a certain number of lesson evaluations to complete in a week or have a regular review in which they focus on some aspect of teaching in order to articulate 'what went well' and how they could develop this further in future lessons. It will be valuable to remind the beginning teacher that while these activities seem to add to workload or even feel like administrative tasks (Owen-Jackson 2015), that the effective and thoughtful engagement will increase the capacity to improve practice. It will also embed a professional practice, which will support throughout teaching. The degree to which the mentor's post lesson discussion encourages the beginning teacher to reflect will affect their responsivity to future planning and teaching; reaffirming that they are both inter-related and dynamic (John 2006; Task 8.5).

Task 8.5   Focusing on D&T during post lesson discussions

- How did the mentee respond to your questions? What aspects of subject knowledge and pedagogical understanding are you able to discern at this point? Can you relate to professional standards (such as the English Teachers' Standards TS3, 4, 5 and 6) and consider progress over time?
- What do responses tell you about targets to move forward from this point and what do you need to do in order to support this development?

The table below is a suggested process for structuring responses. The important factor is that the beginning teacher is given a clear structure to enable them to develop and embed the skill of reflective practice.

1. Personal Objectives

My personal developmental objectives were:	Were they achieved?	What evidence do I have for this?

2. Pupils' learning objectives

Objectives:	Evaluation techniques:	Was the learning achieved?	Notes/evidence

3. Development points for my teaching

My own ideas:
My mentor's feedback:
My subject tutor's feedback:

Using data and assessment to inform planning and teaching

The beginning teacher can be overwhelmed with a plethora of data. Effective mentors model how this is managed and used over time. In many instances, stepping out of the day-to-day life of planning and entering into a reflective and mutually transactional exchange can be refreshing for the mentor. As the training progresses, mentors will often find that they are learning another level of insight about personal practice and that this would not have happened without the ongoing dialogue with the mentee (Rekha and Ganesh 2012).

Most departments will have in-built assessments which will give a focal point to the planning or require 'planning backwards' (Owen-Jackson 2015). Even if this is not the case, this often offers a transparent view of the learning, and will enable the beginning teacher to consider why aspects of the lesson are necessary or valid.

While schools will have whole school marking policies and protocols, this often does not include the assessment of practical work. The mentor can model how marking of practical outcomes becomes meaningful data which feeds directly into the next lesson plan. A mentee will see many disparate parts of the role of being a D&T teacher and the mentor can quickly show how many are interlinked and inform the next stage. For example, it would be possible to list marking, assessment, planning and teaching as a variety of tasks that a teacher undertakes. Rather the mentor's role will be to constantly show how one affects the other and all are interlinked. How the next lesson plan needs to be refined after marking a set of books, or reviewing assessments of practical lessons, is a valuable lesson for the mentee in managing data and ongoing assessment.

Likewise, how the mentor engages with some of the data in order to arrange classes, plan for a variety of learning activities and interact with pupils will be significant aspects of your practice to focus on in your discussions with the mentee in the early weeks. Once again, the mentor needs to crystallise the many skills that she has and be explicit about how these permeate every aspect of her day and therefore inform 'a lesson plan'. Without this guidance in situ, the mentee may still perceive planning as the lesson plan template as opposed to an intricate skill which they are hoping to develop. It is this 'relational authenticity' (Ragins 2016) which compounds much of the learning that the beginning teacher is processing. They will listen to and absorb your own real-time commentary. Being honest and open about what has worked (or not worked) in some of your lessons this week will be a way of conveying a real sense of your role as a teacher and should positively impact on the trust being built between the mentor and mentee (Task 8.6).

Task 8.6   How do you interpret and use data to inform your teaching?

- Think about the basic questions that you ask yourself when setting the learning objective which involves some of the data that you have on groups of pupils or individual pupils? What do you do when the data is not subject specific?

- What would be your three top tips for a beginning teacher when they collect a pack of data for a class?
- What key signs of engagement are you looking for when you read your mentee's lesson plans?
- How does this skill develop? What would you expect to see from a beginning teacher in the first term compared to the second term?

Moving from individual lessons to planning sequences of lessons

The concept of the beginning teacher moving towards planning a sequence of lessons is one that mentors can often worry about. There is an irony here, in that the beginning teacher can only begin to understand how to plan an individual lesson if she understands how it fits into the overall plan for learning. Just as we began this process with considering the interaction with the department's schemes of work or medium-term plans, there comes a point at which the mentee will be best able to meet the needs of the pupils if she has a clear overview of the learning over a sequence of lessons (Owen-Jackson 2015). This may happen quickly with some teachers. Others may take longer to begin to see the links and the fusion between lessons and the learning which is taking place.

From the mentor's point of view, there is no fixed time in the training year when this will become the next step in the beginning teacher's practice. As noted by Maynard and Furlong (1995) in Chapter 1, the professional learning of the beginning teacher will progress at different speeds. The key to this transition will be the mentor's knowledge of her mentee and the rate of their progression. Review meetings will give a clear indication of the beginning teacher's understanding of the pupils' progress and teaching to move towards end of unit assessments. There will be signs for the mentor to look for, such as, a greater degree of ownership of the classes, a more proactive approach to the planning and marking cycle and a more confident and thorough exploration of this, by the mentee, in the review meeting. The mentor will need to plot this progression carefully, challenge where appropriate and ascertain when the learning will be better in a plan which shows progression in a sequence of learning rather than disparate lessons.

How can beginning teachers promote learning over time?

This question sounds onerous to say the least to a beginning teacher. Keeping the mentee focused on getting to know pupils and planning effective lessons will be key in considering how they are able to contribute to this in school. In D&T, this is exasperated as different material areas are often taught as a part of a curriculum carousel, when beginning teachers might only see a group for eight weeks before they rota to another material. The limited time available to assess progress can be a challenge. Therefore, mentors need to consider how their own practice promotes learning over time (Task 8.7).

Task 8.7   capturing learners' progress

- Think about a class that are currently midway through a unit of work. Identify the intended learning outcome at the end of the unit and consider how you will assess progress, perhaps through a formalised assessment.
- Now, consider how this class and certain individuals are making progress towards this **at this point in time**. If there was an impromptu parents' evening, what overview and evidence of progress would you be able to highlight for the parents/carers at this point in the term?
- Does this consideration prompt you to think about your planning differently?

Check points for learning over time - thinking about our own practice and consider how you will share this with your beginning teacher.

- How well do you know your pupils and how do you build this picture over time?
- How do you assess prior knowledge and understanding? Is your starting point right? Is the pitch right?
- How do you know if the pupils have learned in terms of 'doing' and 'knowing' in D&T? Do you notice a pupil's explanation, comment to a peer, thoughtful analogy or link to relevant learning?
- Do you understand the continuum for learning in this medium-term plan? Starting point > noticing learning take place > assessing learning over time > achieving intended outcomes.
- How do you use assessment for learning strategies to support this picture of progress?
- How do you use written and oral feedback to build an effective dialogue of assessment of learning with your pupils?

As the mentor of a beginning teacher, you will need to be able to reflect and respond to these questions in order to consider how you are using your own understanding of pupil progress in order to scaffold this process for the mentee. In taking time to use these questions of your own teaching and the mentee's, there will be recognition of progress over time and how it is inextricably linked with the planning process.

Summary

We have reflected on the complex task of planning and how we can break this down. Underpinning the chapter is the dialogic model of planning for the beginning teacher, as proposed by John (2006). The fluidity of this approach will have clarified your own understanding of planning, and how you can best support the beginning teacher through the different phases of the training.

In so doing we have considered:

- The processes that teachers engage in when planning lessons and sequence of lessons, particularly practical ones.
- How you can articulate and model these processes for mentees.

- The craft of becoming a reflective practitioner in order to plan the most effective lessons and how this reflection needs to take a graduated approach depending on the stage of development of the mentee.
- How the beginning teachers needs to move from solo lesson planning to planning over time using an assess, plan, do, review approach so that planning is part of a process and not a product.

References

Brockbank, A. and McGill, I. (2007) *Facilitating Reflective Learning in Higher Education*. Maidenhead: McGraw-Hill.

Clutterbuck, D. and Lane, G. (2004) *The Situational Mentor: An International Review of Competencies and Capabilities in Mentoring*. Hants: Gower.

Daloz, L. (2012) *Mentor: Guiding the Journey of Adult Learners*. San Francisco, CA: Jossey-Bass.

Fautley, M. and Savage, J. (2013) *Lesson Planning for Effective Learning*. Maidenhead: Open University Press.

Griffith, A. and Burns, M. (2014) *Teaching Backwards*. Carmarthen: Crown House Publishing Limited.

John, P. (2000) Awareness and intuition: how student teachers read their own lesson, in Atkinson, T. and Claxton, G. (eds.) *The Intuitive Practitioner*. London: OUP, pp. 69-83.

John, P. (2006) Lesson planning and the student teacher: thinking the dominant model. *Journal of Curriculum Studies*, 38:4, 483-498.

Katz, L. (1995) The developmental stages of teaching. Available at: http://ecap.crc.uiuc.edu/pubs/katz-dev-stages/index.html (Accessed: 23 October 2018).

Maynard, T. and Furlong, J. (1995) Learning to teach and models of mentoring, in Kerry, T. and Shelton-Mayes, A. (eds.) *Issues in Mentoring*, London: Routledge, pp. 10-14.

McCann, T. (2013) Mentoring Matters. *English Journal* 102:6, 88-90.

Owen-Jackson, G. (2007) Planning your teaching, in Owen-Jackson (ed.) *A Practical Guide to Teaching Design and Technology in the Secondary School*. Oxon: Routledge, pp. 103-144.

Owen-Jackson, G. (2015) Planning to teach design and technology, in Owen-Jackson, G. (ed.) *Learning to Teach Design and Technology in the Secondary School*. London: Routledge, pp. 241-266.

Ragins, B. (2016) From the ordinary to the extraordinary: high quality mentoring relationships at work. *Organizational Dynamics* 45, 228-244.

Rekha, K. and Ganesh, M., (2012) Do mentors learn by mentoring others? *International Journal of Mentoring and Coaching in Education* 1:3, 205-217.

Tyler, R. (1949) *Basic Principles of Curriculum and Instruction*. Chicago, IL: University of Chicago Press.

Wallace, S. and Gravells, J. (2007) *Mentoring in the Lifelong Learning Sector*. Exeter: Learning Matters Ltd.

9 Helping design and technology teachers to plan practical activities (including health and safety)

Jane Burnham

Introduction

Practical work is a wonderful way to motivate and engage pupils. The opportunity to be out of a seat and moving around for an hour is one which will stimulate many pupils who arrive at the design and technology (D&T) classroom door bursting with enthusiasm to start. Lesson observers impressed by pupils' eagerness to enter the room and begin work often notice this.

Planning is essential in order for practical activities to take place efficiently, effectively and most importantly, safely. This chapter will explore the value of practical work, and discusses statutory requirements and specialist advice regarding health and safety considerations to give mentors the confidence to support beginning teachers to plan purposeful practical activities.

Objectives

By the end of this chapter, you should be able to

- Share the benefits of practical work in a D&T setting.
- Identify strategies needed to support beginning teachers manage practical activities.
- Be familiar with the statutory requirements guiding general health and safety legislation in schools and specifically in D&T classrooms.
- Guide beginning teachers to work with support staff to prepare and manage practical activities.

What to make

As we saw in Chapter 2, the D&T curricula vary internationally but at the core is the design process requiring pupils to design, plan and ultimately make a product. This supports the development of a variety of cross-curricular transferable skills, which include developing pupils' creativity, independence, communication, teamwork and resilience. These skills can support future independence and employability so it is important that opportunities to be designers and makers are available in school. Opportunities for children to complete making activities beyond school are often limited by current lifestyle trends, including increased working hours for parents, the design and layout of homes and the influence of the technological revolution and its associated distractions.

This has implications for beginning teachers who misjudge the capabilities of pupils, and plan lessons that assume pupils have acquired a range of manual dexterity skills and the ability to work independently and clear up after themselves.

In his paper, for the John Eggleston memorial lecture, Barlex (see Chapter 4 for further views by Barlex et al.) argues the importance of practical work in D&T in the curriculum, citing 'man is a singular creature. He has a set of gifts, which make him unique among animals; so that, unlike them, he is not a figure in the landscape – he is a shaper of the landscape' (Barlex 2011, p. 19). He captured the nature of this accomplishment by stating,

> the hand is the cutting edge of the mind. Civilisation is not a collection of finished artefacts; it is an elaboration of processes. In the end, the march of man is the refinement of the hand in action... Design and Technology is the only subject in the current National Curriculum that embodies this activity and provides learners with the experience of 'the hand in action'.
>
> (Barlex 2011, p. 116)

In his book 'The Maker Movement Manifesto: Rules for Innovation in the New World of Crafters, Hackers, and Tinkerers', Hatch (2013) argues, 'Humans were designed to make'. He believes it to be a fundamental activity that humans enjoy and once learned need to share the knowledge. He argues a new way of working, where working in a space where others are working, offers opportunities to upgrade and improve and this way of working can lead to economic change. Few dedicated D&T teachers would disagree. He states, 'you no longer have to be a professional to change the world', and continues 'turning ideas can become a physical activity. If you can imagine it, you can make it' (Hatch 2013, p. 47).

When considering the type and range of practical activities, which need to be taught in schools, a general definition of the term is offered with this definition of 'making' through this statement from the English National Curriculum (DfE 2013a):

- To select from and use specialist tools, techniques, processes equipment and machinery precisely, including computer-aided manufacture.
- To select from and use a wider, more complex range of materials, components and ingredients, taking into account their properties.

This definition gives scope as to what should be taught in the subject and gives staff and pupils the opportunity to personalise learning and enhance pupils' making skills and creativity in a range of technology subjects. By making a range of contemporary products the subject has the capacity to enthuse and motivate future generations of engineers, food specialists and textile artists.

Making, however, is not always viewed as contemporary. Choulerton (2016), HMI and National Lead for Design and Technology for Ofsted discussed the need for an up-to-date D&T curriculum and commented on out-dated focussed practical tasks still in place in some schools. She challenged teachers to provide opportunities for pupils to engage in an iterative design process. By allowing pupils this opportunity they can determine the ways that materials and components will be shaped and combined to realise designs that solve real-life problems. However, when students are given an opportunity to design, it is not unusual for the task to be mainly restricted to designing in two dimensions, tackling design tasks such as logos, surface patterns or the appearance of a clock face.

To provide the curriculum with contemporary currency schemes of work must be updated regularly to follow trends in design development and lifestyle. Traditionally, schemes of work were planned with final outcomes as a focus, this approach not only placed limits on the pupils but led to the mass production of products with slight variation and some personalisation.

Beginning teachers and trainee teachers have often been disappointed by the lack of creativity in departments where the planning is still orientated toward making a specific product. They recognise that pupils need to be enthusiastic about making opportunities and see them as an opportunity to work with specific equipment or materials. Where schools adopt this approach, opportunities for making can be seasonal (giving them true contemporary currency) and still support the development of pupils' skills in working with materials and equipment. If the learning is planned around using specialist equipment, a range of materials ideas for contemporary products are quickly generated and pupils are enthused by the opportunity to make something original and this approach can also delineate the traditional 'subject barriers' that exist in many schools. For example, a sublimation printer might be used to print a pupil's design (either computer generated or on paper) on fabric or the process could be used to print on mugs. A laser cutter might be used to cut Perspex for a phone or tablet stand or a bonded textile to make badges or bag tags. Where pupils are taught to make electronic circuits using LEDs they could use this to make alarms, badges or wearable items for themselves or pets. If the focus is on sustainability, they could make chutneys as edible gifts alongside learning about food preservation or make bags for life from recycled clothing. Where, teachers plan for the learning rather than the outcome opportunities for real D&T start to emerge.

If schemes of work are up to date, the beginning teacher will be also be able to discover a plethora of ideas through online resources and professional teaching groups on social media sites. Membership of the Design and Technology Association (DATA) as well as CLEAPSS (Supporting Practical Science and Technology in Schools and Colleges) offers resources for making in all material areas of the subject. In addition, groups exist that focus purely on teaching food and textiles Examination boards will also include suggested products to make to meet assessment criteria in specifications (Task 9.1).

Task 9.1   Ideas for making

Look at the schemes of work that your school delivers.

Work with your beginning teacher to think about the purpose of the tasks and consider how changes to the 'making' activity might make it more contemporary for the pupils. For example, a 2D to 3D task in textiles making juggling bags could be developed to make mobile phone rests or doorstops. How could making activities in food focussed on using meat or dairy products be adapted in response toward the trend for vegan diets while retaining the development of the same skills.

Supporting beginning teachers with practical work

Beginning teachers will need high levels of support when starting to teach practical activities to ensure the statutory duties of care are followed at all times within the constraints of completing on time. A possible starting point is to provide opportunities to observe a variety of class teachers manage a range of practical lessons, with different groups and class sizes. Within an initial teacher education programme time is usually available for this but this is more difficult to facilitate for a newly or recently qualified teacher. In these instances, it is helpful for a mentor to spend time with the beginning teacher (or provide an opportunity for a technician) to show them how the room is organised and where resources and equipment are stored. Do not insist that it has to be done so, if the colleague is to have their own room they should be afforded the professional freedom to arrange it as they prefer although it may be worth advising to work in it as it is before making any radical changes. Making a new colleague familiar with school health and safety policy should be part of the induction programme and may be the responsibility of the mentor, head of department or possibly a member of support staff.

Where it is possible to arrange a series of observations of practical work choose classes that present significantly different challenges. Observing the standards required of a small group of sixth form students working independently for a course work project illustrates different management techniques to a large class of Key Stage 3 pupils working in a food room to complete a product within an hour. The style and pace of each lesson will demand different teaching and management styles, and it is useful for the beginning teacher to gain broad experience of observation where possible, in order to develop a personal style. Supporting beginning teachers through observation is explored further in Chapter 10 (Task 9.2).

Task 9.2   Case study 1

Share this case study with your beginning teacher recalling your first experience of teaching a practical lesson. What challenges did you experience and what are the challenges for Soraya?

Case study: Soraya

As part of my induction at my first placement as a trainee, I sat and observed a food lesson of a large GCSE group of pupils. The teacher seemed to be very stressed and shouted constantly at the pupils throughout the lesson to hurry them up to finish on time. I have always disliked being shouted at and felt uncomfortable just watching and vowed I would not let the pressure get to me to manage time constraints in a similar way. My own teaching style was quite different. I wanted the pupils to feel relaxed and happy in the same way I would want to be treated. However, at times during observations of my teaching my mentor commented that my lessons lacked pace and I have had to learn how to modify my own behaviour in terms of being firm when pupils need to increase the speed of working to meet the requirements of the timetable.

Beginning teachers should take the opportunity to practise making products themselves and as a mentor you might expect to facilitate this, particularly if the beginning teacher is managing practical activities beyond their subject specialism and expertise. Not only does this support them to pre-empt mistakes the pupils may make, it is valuable to acquire skills in using equipment proficiently, and to seek specialist help if needed. A department technician can be delegated to support this and will have great insight into the difficulties pupils have had in the past and will be able to clarify the order of making.

Managing space time and safety

Whether teaching practical work in a resistant materials workshop, a textiles classroom or a food room, managing space and safety is paramount. If you are managing food lessons, the production of a completed product from start to finish in one lesson has its own challenges as well as the obvious rewards.

Any practical lesson will have different stages and it is useful for a mentor to identify and demonstrate appropriate teaching strategies during each stage, for example spot demonstrations, individual support or a group discussion. The internet offers some brief clips of making which can be used at different stages of the process. The advantages of this resource are many. In an ideal world, technicians and teachers have time and resources to set up for each practical lesson in advance. The reality is more likely to be a case of clearing up after one class as the next is waiting to start, or even having to move to teach in a different classroom altogether. In these circumstances, using the internet to set the scene for the lesson can afford a teacher time to set up well. Examples might be watching a three-minute tutorial while the teacher takes the register and arranges the resources for a textiles class about to use batik or a skills demonstration for a food class. Where teachers choose to use these resources, it is important that they review them in advance to ensure that good attention to health and safety is modelled and that explanations are clear and unambiguous.

One of the greatest challenges of teaching 'making' in D&T is how to manage large groups. Budget constraints may mean that there is not enough equipment for everyone. Sharing is the obvious answer but in a food lesson where the product must be cooked and packaged before the end of the lesson time constraints must be considered. Over time experienced teachers develop meticulous organisational skills to deal with this and teach several lessons in succession. Beginning teachers will not always acknowledge this and mentors need to make them aware and offer the strategies they employ to support them to be successful. For example, half the class might use the electric hand mixer to mix the ingredients while the others prepare tins. At times providing opportunities for pupils to work in groups to complete activities might be appropriate for example, when completing investigative practical work. Examples might include cutting different types of plastic to determine the best type for a template, or making small cakes using various proportions of sugar. Beginning teachers will need some support and ideas from a mentor to anticipate the problems and plan to manage the learning with the resources available.

Beginning teachers do not always consider the impact of the length of lessons on practical work. Timetabling can be a contentious issue where D&T teachers desperate for double lessons may well be at odds with colleagues teaching other subjects who may struggle to keep the momentum for a prolonged period. Careful planning and preparation is essential when anticipating what can be achieved in a lesson to ensure pupil progress. Many lessons are of one-hour length, some only 50 minutes. Keeping a sharp focus on the purpose of the learning is critical and invites different approaches to completing tasks within limited lesson time. Why plan individual work if group work can secure the same learning outcomes? Strategies to hurry pupils along such as using face paced music and setting ambitious time targets can make learning challenging and contribute to pupils' sense of accomplishment. Lessons of a longer length are not necessarily a panacea, they can lend themselves to a more relaxed approach, but can also lack pace and challenge and consequently may lead to less focussed learning behaviour and no more successful outcomes (Task 9.3).

Task 9.3   Time and practical work

- Choose a practical activity and break down the elements of the task into chunks of time. Ask your beginning teacher to do the same.
- Compare notes and see if there are discrepancies. An inexperienced teacher may underestimate the time needed for each step. For example, the setting up time at the beginning of the lesson can take almost 15 minutes. This useful activity really does give an insight into the pace required for much practical work.

Supporting beginning teachers with health and safety requirements

It is part of the professional duty of a teacher to ensure a safe working environment in all subjects but this is especially pertinent in D&T. The English Teachers' Standards (DfE 2013b) require beginning teachers to TS1a *establish a safe and stimulating environment for pupils, rooted in mutual respect (TS1a)* and *maintain good relationships with pupils, exercise appropriate authority and act decisively when necessary* (TS7d). Both of these Standards require teachers to be constantly aware of risks and dangers in the classroom in terms of the control and use of resources, procedures and behaviour of pupils.

Statutory requirements for the safe teaching of practical activities in schools are thorough and detailed to ensure the safety of all, in a wide range of situations within a school setting. Additionally, schools have health and safety policy statements and within that, each department will have procedures. It is imperative that all staff are familiar with both, and use them as working reference, rather than something to read during the staff induction process. As a mentor, you will need to ensure that a beginning teacher or new colleague has access to this information.

In England, government legislation and specialist guidance from the Design and Technology Association exist to support staff (British Standard 2014: *BS 4163:2014 Health and Safety for design and technology in educational and similar establishments*). The beginning teacher must not be daunted at the prospect of trying to keep large groups of children safe. However, it is imperative that everything possible is anticipated in order to make certain that the welfare of pupils has been carefully considered whether it be the wearing of dust masks when using hazardous substances or checking medical records for allergies when carrying out a sensory analysis in a food lesson. The Design and Technology Association (DATA) (2013) believes that best practice emanates from teachers who are knowledgeable about relevant aspects of health and safety and who subsequently feel confident in managing and maintaining a healthy and safe working environment. DATA publishes recommended standards for health and safety in D&T departments and provides accredited training. These standards form the basis of many department policies. Some initial training providers include the accredited training within the initial teacher training programmes and where this does not take place, it is likely that trainee teachers will have been made familiar with the DATA standards during training (Leask 2015).

As a mentor whatever the subject within the framework of D&T, you need to work with beginning teachers to ensure the following:

- All pupils should have health and safety training before undertaking **any** practical work. Understanding of health and safety awareness should be evidenced. This can be done in the format of a checklist which is signed and dated by staff and pupils (see Chapter 8 on lesson planning).
- Protective clothing and equipment should be worn at all times when carrying out practical work.
- Equipment should only be used following instruction.
- No running or irresponsible behaviour in the classroom.
- Equipment should be visually checked for safety and annually tested
- The department should have conducted risk assessment reviews on all equipment and hazardous substances.

Practical lessons where pupils are preparing food need additional guidance. Following several incidents of pupils leaving raw chicken in lockers until the practical lesson after lunch (instead of bringing into the food rooms for safe storage in the refrigerator as instructed), one school added explicit information on the storage of high-risk ingredients to its induction lesson which pupils were required to sign and date.

Managing practical lessons safely

The start of a lesson is often hectic with pupils eager to start making, and it can be difficult for the beginning teacher to manage a variety of tasks to include taking the register and giving key information. This can result in some health and safety issues that can affect the welfare of those in the classroom. It is challenging and frustrating for beginning teachers to have to chide pupils to tie hair back or to put on an apron or goggles as well as supervising the use of equipment and machinery in a confined space. Guidance is needed so that clear and effective systems are in place for getting pupils ready to carry out practical work to increase independence and decision-making skills. Some schools have developed approaches to support this such as acronyms that remind pupils what to do, or green cards prominently displayed that list what to do to be ready to go! An emerging issue in some schools is the increasing number of pupils who wear artificial nails. These can hinder the use of tools, and machinery and the capacity to work safely. This highlights the need for department policies to be dynamic to enable teachers to use sanctions with pupils if they continue to be worn in practical lessons, as they do for when the behaviour or presentation creates a risk in a practical setting (Task 9.4).

Task 9.4   Health and safety checklists

Following from observations of experienced staff teaching practical lessons, ask your beginning teacher to produce a quick checklist of health and safety rules to be repeated at the start of each lesson so that it becomes a mantra. For example, 'aprons on, bags away, stools tucked under, hands washed, hair tied back.' One teacher I know makes a point of pretending to get the instructions muddled up *'hair washed, hands tied back'* which always catches the attention of the class and is a quick affirmation that the instructions have been heard.

It is important to be consistent. Goggles are clearly a necessary but not attractive item of protective wear required in a resistant materials lesson. Pupils may wish to rebel and avoid wearing them 'But miss, they mess up my hair!' The beginning teacher must make it clear from the outset that rules for protecting pupils from damage or danger are inflexible and sanctions will be taken against those who will not comply. However, it is important to be aware of pupils with individual needs. This is illustrated by Liam's story

Case study: Liam

It was a particularly hot day and the workshop was uncomfortably warm. In a previous lesson, several pupils had complained of feeling unwell, and I was particularly careful to monitor pupil well-being in subsequent lessons. Following my simple request that pupils were to remove blazers before putting on aprons for the soldering activity, I was surprised and disappointed to notice a quiet and usually well-behaved pupil ignore my instruction and become argumentative and confrontational when I pursued the issue. I felt angry and frustrated at this defiance, which was wasting valuable making time. I asked her to come outside the room into the corridor and asked her why she was behaving in such a manner over such a reasonable request. She broke down in tears saying "Sir, I can't! Look at my arms!" She pulled up her sleeves to show an array of cuts and scarring on each forearm. I was shocked and saddened and told her she could keep her blazer on, subsequently reporting the disclosure to the safeguarding team. This incident really made me think about the patience and sensitivity required when confronted with uncharacteristic behaviour.

Task 9. 5   Barriers to learning

Work with your beginning teacher to consider the barriers to learning in a practical lesson. By anticipating these consider how they could be overcome (Task 9.5).

The greater the class size, the more challenging it can be to supervise the safe use of tools equipment and materials. When considering statutory requirements regarding the safe management of practical activities, space and class numbers are a primary consideration. Heads of subject may well be encouraged to agree to teach with large numbers due to the demands of budget cuts and timetabling. Many children do little or no practical work at home. Learning how to use a screwdriver, threading a needle or even using a can opener may be a wholly new experience. Alongside a trend for 'learned helplessness', where if pupils cannot see or find equipment instantly, they seek help from the teacher, the prospect of managing practical work with large groups can be daunting, and exhausting for beginning teachers. Whatever the class size, pupils 'welfare is paramount and a whole department responsibility. As a mentor a beginning teacher may require your encouragement if things go wrong. A reminder of the pupils' sense of accomplishment when making and the clear progress that can be shown through using new materials and equipment can support them to recognise the complex nature of managing a class successfully particularly in a practical setting.

Skilful teachers pre-empt pupils' responses. In a practical situation, this involves anticipating what might go wrong and taking measures to ensure it does not. Risk assessments are based on careful thought and anticipation of the hazards presented in the classroom with a combination of pupils, materials, equipment and activities. A school should have a range of completed risk assessment proformae to use as a reference point when lesson planning. These should be seen as working documents and not just completed then filed away. Risk assessments should be regularly updated as new schemes of works and activities are planned and developed (Task 9.6).

Task: 9.6   Risk assessment

Working together with your beginning teacher, look at a recent lesson plan and identify possible risks surrounding the layout of the room as well as the activities. Look at the corresponding risk assessment paperwork on record and see whether there are any omissions and if it requires updating.

Working with support staff

Support staff provide a vital role to a department. These might include technicians and specialist teaching assistants. They often possess a lot of specialist knowledge and can be a great ally to a beginning teacher. As a mentor, you may decide to delegate some of the induction activities to these colleagues. Key personal qualities to work in a D&T department include the ability to be resourceful and adaptable, excellent communication and interpersonal skills and the ability to use initiative as well as being a member of a team. A thorough knowledge of health and safety, ideally with COSHH is essential. Each department has its own style of utilising support staff and it is important for the new colleague to understand the roles of individuals within the school system (Task 9.7).

Task 9.7   Working with support staff

- If you have a department technician, share the job description with your new colleague.
- Facilitate an opportunity for them to meet together to discuss the role and ask the technician to identify key areas where teachers require support and how they communicate requirements. Has this changed over time?
- Following the meeting it might be useful for the beginning teacher to identify any specific help they may need to work successfully within the department that the technician could support.

If the school has specialist teaching assistants this task could be repeated with them.

A culture of 'learned helplessness' is increasingly being observed in classrooms, for example a pupil with a can of kidney beans without a ring pull lid recently called for help in a food practical saying *'How on earth am I supposed to open this?'* On another occasion, a pupil declared *'Miss, I'm kind of scared of ovens'*. To an experienced teacher this may be shocking and the additional support of an extra pair of eyes and hands can make the difference between the class completing work on time or not. Those who choose to work in schools enjoy working with children. A teaching assistant described the enjoyment and job satisfaction she achieved when supporting a classroom teacher in a food lesson, highlighting an example of demonstrating how to break an egg in a shallow bowl and whisk with a fork, in preparation for making chicken goujons *'Wow! Look how she's done that!'* was the amazed response. Experienced teachers can be surprised by such examples, which exemplify pupils' experience beyond school. This may be less surprising to a beginning teacher who may be equally astonished by an experienced (older) colleague's lack of proficiency at using a mobile phone or tablet. The benefits of working collaboratively in the classroom with technicians and teaching assistants cannot be underestimated when considering how to establish a safe practical learning environment in D&T, and serve to remind us that pupils and colleagues come to the lesson with differing experience and skills (Task 9.8).

Task 9.8   Daniel and Simon

Ask your beginning teacher to refer back to Task 9:2 where elements of the tasks in a practical activity have been divided into chunks of time. Look at the case studies of Daniel and Simon to identify where additional support would be useful.

Case Study: Daniel

Having struggled to manage increasingly large group sizes in GCSE Resistant materials classes, I now deploy my technician differently in these lessons. I will ask him to supervise pupils using a specific piece of machinery while I am then able to move around the classroom guiding and supporting where necessary.

Case Study: Simon

My Food classroom is very small and badly designed. My predecessor consequently did very little practical work and this was having a detrimental effect on pupils' motivation and behaviour in lessons as well as subject take up at GCSE level. Having reviewed the scheme of work I realised it would be possible to do more practical work if some adjustments were made. For example, products are put in and taken out of the oven by support staff on a rota basis with pupils completing a chart to show what shelf/ time they need. Although this took time to implement, it really has worked well and numbers are beginning to creep up.

In conclusion, support staff are a valuable asset and make a tremendous difference to the department.

Summary

This chapter has emphasised the importance of practical work in the teaching of D&T to educate pupils in a wide range of materials, together with information on some of the key health and safety legislation and guidance in order to support teaching in this subject.

At its most challenging, managing practical activities can be demanding-

> after a quarter of a century teaching D&T I am still filled with dread when entering a strange workshop to meet a class of energetic students eager to start 'making'. There are so many variables and complexities from operating machinery you are not familiar with to finding where the hand tools are stored. Trust me, it's a darn sight more demanding than trying to find text books and lined paper.
>
> (Woodward 2016)

The beginning teacher needs to be guided to ensure that practical activities are stimulating, relevant, and can be completed within the timeframe, using available resources and equipment. Pupils gain a great sense of accomplishment through making things well. Above all, they need to know how to keep pupils safe. Time after time, activities which teachers perceive to be straightforward will prove challenging but this is not a reason not to try.

The benefits of teamwork cannot be exaggerated; teaching colleagues, technicians and specialist teaching assistants have a great deal of expertise to share with a beginning teacher. Working as a team and acknowledging each other's strengths and areas of expertise and where and when to seek assistance is a professional responsibility. As a mentor guiding a beginning teacher to recognise this and supporting them to contribute to the team, you have the potential to make a difference to all of your colleagues.

Further resources

CLEAPPS (2015) *Supporting Practical Science, DT and Art in Schools and Colleges. PS68- Design and Technology and Class Sizes, Room Sizes and Possible Effects on Safety.* Uxbridge: CLEAPPS.

CLEAPPS (2017) *Auditing Health and Safety in Design and Technology and Art and Design Departments.* Uxbridge: CLEAPPS.

Health and Safety Executive (2004) *A Step by Step Guide to COSHH Assessments* www.hse. gov.uk/coshh/basics/assessment.htm (Accessed: 28 August 2018).

Health and Safety Executive (2007) BS 4163:2007 Health and safety for design and technology in schools and similar establishments – Code of practice. Available at: www.hse.gov.uk/ services/education (Accessed: 28 August 2018).

Health and Safety Executive (2018) *Health and Safety Checklist for Classrooms.* Available at: www.hsegov.uk/risk/classroom checklist.pdf (Accessed: 28 August 2018).

Owen-Jackson, G. (2015) Planning to teach design and technology, in Owen-Jackson, G. (ed.) *Learning to Teach Design and Technology in the Secondary School.* London: Routledge, pp. 241-266.

Websites

www.data.org.uk
www.cleapss.org.uk
www.tes.com/teaching-resources/hub/secondary

References

Barlex, D. (2011) John Eggleston Memorial Lecture, 'Dear Minister, This is why design and technology is a very important subject in the school curriculum', *Technology Education: An International Journal* 16(3) pp. 9-18.

British Standards Institution (2014) BS *4163:2014 Code of Practice for Health and Safety for Design and Technology in Educational and Similar Establishments, Code of Practice.* London: BSI.

Choulerton, D. (2016) *Challenges and Opportunities in D&T.* Available at: www.data.org.uk/ news/challenges-and-opportunities-in-dt/ (Accessed: 09 November 2018).

DfE (2013a) *National Curriculum in England: Design and Technology Programmes of Study.* London: Department for Education. Available at: www.gov.uk/government/publications (Accessed: 09 November 2018).

DfE (2013b) *Teachers' Standards: Guidance for School Leaders, School Staff and Governing Bodies.* London: Department for Education. Available at: www.education.gov.uk/publications. (Accessed: 28 July 2018).

DfE (no date) *Risk Assessment in Secondary School Design and Technology Teaching Environments.* Available at: www.data.org.uk (Accessed: 09 November 2018).

Hatch, M. (2013) *The Maker Movement Manifesto: Rules for Innovation in the New World of Crafters, Hackers, and Tinkerers.* New York: McGraw-Hill Educational.

Leask, D. (2015) 'Health and safety in design and technology', in Owen-Jackson, G. (ed.) *Learning to Teach Design and Technology in the Secondary School.* London: Routledge, pp. 37–56.

Woodward, P. (2016) 'What makes a design and technology teacher?', *TES blog*, 21 April. Available at: www.tes.com/news/blog/what-makes-a-design-and-technology-teacher (Accessed: 09 November 2018).

10 Observing design and technology teachers' lessons: tools for observation and analysis

Sarah Davies

Introduction

We often take the human capacity of observation for granted. Our ability to observe the social world around us in repeated and varied ways allows us to learn: how to act; how things work and what other people do. In Wragg's (2011, p. vii) seminal book, *An Introduction to Classroom Observation*, he wrote that:

> [i]t is because we have crossed the road thousands of times that we know what to look for, though the context will be different on each new occasion. We have the means of recognising what is familiar and what is novel, and this puts us in a position to make decisions rapidly about the speed of vehicles, their distance away, likely position in a few seconds, our capability of walking or running at a certain pace and in a particular direction.

Wragg was using this passage to highlight the way we use observation as a map for human activity and the rules of the game, as they apply, within a variety of contexts. By observing the social world around us we become familiar with that world and the way that people behave within it. Mentors of beginning design and technology teachers use observations of lessons, to support their teacher's development.

This chapter focuses on the mentor's role using classroom observation. Classroom observation is a simple and vital part of the developmental process and mentors, i.e. you, are required to record observations of lessons for the combined purposes of teacher judgments and progress. You will use feedback from observations to scaffold your teacher's developing growth through your analysis of the evidence the lessons provide. To do this job well, you need a general knowledge of how and why observation became such an essential tool in the process of teacher development and more importantly, how you can effectively carry out this crucial task using traditional and innovative tools. This chapter is for anyone new to the use of classroom observation as a tool for teacher development and those that would like a refresher or advice on how to move practice forward.

Objectives

At the end of this chapter, you should be able to:

- Have a greater understanding of the role of observation in developing beginning design and technology teachers.

- Have an awareness as to how different tools can be used to support the processes of classroom observation and analysis.
- Have a knowledge of alternative ways to use classroom observation within ongoing professional learning.

The role of lesson observation in the development of beginning teachers

Observation helps us to learn about the classroom. How teachers act in the classroom and how the pupils respond to those actions, gives us information about effective and less effective behaviours for teaching and learning. Experienced and novice teachers use observation to analyse their own and others' teaching and learning. The Sutton Trust Report – What Makes Great Teachers? (Coe et al., 2014, p. 25) identified that:

> Classroom observations are the most common source of evidence used in providing feedback to teachers in OECD countries, whether American (e.g. Canada, Chile, United States), European (e.g. Denmark, France, Ireland, Spain) or Asian-Pacific (e.g. Australia, Japan, Korea).

When we use observation in the social context of the classroom we can find out how teachers behave, what actions promote or restrict learning and what pupils do in response to the teacher's actions. This information helps you and whomever the information is shared with, to evaluate teaching and learning better. This makes classroom observation an invaluable tool for collecting the kinds of data that you will need for your work with teachers.

Goldstein (2007) found that traditional teacher evaluation transformed when an experienced – master teacher – conducts the summative as well as the formative assessments of beginning teachers. Her research also identified six features of active observation, including: time, professional development, transparency, work relations, decision making and accountability. We will look at each of these as the chapter progresses, but, at this stage we are concentrating on the role that classroom observation plays in gathering formative and summative assessments by you, the experienced teacher. Summative assessments get used to make a pass or fail decision about a teacher's competencies to teach. Appraisal sounds harsh, but observation has historically been used to measure teachers work in the classroom the spending of public money on education (Grubb, 2000). It also emphasises the importance of your expertise in making judgements about the teacher's ongoing progress through the developmental process that eventually leads to summative decisions. The formative process is the major purpose for classroom observation in work developing teachers because we know that learning to teach is more than meeting set competency criteria. The Department for Education (DfE) guidelines (2018) for England identify classroom observation as a tool to help beginning teachers with:

- the role of the teacher;
- planning and assessment to ensure pupil progress;
- national assessments and examinations;

- child development and learning;
- priorities, such as managing pupils' behaviour, early reading and special educational needs and disability;
- assessing and evaluating teaching;
- the use of evidence and research to inform teaching.

These teacher behaviours and duties are developed during practice in the classroom. Eraut (2007) contends that people learn in the workplace. The workplace for design and technology teachers is the subject department and this is the place where academic knowledge, discovered during the taught parts of a beginning teacher's education, is put into practice or you could say, made concrete. These real experiences help the teacher to make sense of personal academic knowledge about teaching. This is not an easy process. Eraut also asserts that workplace learning is only useful when feedback is used to support a teacher's reflections about practice. Data from classroom observations goes on to create the formative feedback that you can provide for your teacher to encourage dialogue about practice, which is vital for helping the teacher to evaluate and analyse practice for improvement. Your expertise in the process of teaching becomes invaluable to the teacher as you can help them to recognise the dynamic and complex nature of teaching and learning.

In summary, we have considered the purpose of classroom observation about gathering formative and summative data as part of a beginning design and technology teacher's development. We have also looked at the role your expert judgement plays in improving the work of your teacher through ongoing formative assessments that guide dialogues about the practice and how it links to theory and policy. This helps us to see that classroom observation is an essential tool in a beginning teacher's early development (Task 10.1).

Task 10.1   Expert and novice?

- Personal reflection: come up with a variety of terms that you associate with classroom observation.
- Research the terms 'expert' and 'novice' teacher. List common and unique characteristics for both.

The relationship between the experienced and novice teacher is vital for active teacher development. Goldstein (2007) identified the importance of work relations in the progress of valid observations. Observation is a personal thing and a relationship of trust between the observer and observee is imperative. These two purposes of observation: to assess competencies and create data for analysis and reflection can lead to tensions concerning the use of the observation for the observer. If the focus is too much on assessment judgements then the teacher might become resistant to the developmental feedback. This might also lead to situations where the beginning teacher fails to take risks with teaching for fear that they will not meet the identified standards for the job (O'Leary, 2013; Puttick, 2017). Westerman

(1991) argues that classroom observation can be a stressful experience, which relies on your performance and judgements as an observer. Beginning teachers, on the other hand, see observation as an essential tool for action planning and reflection on progress. This tool might lead to an over-reliance on the observer's comments rather than personal thoughts and analysis of how the pupils behaved in response to an instruction. Managing this relationship is therefore crucial. It is important that as the observer you take precautions to ensure that observations and the following dialogue focus on developing the teacher and that getting things wrong is part of the process (Task 10.2).

Task 10.2   Learning departments

- Think about the subject department that you work in. How is the department a learning environment? Do teachers openly discuss practice in relation to pupil learning and are there opportunities for experienced colleagues to share continuing professional development issues with less experienced colleagues?

The process of classroom observation

The way you carry out observations of your beginning teacher will depend on the purpose of your classroom observation and organisational protocols or guidance which apply. Accountability is vital to active observation and protocols can vary. If an assessment is part of the role of the observation, then you are likely to be using a more structured system that will guide your decision making. For example, a beginning teacher studying for an Initial Teacher Education (ITE) qualification will need to evidence how they are meeting the criteria of the requirement. For this to happen, your classroom observation paperwork is essential to this process. Goldstein (2007) refers to this as transparency. Observation paperwork allows all members of the organisation to share the process and findings. In the ITE example, your work and that of the external or internal ITE provider, school or local authority with whom you will share your decision and the process you took to make them, are linked. The shared paperwork guarantees transparency. Guidelines are likely to be informed by national policies, such as the Teachers' Standards (DfE, 2011) concerning the extent and focus of observation. Knowing which protocol to use is key to successful observation and can support the inherent tensions discussed above in the expert/novice work relationship. Using the wrong protocol for observation might lead to the collection of incorrect data and put strains on your developing relationship with your teacher. The way a specific organisation does things will link to other aspects of the beginning teacher's training programme, be that initial teacher education or newly qualified status. Communicating these procedures to your beginning D&T teacher enables both parties to feel in control of the situation. Remember that it is your job to ensure that all the stages of the classroom observation, in line with the appropriate third-party guidelines, have been prepared and set up before recording your actual observation (Task 10.3).

Task 10.3   Recording observations

- Reflect on the context in which you carry out your observation duties.
- Make yourself familiar with any internal protocols for classroom observation and any additional documents linked to your beginning teacher's external providers.
- Ask yourself: What aspects of the documents will be of most use to your work and why?

Preparing for the observation

Once you are familiar with the appropriate system of observation for the teacher you are working with you will need to consider what needs to be done before, during and after the observation.

Before the observation, observers need to get organised and become familiar with certain aspects of the lesson to be observed. Ensure you arrive in good time for the lesson observation and are fully conversant with assessment criteria against which you are required to comment on during the observation (see the section above). Ensure you are familiar with the teacher's lesson planning and particularly the lesson objectives for pupils and how they have planned to meet these. Through a request to make available a copy of the lesson planning for the session, the observer can ensure they are familiar with the lesson beforehand. It is also vital to understand the trainee's developmental focus for the lesson observation, what they need to work on and where they require feedback. Either a prior meeting or the sharing of a teaching journal can clarify the developmental focus across both parties. All this preparation will enable the observation to run smoothly and ensure that you are clear about the steps the teacher has taken to prepare for the lesson. Otherwise, you run the risk of having no focus or too many areas of focus. By getting yourself well prepared, you will feel in control and be able to focus on the observation stage of the process (Task 10.4).

Task 10.4   Focusing observations

- Think about ways to make the process effective for your beginning teacher.
- Ask your beginning teacher, before the observation, to identify: what they think the strengths are and what they need to work on next.
- You will then be able to focus the observation on affirmation of strengths and steps to improve weaknesses.

During the observation

During the observation, you will need to record what you observe while evaluating teaching and learning for assessment and later reflection. This requires you to record a description

Table 10.1 Bocquillon and Derobertmasure 'aspects of practice' (adapted from Bocquillon and Derobertmasure, 2017, p. 04)

Aspects of practice	Summary description
The instruction area ('didactic area')	Consists of actions and interactions relating to the educational content. It includes four types of actions implemented by the teacher: • selection and organisation of content; • didactic speech; • reference to lesson plan; and • teaching materials.
The management area ('psycho-pedagogical area')	Consists of actions and interactions relating to managing a group of individuals. It includes seven types of actions performed by the teacher: • linguistic acts by the teacher (formal aspects of discourse such as tics, clarity etc.); • content-based activities presented to the pupils; • classroom atmosphere; • body language; • learning management (what the teacher says or arranges to enable the pupils to progress, whether by helping them make conceptual progress, using responses as a springboard, etc.); • adherence to lesson plan; and • pace management.
The cognitive area	Consists of information about the pupils' cognitive characteristics. It includes two types of student characteristics: • pupils' learning/motivation; and • their level/profile.
The objectifying area	Consists of pupils' actions that inform the teacher about thinking (e.g. oral responses, written responses, handling of objects, etc.) The 'objectifying area' has two types of actions: • pupils' actions; and • pupil's responses to content.

of the teacher's actions in the classroom alongside a commentary that interprets what you see. This is not an easy task. Bocquillon and Derobertmasure (2017) offer a model of teaching-learning practice that can be helpful in your categorisation of the behaviours that you observe in the lesson. They identify four 'aspects of practice' that can be used to structure feedback in support of your teacher's professional development (Table 10.1).

To help you judge the teacher's effectiveness on pupils' progress, you can record the pupils' observed actions and responses, for later discussion (Table 10.1). To supplement this, you might also use suggestions from the TeacherToolkit website (www.teachertoolkit.co.uk/) about questions to ask pupils in the lesson. This recording of actions and responses will inform the observer's judgements about pupils' learning and motivation:

• What are the lesson objectives?
• Why are you doing this?
• What does success look like?
• How do you know?
• What is your teacher looking for?

- Can you tell me any keywords for this lesson?
- What is your current target?
- How often is your own design and technology work marked?
- Do you receive feedback? Give me an example...
- Are you allowed time to improve (iterate) your work?
- Do you enjoy the lesson? Why?
- Describe a typical lesson to me?

All these different things to do within the space of one observation makes preparation even more key and the tools with which you will systematically record this information essential.

Recording the observation

Recording classroom observation for assessment and teacher development can be carried out in a variety of ways. O'Leary (2013) suggests three methods of note-making during observation: (1) unstructured; (2) semi-structured and (3) highly structured.

The completely unstructured model involves a blank piece of paper on which to record notes as a 'running' log of events. This 'stream of consciousness' allows the observer to objectively write 'what' they see by precisely describing what they observe through specific examples of the teacher's behaviour and student-teacher interactions. A record sheet model (Table 10.2) with space for timings could be used to capture this form of unstructured note making. It is worth considering the implications of this approach when observing a busy practical design and technology lesson. This 'stream of consciousness' method may be useful as a tool to support your beginning teacher's self-evaluation; however, it may prove challenging when you are aiming to record assessment and teacher development information.

The semi-structured model might include a combination of blank space for unstructured observations plus a set of pre-established categories for comment (Table 10.3). The pre-established categories are likely also to need the observer to refer to a set of assessment criteria to help complete. For example, one ITE provider requires classroom observers to record lesson observations on a form that offers space for unstructured descriptions of the teacher's behaviours and interactions, alongside space to record evaluative comments about the trainee's intentions and the effect on pupils' learning. The right-hand side of the reporting form is designed to prompt further reflection about strategies/ideas that the trainee might consider improving. Importantly, for design and technology teachers, health and safety points can also be recorded within this column. The rest of the form also guides observers in making overall judgments about the teacher's progress against the appropriate assessment criteria and actions that need to be taken to support further improvement and development. An example of assessment criteria for ITE is the NASBTT (2017) Training and Assessment Toolkit: A guide to accuracy in the assessment of trainees.

Table 10.2 Unstructured note-making model

Time	Observed evidence

Table 10.3 Semi-structured note-making model

Student teacher name		Date	
Observer name		Class details	
Time	Observed evidence	Impact on learning and progress/points for discussion/health and safety/commentary	
The learners: what evidence is there of learning and progress made by individuals and groups of learners during this lesson and/or over time?			
Key strengths that have contributed to learners' progress:		**Areas for development to ensure greater impact on learners' progress:**	
Professional development target			
Summary of student teacher progress against the Standards			

The highly-structured model shares many features of the previous type but divides the assessment of the lessons into individual performance indicators. Feedback is focussed on each performance indicator (Table 10.4).

can stimulate conversations with your beginning teacher about practice, however, they are limited in what they can tell us about 'why' the teacher behaves in such a way and why the teacher–student interactions are happening or not. Therefore, it is crucial either during or after the observation to gather data from the teacher about why they took specific actions and why the pupils asked particular questions or did certain things. Ultimately it is the impact that the teacher has on pupil progress over time that count and that makes the lesson assessment and evaluative comments reliable and valid (Task 10.5).

Table 10.4 Highly-structured note-making model, based on extract from NASBTT (2017) training and assessment toolkit

Set high expectations which inspire, motivate and challenge pupils	• establish a safe and stimulating environment for pupils, rooted in mutual respect • set goals that stretch and challenge pupils of all backgrounds, abilities and dispositions • demonstrate consistently the positive attitudes, values and behaviour which are expected of pupils.	
Promote good progress and outcomes by pupils	• be accountable for pupils' attainment, progress and outcomes • be aware of pupils' capabilities and their prior knowledge, and plan teaching to build on these • guide pupils to reflect on the progress they have made and their emerging needs • demonstrate knowledge and understanding of how pupils learn and how this impacts on teaching • encourage pupils to take a responsible and conscientious attitude to their own work and study.	

Task 10.5   Making notes

• Consider which of the three note-making styles you feel most comfortable with using for classroom observation of beginning design and technology teachers and why?
• Which do you use the least often and/or feel the least comfortable with and why?
• How might you adapt the note-making examples to better suit the needs of your beginning teacher?

After the observation

After the observation, you will need to create a space to share your summary of the lesson and allow time for thoughtful dialogue about the beginning teacher's progress (see Chapter 11 on holding learning conversation). For the post observation discussion to support professional development, it needs to link to the teacher's ongoing progress. You will need to summarise the main points of the feedback on the teacher's growth by sharing your evaluation of the lesson, which might involve confirming, clarifying and challenging the teacher's assessment. Remember to include strengths alongside weaknesses to inform action planning. This summary is where the specific examples you note in the reporting forms will help extrapolate the teacher's intentions and impact on pupils' learning. Westerman (1991, p. 301) uses Veenman (1984) to argue that 'teachers at different developmental stages perceive and process classroom problems in different ways'. It is through conversations, with experienced teachers, about classroom practice that the expert teacher can help the novice teacher to see the complexity and dynamic nature of the decisions a teacher makes within the process of teaching and learning. In assisting the teacher to do this, you can agree on areas for development that will inform the next phase of the teacher's development (Task 10.6).

Task 10.6   Questioning

• Think about ways that you might help your teacher to gather thoughts about the lesson.

Consider asking your teacher to evaluate the teaching objectively, by reflecting on the strengths and weaknesses of the lesson. It is important to follow-up these questions with further questions about why these behaviours came about and what alternative approaches the teacher might have taken. This questioning will help the teacher to identify the next areas for development and gives the teacher a focus for the following discussion.

Alternative approaches

Considering alternatives to the observation process discussed above can shift the balance of power within the expert/novice relationship and provide more accurate information on observation. This change can be done through teacher collected videos via various innovative systems that use camera kits and online video storage. Beginning design and technology teachers can take responsibility for recording lessons and then choosing which experiences to submit for formative and summative assessments. The video that is collected can be labelled at points in the lesson to pinpoint areas for discussion during the feedback. For example, if the focus is on behaviour management, the mentee can tag or label the video at points when positive behaviour management occurs. Barnett (2006) has asserted that professional development and the education of pre-service and practicing teachers ought to be moving to a more collaborative process. The use of camera kits and online video storage systems enable teachers to share lesson observations across learning communities and connect with different teachers within a range of settings, for example, with other beginning design and technology teachers or external experts. This form of observation offers higher precision and capacity for collaboration that might counteract the current observer dominance. Through the pinpointing of behaviours observed, evaluative feedback can become concrete and render more explicit meaning between the beginning teacher and their mentor. Thus, potentially counteracting the fear of risk taking on the part of the observed teacher, highlighted by Wright (2016). Through a shift in power relations you can take an equal relationship with your teacher.

This balanced relationship creates shared ownership of observation that can stimulate reflection on practice and greater engagement with future professional development. Brown (1993, p. 10) reflected that:

Ownership of observation needs to be devolved down as much as possible to the participants in the teaching process. The closer the ownership of the process is located to the actual participants, the more likely it is that the aims will be achieved and the outcomes accepted by all concerned.

The Best Foot Forward Project (Kane et al., 2016) identified that teachers involved in the collection of video observations were more self-critical and started to notice previous un-seen pupil behaviours. They also perceived that the experienced teachers that they worked with were more supportive, leading to fewer disagreements over assessments and an increased likelihood of specific changes in practice. A higher capacity to analyse and evaluate practice is essential for the teacher. Research from Lofthouse and Birmingham (2010) says that teacher-captured video opens professional dialogues that are more authentic and facilitating of reflection. We need our beginning teachers to be self-critical and use observation feedback to understand the complexity of teaching better. If video can provide an additional tool for professional dialogue about practice, then it needs to be considered as part of the observation process because as we have seen above the shift to greater collaboration and ownership of classroom observations is imperative for active professional development (Task 10.7).

Task 10.7   Effective observations

- Considering the role of observation, observation processes and alternative approaches outlined in this chapter, reflect upon what you think the characteristics of effective classroom observation are.
- Having identified the characteristics of effective classroom observation, consider the best tool for you and your beginning design and technology teacher at different stages in the relationship.

Summary

As noted in Chapter 1, effective mentoring is a complex and demanding task, but, as with any role that enables you to have a positive impact on the development of others, it is hugely rewarding. In this chapter, we have looked at the part of observation in developing beginning design and technology teachers, how we might use different tools to support the processes and alternative ways to use observation within ongoing professional learning. In looking at the role of observation we have been able to:

- discuss its importance as a tool for professional development and your role in the relationship between yourself and your beginning design and technology teacher;
- identify the importance of preparation and the use of shared assessment criteria to support transparency and decision making about lesson assessment and feedback;
- exemplify a range of note-making strategies that can be used to support post-observation feedback and
- look at how video can be used to enhance our work with beginning design and technology teachers.

Further resources

O'Leary, M. (2013) *Classroom observation: A guide to the effective observation of teaching and learning*. London: Routledge.

   Classroom Observation explores the pivotal role of lesson observation in the training, assessment and development of new and experienced teachers. Offering practical guidance and detailed insight on an aspect of training that is a source of anxiety for many teachers, this thought-provoking book offers a critical analysis of the place, role and nature of lesson observation in the lives of education professionals.

Wragg, T. (2013) *An Introduction to Classroom Observation (Classic Edition)*. Oxon: Routledge.

   This highly regarded and authoritative text, with a new preface from Professor Richard Pring, introduces a new generation of education professionals to E.C. Wragg's straightforward and essential guide to observation. The book includes a combination of case studies, photographs and illustrations to show how various people study lessons for different purposes and in different contexts. It outlines a range of approaches in clear language and gives examples of successful methods.

References

Barnett, M. (2006) 'Using a web-based professional development system to support preservice teachers in examining authentic classroom practice'. *Journal of Technology and Teacher Education*, 14 (4), p. 701.

Brown, S. (1993) *Observing Teaching. SEDA Paper 79*. Birmingham: United Kingdom.

Coe, R., Aloisi, C., Higgins, S. and Major, L. E. (2014) *What Makes Great Teaching? Review of the Underpinning Research*. Millbank, London: The Sutton Trust.

Department for Education (2011) *Teachers' Standards*. Available at: www.gov.uk/government/publications/teachers-standards (Accessed: 01 September 2017).

Department for Education and National College for Teaching and Leadership (2018) *Initial Teacher Training (ITT): Criteria and Supporting Advice*. Available at: www.gov.uk/government/publications/initial-teacher-training-criteria (Accessed: 13 March 2018).

Eraut, M. (2007) 'Learning from other people in the workplace'. *Oxford Review of Education*, 33 (4), pp. 403–422.

Goldstein, J. (2007) 'Easy to dance to: Solving the problems of teacher evaluation with peer assistance and review'. *American Journal of Education*, 113 (3), pp. 479–508.

Grubb, W. N. (2000) 'Opening classrooms and improving teaching: Lessons from school inspections in England'. *Teachers College Record*, 102 (4), pp. 696–723.

Kane, T. J., Gehlbach, H., Greenberg, M., Quinn, D. and Thal, D. (2016) *The Best Foot Forward Project: Substituting Teacher-Collected Video*. Cambridge, MA: Harvard University.

Lofthouse, R. and Birmingham, P. (2010) 'The camera in the classroom: Video-recording as a tool for professional development of student teachers'. *Teacher Advancement Network Journal*, 1 (2). Available at: https://ojs.cumbria.ac.uk/index.php/TEAN/article/view/59/70 (Accessed: 22 May 2019).

The National Association of School-Based Teacher Trainers, (NASBTT) (2017). *Training and Assessment Toolkit: A Guide to Accuracy in the Assessment of Trainees (Third Edition December 2017)*. Available at: www.ucet.ac.uk/?s=NASBTT (Accessed: 26 May 2018).

O'Leary, M. (2013) *Classroom Observation: A Guide to the Effective Observation of Teaching and Learning*. Oxon: Routledge.

Puttick, S. (2017) 'Student teachers' positionalities as knowers in school subject departments'. *British Educational Research Journal*, 44 (1), pp. 25–42.

Westerman, D. A. (1991) 'Expert and novice teacher decision making'. *Journal of Teacher Education*, 42 (4), pp. 292–305.

Wragg. T. (2011) *An Introduction to Classroom Observation (Classic Edition)*. Oxon: Routledge.

Wright, V. (2016) 'Giving lesson observation feedback'. *Teacher Education Advancement Network Journal (TEAN)*, 8 (1), pp. 116–127.

11 Supporting the beginning teacher through professional conversations

Alison Winson

Introduction

Professional conversations can support a beginning teacher to progress and develop in any subject but in Design and Technology (D&T) lessons the nuances of pedagogy linked with health and safety make the planning for delivery crucial. Winson and Wood-Griffiths (2018) noted that that the feedback given, the language chosen and the questions posed are crucial to beginning teachers' development and successful mentoring. In this chapter, we explore both the role you play as a mentor in these conversations and the role the beginning teacher plays.

The chapter will consider when these conversations could take place, what the focus might be, management of the conversations and how the conversations might engage both yourself and the beginning teacher in the reflective practice process.

Monitoring and reviewing, the progress of the beginning teacher will also be considered. Finally, the chapter will consider the ways in which you might support the beginning teacher to achieve more immediate and future aspirations.

Objectives

At the end of this chapter, you should be able to:

- Consider the ways in which you can best support the beginning design and technology teacher through professional conversations;
- Feel confident to develop effective conversations which benefits practice;
- Ensure that progress is made and maintained, and that the future aspirations of the beginning teacher are supported.

The professional conversations you have will be different depending on the career stage of the beginning teacher. For example, if you are working with a trainee teacher the conversations will probably be more frequent than with someone in the induction year. When working with a beginning teacher in the early stages of training you might be discussing planning and teaching on a regular, often daily basis. This is also likely to be true in terms of the level of sophistication and content of the conversations you have with a newly or recently qualified teacher. For those beginning teachers who have just taken up a first teaching post the shift away from having frequent, often daily, conversations can be challenging as they can become reliant on regular feedback, indeed many early career teachers have remarked that they miss the continual dialogue about lessons and the reassurance that they are making the necessary progress.

Experienced mentors often note that having professional conversations with the beginning teacher benefits their own practice. These benefits are highlighted by Hudson and Hudson (2018) who note that benefits can include positive professional development, critical self-reflection resulting in enhancement of personal teaching skills, an increase in confidence and improved communication skills. You will undoubtedly have to reflect and then unpick the things you take for granted in your own teaching in order to support your mentee. You will observe lessons where you think, 'What a brilliant idea, I'll try that out' and others where your reaction will be, 'How on earth can I support her to get this right?' The conversations that take place between the mentee and the mentor are vital in supporting the beginning teacher to develop their confidence and their future development. They are also important in terms of shaping your future working relationship. Wright (2018a) emphasises that no one else can equal the mentor's role in the partnership and the resulting influence is the major determiner of the success, nature and quality of the new teacher.

Initial professional conversations

Task 11.1   Where to begin?

Imagine you are a beginning teacher. What information would you need to gather in an initial conversation? Write a checklist and add to this as you read the information below.

Scheduling some time to meet in school to have an initial conversation in advance of the beginning teacher starting will be of great benefit to you building a positive relationship. Hudson and Hudson (2018) share this opinion and state that a positive mentor–mentee relationship is a two-way experience where both have essential roles in forming and sustaining the partnership. They continue by noting that the mentor–mentee interaction should be mutually beneficial, which allows for the relationship to be maintained. A good starting point is to find out about the career journey of the beginning teacher to date. Questions might focus on the degree they studied, prior employment, prior teaching experience, strengths and interests in terms of subject knowledge and skills. Equally important is to share your career. These early conversations will help alleviate any anxiety that the beginning teacher might have. Prior to first meeting you might have an opportunity to ask the beginning teacher to send you any questions they have. This will help you to plan the conversation and gain the most out of the time you have together. It should be acknowledged that if you are working with a trainee teacher, you might not have an opportunity to meet with them before they begin their placement with you. If this is the case, it is still worthwhile putting some time aside on day one to have a conversation. Cuerden (2018, p. 148) offers some helpful advice around working with newly qualified teachers which could be applied to working with any beginning teacher. She advises try and find some time at the end of the first day for an informal chat with you new teacher. This will allow her to ask all the questions that she has thought of during the day. Try to give her your undivided attention at this point: she needs to feel that you are going to be approachable and willing to support her.

These initial conversations will facilitate questions to be asked and answered in a timely manner, which, in the case of someone about to begin induction, will then allow some time for planning before a busy start of year or term. If it is possible to schedule more than one meeting, this will avoid information overload. You could also arrange an opportunity to meet the department perhaps through a social activity (Task 11.2).

These initial conversations might include;

* sharing information about the staffing structure in the school,
* explaining who key people are, as well as the roles they perform, within the department (e.g. technicians and specialist teaching assistants),
* sharing and explaining some of the school and department policies,
* details of the subjects and groups to be taught as well as sharing schemes of work,
* touring the department and perhaps introducing them to how the rooms are organised,
* available curriculum time e.g. length of rotations etc.

Task 11.2   Setting expectations

As a mentor what expectations might you have of a beginning teacher and what expectations might the beginning teacher have of you as the mentor? Make a list of expectations. You might want to share your list with an experienced mentor or head of department to check your expectations are realistic.

It is important to establish what you expect from each other. Beginning teachers will appreciate knowing what is expected of them from the start and as time progresses and they become more familiar with the school, these expectations will shift and change. Take time to have a conversation about what the support might look like from your point of view and at the same time explore what the beginning teacher thinks would be most useful to them? See Chapter 13 for examples of stakeholder views on this topic. This might be a weekly scheduled meeting, for example, or planned lesson observations followed by a conversation. Whatever you decide the 'package' should be supportive and realistic. Hughes (2018) discusses a helping relationship continuum. He believes that trainees and new teachers need help in different ways. Downey (2001, p. 48) describes a directive and non-directive continuum. *'Being directive involves telling, the giving of instructions, whereas non-directive involves supporting learners to come to an understanding of where they stand and to reach their own conclusions'.* He goes on to suggest that mentors reflect on where they see themselves on this continuum. Are you directive (pushing) or non-directive (pulling)? (Task 11.3).

Directive (push) ——————————————————————— Non-directive (pull)

Task 11.3   The relationship continuum – where are you?

Using the diagram above where would you place yourself on the continuum? Consider the beginning teacher that you mentor. Do you believe you are working at the right point on the continuum? Has this moved as the beginning teacher has gained more experience?

It is worth noting that if you are supporting a trainee some of these expectations and indeed entitlements will be outlined by the training provider.

Beginning teachers will have many questions about logistic details of teaching. They will want to know the number of pupils in each of the groups they will be teaching, pupil abilities including individual needs and how the group or individuals within the group are best managed in terms of behaviour. They also need to know resources available and the logistics of managing equipment and machinery. It is also helpful to focus on what the group has achieved previously. Sharing schemes of work that have already been taught and those that need to be taught should be a priority. Remember that teaching schemes written by someone else can be challenging, as the beginning teacher will not know the thought processes of the person who wrote them originally. Explaining how much freedom there is to deviate from the scheme is useful to know. It might be that the scheme has been in existence for a while and is in need of refreshing or even rewriting. If no schemes of work are available and this is not unheard of, then the beginning teacher will need clear guidance and support from you as well as advice about pupils' capabilities.

As noted in Chapter 8, the craft of lesson planning needs a graduated approach. In the initial phase of mentoring initial conversations might include timetables and working environments. Beginning teachers will ask questions such as whether they have sole use of a D&T specialist room. What are the expectations around managing the room? Is there a particular routine that works well? Is there freedom for the person to rearrange the room? Will there be any technician support? How are materials and ingredients procured? What health and safety regulations need to be followed? What resources are available? Is there a budget for resources?

If the beginning teacher is newly qualified another useful starting point is to ask them what targets were highlighted for the induction year. This may be documented and the school may have been sent details from the training provider. This provides a useful starting point for the early conversations, and will help build on what has gone before to structure the next stage in the mentee's career. In the initial conversations it is recommended that you ask the mentee about short-term and long-term aspirations, as a mentor you need to support career development and once they are established in school you will be better placed to fulfil this responsibility.

Post lesson conversations – when is the best time to have a conversation?

Chapter 10 explores the need, before you observe a lesson, to negotiate with the beginning teacher the timing for the post lesson conversation. Some prefer a conversation straight after the observed lesson, others the same day, or within a few days. Often the timing of the conversation will be determined by practicalities, for example, when you are both available. Beginning teachers do comment that, if the gap between the lesson and feedback is too long they forget the aspects of the lesson, and the developmental value is reduced. You should also consider that when an observed lesson has not gone to plan waiting to have a conversation might add to the anxiety of the mentee.

Having a conversation immediately can prevent enough time elapsing for reflection. Where possible you might suggest the mentee notes some brief reflections on the lesson before you meet. You might even be directive and provide some suggested headings for reflection. O'Leary (2014) emphasises that classroom observation represents a medium through which the process of reflection can be actively nurtured. This is true for teachers at all stages of their careers, from preservice to in-service, NQTs to highly experienced practitioners.

Starting the conversation with positive prompts, for example 'what did you enjoy about the lesson?' Or 'what went well?' Or 'what would make the lesson even better?' can set an expectation for the mentee to lead the direction of the discussion. These prompts are a good starting point for reflecting on practice especially for someone at the beginning of their career. Whatever you negotiate, scheduling the feedback conversations, in advance is as important as carrying out the observation.

What should a post-lesson conversation look like?

Too often, I have observed a post-lesson conversation between a mentor and beginning teacher which in reality turns out to be one-way feedback. The mentor begins with good intentions often asking the question *'How do you think the lesson went?'* which after the initial response then switches to one-way feedback where the mentor sequentially dissects the lesson providing little or no opportunity for discussion.

A two-way professional conversation has greater benefit to both participants. You will have to lead the conversations early on, for example if working with a trainee but ultimately the aim is for a balanced professional dialogue. It is helpful to establish the purpose of the conversation and what each party hopes to gain from it. The language you use and the questions you pose are crucial to successful mentoring, as is the tone and content of the discussions. Getting this right will promote a more collaborative, collegiate and supportive relationship.

Conversations will promote reflection if you pose the right questions. Planning questions to promote reflection for the beginning teacher and offering the opportunity to respond with further questions will support reflection on your own practice alongside the mentee (Task 11.4).

Task 11.4   Reflective questioining

In your role as mentor, what questions could you ask a beginning teacher to encourage reflection following a lesson observation? Think about the questions you might ask after a successful lesson that went to plan and then consider the questions you might ask after a lesson that did not go well. Write down these questions and add to them as you read the information below.

Below are some questions you could ask during post lesson conversations. You might find it helpful to list these questions and use them as an aide memoire when observing, and to frame your subsequent discussion. Alternatively, you might negotiate, beforehand which questions you will focus on. The choice of questions might be informed by the previous lesson or be based on current targets.

Here are some exemplar questions that might scaffold a post-lesson conversation.

- In which part of the lesson did you feel most confident/least confident? Explain why.
- What was the impact of your teaching on the students' learning? How do you know?
- How did you meet the learning needs of the group? Were the strategies used successful? How do you know?
- How was the learning assessed? How effective was the assessment strategy? How do you know?
- Are there any other strategies you could have used to assess the learning?
- How would you rate your explanations during the demonstration? Why?
- How did you ensure the pupils managed their time well? Can you think of alternative strategies to manage the lesson time in a busy practical lesson?
- Can you suggest how you might have managed the resources more effectively?
- What strategies did you use to manage behaviour? Were these methods effective? What would you do differently next lesson?
- How did you manage the transitions between tasks? Could this have been more effective?
- How did you manage the clearing up? What might you do differently?
- Did the resources you used promote learning? How do you know?
- Who made the most progress with practical work?
- What key targets would you set yourself, having planned, taught and assessed the lesson?
- What would enable you to progress further in your teaching?

The asking and answering of questions demand serious thinking from beginning teachers. Throughout training, and particularly early in the process, they are likely to need support in developing questions about their own and observed practice. In the early stages, the mentor will fulfil a role in training the beginning teacher to assess herself. Winson and Wood-Griffiths (2018) support this notion explaining that it is through skilled questioning that a two-way dialogue about teaching and learning can take place.

The conversation does not always need to be specifically about one lesson. Indeed, when working with a beginning teacher in the induction year it might be that you both decide to have a conversation about a particular group of students who have been taught over a longer period of time. This approach really supports a discussion about the pupils' progress over time and the subject knowledge and skills they have acquired.

As beginning teachers move on, the questions can become more challenging in scope and serve to shift thinking toward pupils and pupils' learning and away from themselves as teachers.

Target setting

Targets give direction for both the beginning teacher and the mentor. Negotiating, refining, setting and recording targets will support the development of the beginning teacher. The importance of target setting is discussed by Winson and Wood-Griffiths (2018, p. 56).

target setting is at the heart of this personalised development. At the end of each feedback, a summary of the targets that have emerged during the conversation will help clarify areas for further development for both the trainee teacher and the mentor.

Target setting is a skill to be learned. It is crucial that targets you negotiate include appropriate strategies. It is not appropriate to write vague, abstract targets, such as 'you need to give clear instructions'. This target is difficult for the beginning teacher, especially a trainee teacher, to unravel. Sometimes she will not understand or have developed enough experience to know how to achieve this. Strategies indicating *how to give clear instructions* need to be given. These might include, keep instructions short but concise, repeat them several times in different ways, put the key things pupils need to do on the board to reinforce the instruction, use questioning to check understanding, judge the number of instructions that you give- not too many at once, ask pupils to repeat instructions to check they have understood. In other words, what looks like a simple target arising from a straightforward observation may well be complex and needs careful analysis by the mentor as well as the beginning teacher (Tasks 11.5 and 11.6).

Task 11.5   Strategies for meeting targets

Work collaboratively with your mentee to list strategies to address these two areas;

- checking progress of learners during practical lessons in episodes and over time
- using questioning to challenge pupils understanding of materials or ingredients

---

Task 11.6   Learner focused target setting

Targets should be learner focused. Work with your beginning teacher to rewrite these targets to ensure they focus on the learner. Choose two targets (the what) and decide on 3-4 specific strategies (the how).

- use the voice more effectively;
- give clearer explanations;
- use praise more constructively;
- ensure full and successful transitions between activities;
- show more enthusiasm;
- be more assertive.

Alternatively choose two areas that you are currently focusing on.

Table 11.1 adapted from Winson and Wood-Griffiths (2018, pp. 58-60) exemplifies how key targets may be broken down into component parts to make them accessible to a beginning teachers. It provides examples that a beginning teacher might need to work on with measurable strategies to action.

It might be that when you have identified a target you suggest that your beginning teacher watches how you address this in your teaching.

Table 11.1 Suggested strategies for target setting

Area to work on	Suggested strategies
Use of voice	Ensure that you vary the volume and the pitch of your voice; along with the speed of delivery (think of sports commentaries).
	Avoid shouting, which can lead to your voice sounding shrill. Aim to breathe from your diaphragm and project your voice. Imagine yourself yawning in order to get a deeper sound.
	Use the word 'stop' during practical lessons making sure you take a deep breath and then lowering the tone to make sure the word is projected across the practical classroom.
Give praise	Give lots of praise, but make sure that it sounds sincere -establish a 'chef of the day' award or 'practical engineer of the week. Share the success criteria with the pupils
	Using praise before a reprimand can be very effective (e.g. I know that you can be sensible, but I don't like the way you are ...).
Ensure smooth transitions	Give out the next task before pupils have finished or while they are working.
	Use your learning objectives as a map for the lesson to avoid pauses while you look at your lesson plan.
	Have a clear start, middle and finish to a lesson.
	Organise resources and equipment prior to the lesson to ensure everything is to hand.
	Use assertive delivery by writing a script for when you want pupils to move from one activity to another 'when I say, and not before, I want you to...'
	Gain pupil attention before giving the next instruction.
	Refer to the previous task so pupils see the link between tasks.
	Arrange furniture to suit the activity by planning for this n your lesson plan
	Use recap – activity – recap.
Show enthusiasm	Smile and have an open body language – avoid crossing your arms
	Focus on the positive aspects of the topic you are teaching.
	Use encouraging gestures such as thumbs up or putting merit marks on the board
Set appropriate challenges	Encourage pupils to go 'one step further' using explicit success criteria.
	Always have extension tasks ready and set them in advance (possibly with a menu of activities to work through on the board).
	Provide a choice of tasks.
Be assertive	Aim to be assertive rather than aggressive. Prepare key phrases on your lesson plan
	Be decisive, e.g. when setting tasks, choosing pupils to do things, collecting in materials, etc.
Cut out peripheral chat/ low-level disruption	Do not talk over pupils.
	Use a click, stare, etc. in the first instance.
	Use pupils' names to correct individuals.
	Wait for silence (and tell them what you are waiting for!)
	Move pupils who continue to talk.
	Set up a seating plan and annotate this as applicable
Avoid confrontation	Focus on the ground rules and reasons, especially in relation to health and safety
	Don't punish whole classes – be firm and fair. If a pupil misbehaves tell them what they have done and what they need to do correct their actions.
	Give pupils a good choice option and a poor choice option. Plan in advance how to reward the good choice and the consequences of the poor choice.

How many targets are too many?

Overloading a beginning teacher with too many targets is likely to be overwhelming; they will not know which ones to address first. If the beginning teacher is going to be able to demonstrate progress, limiting targets to a manageable two or three is probably best practice. If a significant number of targets are emerging from lessons, you will have to decide or indeed negotiate which should be a priority. It is important to follow up on targets set.

Wright (2018b, p. 18) makes an important point about the number of targets, and that they should not be lost but once met should be acknowledged. He explains

> Targets are set. A week or a month later, more targets are set. The trainee may, after a few months, be carrying fifty to sixty targets around with her. No one has ever returned to any of these targets, to disapply them as now achieved, or to reinstate them as still pending.

Focusing and commenting on these targets in subsequent lessons is helpful to the beginning teacher or asking them to reflect on them in the next conversation can serve to close the feedback loop. The original target can then be developed or acknowledged as having been met. Remembering to praise the beginning teacher for achieving targets successfully is important to ensure they have a sense of achievement and feel they are making progress. If a target is proving difficult to address, then breaking it down into smaller sub-targets might be a useful strategy to render it more realistic.

Providing challenge and supporting future aspirations

A good mentor will want to inspire the beginning teacher to encourage and support the aspirations and career development. A good starting point is to share your career journey and ask colleagues to do the same. Beginning teachers want to know how to develop their careers, and want to hear positive success stories. Too often teachers become disenchanted by the workload which is often given as the main reason for the current high attrition rates of teachers, recently debated at government level in England (DfE 2016a, 2016b, 2016c, 2018). Beginning teachers need nurturing and if as a profession we can offer new developmental opportunities to those in their early careers we might curtail the high attrition of teachers to other careers (Task 11.7).

Task 11.7   Targets to motivate

You are working with a high performing trainee who has plateaued towards the end of the training or a recently qualified teacher who seems to have become disenchanted. They need to be challenged not with more work but with different opportunities. What might these opportunities look like?

Chapter 10 of this book explores the specific challenges associated with setting risks to move beginning teachers beyond their comfort zones to improve their practice and to inspire and motivate. Make time to discover what hopes and aspirations, in the short- and longer-term, your beginning teacher has. Ask for ideas about how these aspirations might be realised and how you might support these. Take time to explain the promotion system or additional opportunities that exists for teachers in your school. This often lacks clarity and a beginning teacher will hear different advice. Support the beginning teachers to draw up an aspirational two- or three-year plan to share with school leaders and remember to revisit this periodically over time as early aspirations often change (Task 11.8).

Task 11.8   Aspirational targets

A beginning teacher is keen to assume a head of department role within 5 years. How would you support them in meeting this aspiration?

Ideas to include on a plan might comprise some of the following:

- teaching across the whole age range including post 16,
- developing skills across different D&T material areas,
- involvement in subject-specific careers education including D&T vocational options,
- working on D&T primary/middle school transition,
- shadowing a head of department,
- reading a subject related book or article and sharing the key messages in a department meeting,
- encouraging engagement with subject associations such as the Design and Technology Association,
- carrying out small scale classroom action research and sharing outcomes with colleagues within the department,
- attending external Continuing Professional Development (CPD) and sharing outcomes with colleagues,
- delivering CPD in the department,
- delivering CPD to a group of subject specialists from other schools,
- designing a new scheme of work,
- assuming responsibility for a key stage or material area,
- becoming a mentor to beginning teachers,
- delivering a subject session for a group of beginning teachers,
- registering for a Master's or leadership qualification,
- moderating and marking D&T work for an examination board,
- involvement in whole school initiatives/working groups.

Encourage your beginning teacher to keep a record of all the 'extras' they have engaged in so that they can draw on these when making applications for new roles or positions.

Summary

In this chapter, we have considered how important professional conversations are in support-ing the development of the beginning teacher. We also acknowledge that these conversations provide valuable opportunities for reflective practice with mutual benefit for both the mentee and mentor. We have also focused on how professional conversations can build positive collegiate relationships and how these conversations will change according to the career phase of the mentee.

In summary,

- Invest time in planning and having early conversations with your beginning teacher. This will help you to plan how to support progress and development as a teacher.
- Where possible negotiate to set the correct tone for the relationship between the mentor and mentee. This negotiation might concentrate on the best time to meet, agendas for meetings, the focus of observations and the framing of targets.
- Have empathy for the beginning teacher by listening, nurturing and supporting development to be the best teacher they can while maintaining a healthy work life balance.

Mentoring is a privilege, show a real interest in guiding the beginning teacher to meet professional aspirations and support them to do this.

References

Cuerden, J. (2018) 'Mentoring the newly qualified teacher', in Wright, T. (ed.) *How to be a Brilliant Mentor*. Oxon: Routledge, pp. 147-161.

Department for Education (2016a) Eliminating unnecessary workload associated with data management. Available at: https://assets.publishing.service.gov.uk/government/uploads/system/uploads/attachment_data/file/511258/Eliminating-unnecessary-workload-associated-with-data-management.pdf. (Accessed: 21 November 2018).

Department for Education (2016b) Eliminating unnecessary workload around marking. Available at: www.gov.uk/government/publications/reducing-teacher-workload-marking-policy-review-group-report. (Accessed: 21 November 2018).

Department for Education (2016c) Eliminating unnecessary workload around planning and teaching resources. Available at: www.gov.uk/government/publications/reducing-teacher-workload-marking-policy-review-group-report. (Accessed: 21 November 2018).

Department for Education (2018) Addressing teacher workload in Initial Teacher Education (ITE). Advice for ITE providers. Available at: www.gov.uk/government/publications/addressing-workload-in-initial-teacher-education-ite. (Accessed: 21 November 2018).

Downey, M. (2001) *Effective Coaching*. London: Orion Business Books.

Hudson, P. and Hudson, S. (2018) 'Mentoring preservice teachers: identifying tensions and possible resolutions', *Teacher Development*, 22:1, 16-30.

Hughes, S. (2018) 'Mentoring the newly qualified teacher', in Wright, T. (ed.) *How to be a Brilliant Mentor*. Oxon: Routledge, pp. 120-135.

O'Leary, M. (2014) *Classroom Observation: A Guide to Effective Observation of Teaching and Learning*. London: Routledge.

Winson, A. and Wood-Griffiths, S. (2018) 'Mentoring the newly qualified teacher', in Wright, T. (ed.) *How to be a Brilliant Mentor*. Oxon: Routledge, pp. 46-62.

Wright, T. (2018a) 'Inputs and outputs', in Wright, T. (ed.) *How to be a Brilliant Mentor*. Oxon: Routledge, pp. 16-27.

Wright, T. (2018b) 'The pivotal importance of the mentor', in Wright, T. (ed.) *How to be a Brilliant Mentor*. Oxon: Routledge, pp. 1-15.

12 Risk taking in the classroom – moving teachers forward from pedestrian to innovative practice

Dawne Irving-Bell

Introduction

We have seen in earlier chapters that mentors play a crucial role in supporting those new to the teaching profession, but often the challenges encountered, and the vital part mentors play in encouraging beginning teacher to engage in activity outside of their comfort zone, are overlooked.

With comprehensive support, successfully challenging a beginning teacher to move successfully into previously unexplored activity is beneficial for both efficacy and motivation. This also provides the opportunity for longer-term management of personal growth and development. Unsupported however, rather than boosting confidence, challenge can become a counterproductive experience that inhibits a beginning teacher's development.

In this chapter, we explore both the opportunities and challenges that are presented in supporting beginning design and technology (D&T) teachers to move beyond the 'comfort zone', and the inherent benefits of moving from pedestrian to an innovative practitioner.

Having presented a clear rationale of the benefits risk taking can bring, the chapter begins by defining, activities considered to be 'challenging'. It examines strategies that you can use to encourage beginning teachers to take a risk, to identify and set appropriate challenges, and suggests practical ways that you can scaffold a beginning teacher's development.

The chapter moves to discuss how you can help to create an environment within which the beginning teacher feels confident, and emotionally safe to explore new pedagogical approaches, to examine the benefits of alternative approaches to assessment, and experiment with innovative techniques and technologies.

Drawing upon personal narratives the recollections of both novice and experienced mentors are interwoven throughout the chapter. Designed to contextualise the content it also presents a series of practical tasks designed to help support you, in your role as a mentor, to work with beginning D&T teachers at all career stages.

Objectives

At the end of this chapter, you should be able to:

- Work with beginning teachers to help them to identify potential capacities for personal growth and development.

- Support beginning teachers to explore and engage with potential aspects of new practice, including alternative approaches to pedagogy, planning, assessment and new technologies, and to set, by mutual agreement, appropriate risks and challenges.
- Select and use appropriate strategies to scaffold beginning teachers to engage in honest and open self-reflection, and to challenge, for the purposes of development, aspects of practice.

The benefits of successful risk taking

Difficulties and challenges are part of everyday academic life, but they have the potential to impact negatively upon a beginning teacher's development. Supporting your beginning teacher to develop the ability to overcome common setbacks, to build academic resilience and to become *'academically buoyant'* (Putwain et al. 2012) is an important aspect of the mentor's role.

One way that you, the mentor, can support a beginning teacher to develop resilience is to facilitate the ability to understand the importance of, and be able to identify opportunities for personal growth, while practicing within the context of a safe and supportive working environment early in their teaching careers.

The benefits to a beginning teacher of successfully undertaking a risky activity are significant and include increased efficacy, self-confidence and motivation. As a result, the beginning teacher is more likely to develop resilience, and in turn their ability to cope effectively with distressful situations. They will become emotionally stronger, which in turn will lead to increased feelings of satisfaction and wellbeing.

Successful engagement in previously uncharted activity can encourage the beginning teacher to challenge assumptions (including experience-related beliefs) that may not always be helpful to the formation of professional identity. Mentors need to inspire beginning teachers to think in new and diverse ways, and help to shape how they approach, sustain and develop a *'sense of self'*. Research shows that the longer a teacher has been in post, the less likely they are to adapt established pedagogical practice (Herckis et al. 2017). Therefore, it is important to support beginning teachers at the earliest stages to become independent, confident practitioners, with both the desire and capability to explore and embrace innovation

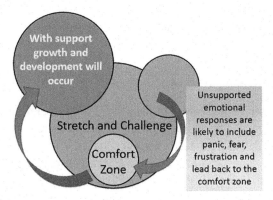

Figure 12.1 Mentoring beyond the comfort zone

and change. Mentors need to support them to build a capacity to foster resilience, and to develop the ability to adapt positively to adverse situations.

With improved levels of skill and increased self-assurance, the successful completion of challenges can help the beginning teacher to become confident to try new things, and to move beyond a comfort zone where the capacity for learning and personal growth may be limited (Figure 12.1).

Defining risk

Having established the benefits, what kind of activity may constitute a risk? Before we begin, it would be useful to define the term risk, within the context of teacher education, the mentor and the beginning teacher.

Within the context of this chapter, risk refers to an orchestrated challenge, undertaken within a carefully structured environment where, within a framework created by the mentor, the beginning teacher undertakes an activity that pushes them to the boundaries of their personal comfort zone. It is important to note that what would be considered as a risk to one beginning teacher may not be to another. In addition, as a beginning teacher develops an activity that they considered as a risk at the start of a teaching placement would not necessarily be so towards the end. Risks should always be discussed and agreed between the mentor and the beginning teacher and suitable activity may include the adoption of innovative teaching, for example the delivery of a lesson using a pedagogy that is new to the beginning teacher or the employment of alternative assessment methods.

Within and specific to D&T as a subject discipline, there are numerous risks which with careful monitoring and supervision would serve as suitable activities designed to further the personal and professional development of the beginning teacher. These may include:

- the delivery of a lesson utilising an approach that is innovative or novel to D&T, for example a pedagogy or assessment method typically associated with another subject discipline. For instance, adopting a scientific method of inquiry approach to the testing of material properties when selecting suitable construction materials.
- the delivery of a D&T lesson outside of the age (or ability) phase of the beginning teacher
- being asked to plan, prepare, teach and assess a D&T discipline that is new or unfamiliar

While to the experienced teacher these activities may not appear to be risky, it is important to remember that what constitutes a reasonable risk to you for a beginning teacher may be perceived as too great a challenge.

Encouraging risk taking

In addition to the general complexities of mentoring, the actual task of encouraging a beginning teacher to engage in an activity that is designed deliberately to take them beyond a comfort zone clearly has the potential to be problematic.

There may be several reasons why a beginning teacher may be reluctant to take a risk, but typically these will include fear, which could be either of the unknown, or of failure.

A beginning teacher in the very early stages may need a gentle nudge to explore a broader range of pedagogies. While at the other end of the continuum the more accomplished beginning teacher may be satisfied with their practice and as such are not overly enthusiastic about trying anything different or unusual. This is a stage that Maynard and Furlong (1995, p.13) akin to hitting a plateau, which may require considerable persuasion by the mentor to move an individual into new and previously unexplored territory (see Chapter 1 for further consideration of Maynard and Furlong's models of mentoring).

However, whatever the reason, it is the mentor's role to unpick the beginning teacher's concerns, support the development of intrinsic motivation, and hence encourage the beginning teacher to take ownership of their professional development. Key factors for consideration include at what point should you encourage a beginning teacher to take a risk? How do you support them to move safely from the current stage onto the next?

In the next section we explore strategies to support you to do just this, to help ensure a carefully structured approach is adopted to get the balance right.

Getting the balance just right

Providing your beginning teacher with the opportunity to grow is crucial, however in setting any challenge it is vital to ensure that the activity is not only appropriate, but within the realistic reach of the beginning teacher's capabilities.

Setting challenging but realistic goals can be difficult for two reasons; first, gaining the agreement and active engagement from the beginning teacher, and second once agreement has been reached there may also be difficulties in balancing the levels of discomfort, to ensure they are acceptable and do not lead to an unintended state of uncontrollable distress or panic.

To encourage the beginning teacher to engage with the task, and to take full ownership of it, it is important to share and make clear the benefits and purpose for undertaking the activity.

You should always also be mindful that what you consider to be an appropriate challenge may be perceived as too big a step by the beginning teacher. This can be particularly precarious when contemplating suitable challenges for those you may consider to be competent. While the beginning teacher may be proficient in numerous aspects of practice, please remember that however accomplished they may appear to be, they will still require support. Having set an activity designed to move a beginning teacher from a comfortable and stable state into one that is uncertain, strategies you could employ are good communication, honest dialogue and careful monitoring (Task 12.1).

Task 12.1   Developing confidence

Reflect on your experience as a beginning teacher. Recall an occasion where you felt vulnerable and outside your comfort zone. Consider the strategies your mentor(s) used to support you or could have used. Write them down and consider those you might utilise to support a beginning teacher to undertake a risk.

Identifying suitable challenges

It has already been noted that what constitutes a risk to one beginning teacher may not be to another. In this section, we examine practical strategies to guide the beginning teacher to identify suitable areas of challenge, an activity that will further an individual's personal development, without pushing them beyond their capabilities.

Within D&T a potentially suitable but rigorous challenge to a beginning teacher, who may be competent in all aspects of subject delivery, could be to apply pedagogical skills to another discipline with which they are less familiar. Within this context potentially there could be:

- risks associated with planning, teaching and assessment
- risks associated with delivery, possibly utilising new equipment and technology
- risks in managing pupil behaviour in an unfamiliar classroom environment

Developing strong, professional relationships

To encourage a beginning teacher to move into uncomfortable spaces, the relationship be- tween the beginning teacher and mentor needs to be very strong. Mechanisms that will help include making clear from the outset that you both agree what the mentoring role is, and what it is not. As discussed in Chapter 11, fostering a non-judgemental approach, where time is set aside to listen, and pose questions, the facilitation of regular points of contact, both formal and informal, where you can make clear shared expectations and nurture a culture of honest and open dialogue are key (Task 12.2).

Task 12.2   Aligning perspectives

In practice, the term 'mentor' is used within many contexts to describe activity that others would perhaps define as counsellor, coach or critical friend. Therefore, it is quite feasible that your perception of your role may be quite different from the expectations of a beginning teacher. Ensuring consensus from the outset is vital in developing a strong working relationship. Within the context of risk taking consider specifically the implications of a 'mismatch' of expectations. List approaches you could use to align any variance in perception. Construct a framework of strategies you can use to build a strong relationship with your beginning teacher.

To help consolidate the work covered thus far in this chapter let us look at an example.

Case study: Tom's story

Tom's story presents a reflective account of mentoring where a poor communication and a 'mismatch' of expectations could have led to a very different outcome:

'During my early teaching practices, I made minimal development in terms of my educational understanding of unfamiliar design and technology subject areas, and with hindsight this made my final practice a lot more challenging than I had anticipated, although ultimately it turned out to be a hugely beneficial experience.

Due to the material areas delivered within the department I had a lot of lessons outside of my own subject expertise. My mentor worked with me consistently to build a strong subject knowledge, but when teaching my biggest fear was something as simple as providing incorrect information to the students. I remember one occasion, during a Resistant Materials lesson. I told the class that the material was PVC, when it was actually HIPS. When my mentor intervened, I felt embarrassed, insecure and that my control over the class had been compromised. Afterwards as we discussed the lesson, and he relayed a similar story from his own practice, so even though I was upset, I came to realise that the decision my mentor made to intervene was positive because it gave me the ability to reflect on my practice as it was happening. Looking back, I think this was the pivotal moment in our relationship, and from then on we had a mutual respect for each other's strengths and weaknesses, from which trust grew over.

I'm still in contact with my mentor, and because of our relationship I feel comfortable asking him for his opinions and advice even now I am a Newly Qualified Teacher (NQT). I'm not a mentor yet, but I feel it is vitally important that the relationship between a mentor and beginning teacher is built upon mutual respect and trust which is essential in helping to create a feeling a togetherness, and the best possible environment for effective personal development'.

Practical strategies

In this section, we explore specific strategies that you, the mentor, could draw upon:

Creating a safe environment

Creating an environment where the beginning teacher feels able to take a risk is integral to effective support. One strategy that can help foster this environment is the adoption of a team or group approach to mentoring. Here the beginning teacher can draw upon the support of the whole department, and in addition to formal mentor meetings and observations, a team approach to mentoring helps to create a culture of 'corridor conversations' which provides constant opportunities for the beginning teacher to access advice and support. However, it is also important not to overwhelm the beginning teacher, particularly with respect to the potential a team or group approach to mentoring support may present in terms of conflicting opinion or advice.

Observation, feedback and reflection

In Chapter 10, the opportunity to facilitate opportunities for the beginning teacher to observe you, the mentor, but also where possible to shadow colleagues working across the department was highlighted.

In advance of any observation, always agree the focus, and ensure you create sufficient space and time after the lesson to engage in meaningful reflection. To support the development of a 'growth mindset', and an environment where the beginning teacher feels it is safe to make mistakes, ensure feedback is empathetic and non-judgemental. Where possible explore innovative approaches, for example joint or group observations, or using technology (Task 12.3).

Task 12.3   Using technology to support reflection

With the beginning teacher's agreement, and for the sole purposes of reflection, using a classroom camera or other suitable secure device, record engagement with the challenging activity. Following the lesson, ensure the beginning teacher has time to review the performance before scheduling a mutually convenient time where you can observe and reflect upon the lesson together. Using your combined reflections, celebrate successes and as appropriate devise plans to support the beginning teacher to move onto the next stage in their development.

Modelling practice and sharing stories

Another strategy you may wish to utilise is modelling. It is no surprise that any form of feedback is better received when the person receiving the advice has respect for, and a belief in the abilities of the person offering the critique. Hence facilitating frequent and regular opportunities for the beginning teacher to observe your practice, and as appropriate other colleagues working within the department is invaluable not only to share aspects of practice but also to support the development of a strong professional working relationships. Alternatively, you may seek to provide the beginning teacher with opportunities to engage in reflective practice, for example via team teaching.

Another strategy you may wish to utilise is to share relevant examples of your experience. Through stories you can empathise with challenges a beginning teacher may face, while also offering potential workable solutions to dilemmas.

Frameworks to support developmental growth

There are numerous scaffolds designed to support the personal growth of others. Some may be specific to scaffold discussion, others to follow more formal steps, but each has the potential to help support the beginning D&T teacher to move logically through a designated activity.

The next section presents a sample of popular frameworks that you, the mentor, may find useful to help plan a programme of support.

The grow model

While this model of personal development aligns with coaching rather than mentoring, it became popular as a developmental tool, where the coach is not an expert in the immediate

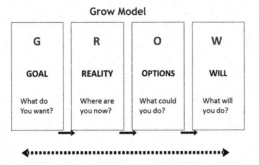

Figure 12.2 The GROW Model: Coaching for Performance (Whitmore 2017, p. 95)

situation. Developed in the 1980s, and popularised following the publication of Coaching for Performance (Whitmore 2017), the GROW model provides a systematic process that uses carefully structured questions. Following identification of a goal, the model could be utilised to support the beginning teacher to examine the current situation (reality), to explore and identify personal options, and to establish the will to undertake the challenge. Within the context of D&T, there may be many occasions where you may be required to guide a beginning teacher outside of your own specialist subject discipline. Under these conditions, utilisation of the GROW model may provide a useful platform from which to structure your support (Figure 12.2).

Setting 'smart' targets

One well-known example of scaffolding is the 'SMART' acronym. This refers to the setting of targets that are: Specific, Measurable, Attainable, Relevant, and Time-bound. Use of a very simple scaffold such as this can help ensure a focused approach when working to achieve an identified goal.

The conscious competence ladder

Emotions play a key role in the formation of teacher identity (Beauchamp and Thomas 2009; Yuan and Lee 2016), and this model can be used to help beginning teachers to navigate emotions. For example, to remain motivated during phases where they are likely to experience discomfort, to manage expectations or to prevent them from trying to achieve too much, too soon. As competence is developed the scaffold may also be used to prevent stagnation. This scaffold supports through the consideration of four stages:

1. Unconsciously unskilled
2. Consciously unskilled
3. Consciously skilled
4. Unconsciously skilled

Distressful situations can have detrimental effects on a beginning teacher's development (Lindqvist et al. 2017), and this scaffold may also prove invaluable in identifying *'hot spots'* where the beginning teacher is likely to require a significant amount of support.

The use of frameworks and scaffolds can be useful in supporting beginning teachers, however whichever mechanism you select, it is essential to remember that the onus to undertake any steps toward a target or goal should, with encouragement, be the responsibility of the beginning teacher (Task 12.4).

Task 12.4   Scaffolding

In your work as a mentor, you may utilise any of the scaffolds, strategies or frameworks suggested within this chapter, however creating your own bespoke scaffold is simple. Using the prompts below as a starting point, try to develop your own.

Setting beginning teacher challenges	*Add your own potential strategies here*
Assess the level of risk	
Identify a suitable focus	
Set meaningful, measurable objectives	
Support the risk	
Encourage authentic reflection	
Provide effect feedback	

Mentoring outside of your comfort zone

As we explore the complexities of mentoring beginning teachers to take a *risk*, an aspect of the role that must not be overlooked are the challenges that you, as a mentor, may encounter, for example working beyond your subject expertise.

The interdisciplinary nature of D&T means the potential for non-subject specialist mentoring is high. Mentoring a beginning teacher who is delivering lessons outside of your subject area can be challenging, but may also present several developmental and mutual enrichment opportunities. In working with a beginning teacher in this way there is the obvious and immediate potential for conflict. For example, the beginning teacher may be less inclined to act upon your advice, particularly if it does not align with personal beliefs (see Chapter 2), or is perceived as critical in nature. One strategy you may utilise in this situation is to ask the beginning teacher to share knowledge with you. This presents an opportunity for you, the mentor, to learn and develop new subject knowledge, but also the beginning teacher is afforded the opportunity to hone teaching skills, while you can provide feedback on knowledge dissemination. Additionally, this process has the potential to lead to the co-construction of new knowledge, which offers a rich and rewarding experience for both parties, and it is through this kind of genuine experience that stronger working relationships, built on mutual trust and respect will grow.

Case study: Rob's story

In this narrative, exploring his perspective as both beginning teacher and mentor, Rob recalls his experience of working beyond subject knowledge boundaries:

'During my first year of teaching I was not greatly challenged and quickly became disillusioned. I wanted to be able to develop personally, and contribute more fully, but as the year progressed I got frustrated, so began to look for a new challenge. Fortunately, my previous placement settings had a vacancy to start the following September, which I secured, even though the subjects they needed me to cover were beyond my mechanical engineering background. I was a bit apprehensive, but was looking forward to the challenge nevertheless. In the period before starting my new post I asked the Head of Department if he could help support me to learn about electronics, which he was pleased to do. In the months before starting my new job I learnt as much as I could about this new discipline. My new Head of Department (mentor) arranged for me to attend a local college where I attended twilight sessions, and running alongside these sessions he would set me bite sized challenges.

This gave me momentum, so I would go away, research and find out as much as I could. He was always supportive and gave positive feedback but then would say '... so right ok why don't you move onto the next step?' This created a cycle of research and feedback, which was great because it gave me the impetus to come back and show him what I'd found out, receive encouragement and then move on. This went on until I guess he felt that he could leave me alone, drawing back, allowing me to take greater ownership for myself, and just ask every now and then how things were going. My mentor was supportive of my need to be challenged, and created a supportive space within which I could develop. He supported me by modelling practice, but also by suggesting alternative ways I might wish to do something.

A few years later, as Head of my own department in a different school, I appointed a member of staff who was also an ex-mechanical engineer. Similar to my own experience, I required him to deliver electronics, of which he had no prior experience. However initially he was very reluctant to do this, because he felt it was completely outside of his comfort zone. So, I needed to call upon everything I could think of to try and ensure that he could deliver the subject confidently the following academic year. I recall introducing virtually the same system that my mentor had undertaken for me all of those years before. I offered the same initial support and guidance, and then slowly withdrew that support as the year progressed, and thankfully he did exactly the same thing that I did and went onto become a brilliant all-round teacher, who now has his own department!' (Task 12.5).

Task 12.5   Working beyond subject expertise

As a subject D&T consists of a diverse range of subject disciplines, and it is feasible that the challenge set could involve a beginning teacher working outside their subject area. Consider the potential issues that could arise, and list strategies that you could take to fully support the beginning teacher.

Summary

This chapter explored the specific challenges associated with setting risks to move beginning teachers beyond their comfort zones. Taking key points from the chapter, in summary:

- Remember, what is *second nature* to you could be perceived as challenging by your beginning teacher.
- Before setting any activity, discuss and agree the scope of the risk being undertaken. Make sure both you and your beginning teacher are comfortable with what is being asked, and are both clear as to what the purpose and intended outcomes of the activity will be.
- In setting an activity ensure you have a scaffold of supportive strategies in place, this will help to build trust. Also ensure that you have discussed, and have strategies in place should things not go quite according to plan.
- Regarding observation, make sure you agree a clear focus with the beginning teacher of what will be covered or observed and when feedback will take place.
- Always set aside sufficient time after a lesson to provide feedback, allow time for reflection and as appropriate revisit the lesson to ascertain any changes in perception.

Further resources

To further support your work in mentoring beginning teachers, particularly regarding supporting stretch and challenge, you may find these resources useful:

National standards for school-based initial teacher training mentors: The national standards provide a comprehensive reference guide to mentoring in schools. National standards for school-based initial teacher training mentors. Available at: www.gov.uk/government/uploads/system/uploads/attachment_data/file/536891/Mentor_standards_report_Final.pdf.

How to be a brilliant mentor

This easy to read, non-subject specific book offers practical information covering the key aspects of mentoring beginning teachers.

Wright, T. (ed.) (2010) How to be a brilliant mentor: developing outstanding teachers. Oxon: Routledge.

Resolving feelings of professional inadequacy

This paper examines for analysis the emotional aspects of the beginning teacher journey, explores the notion of professional inadequacy journey and explores how they may cope with distressful situations

Lindqvist, H., Weurlander, M., Wernerson, A. and Thornberg, R. (2017). Resolving feelings of professional inadequacy: student teachers' coping with distressful situations. *Teaching and Teacher Education*, 64, pp. 270-279.

'I need to be strong and competent'

This paper in useful in developing our understanding of the dichotomous role of the beginning teachers, who as novice practitioner, is also expected to exhibit attributes of expertise.

Yuan, R. and Lee, I. (2016) 'I need to be strong and competent': a narrative inquiry of a student-teacher's emotions and identities in teaching practicum. *Teachers and Teaching*, 22, pp. 1-23.

References

Beauchamp, C. and Thomas, L. (2009) 'Understanding teacher identity: an overview of issues in the literature and implications for teacher education', *Cambridge Journal of Education* 39 (2), pp. 175–189. Research Papers in Education 489.

Coaching for Performance (2017) The GROW model: coaching for performance. Available at: www.coachingperformance.com/ (Accessed: 15 August 2018).

Herckis, L., Scheines, R. and Smith, J. (2017) 'Failure to embrace new teaching techniques not just about fear of embarrassment', *Times Higher Education*, July 12, 2017. Available at: www.timeshighereducation.com/blog/failure-embrace-new-teaching-techniques-not-just-about-fear-embarrassment.

Lindqvist, H., Weurlander, M., Wernerson, A. and Thornberg, R. (2017) 'Resolving feelings of professional inadequacy: student teachers' coping with distressful situations', *Teaching and Teacher Education*, 64, pp. 270–279.

Maynard, T. and Furlong, J. (1995) 'Learning to teach and models of mentoring', in Kerry, T. and Shelton-Mayes, A. (eds.) *Issues in mentoring*, London: Routledge, pp. 10–14.

Putwain, D. W., Connors, L., Symes, W. and Douglas-Osborn, E. (2012) 'Is academic buoyancy anything more than adaptive coping?' *Anxiety, Stress & Coping*, 25 (3), pp. 349–358.

Whitmore, J. (2017). *Coaching for performance: the principles and practice of coaching and leadership*. 5th Edition. London: Nicholas Brealey.

Yuan, R. and Lee, I. (2016) 'I need to be strong and competent': a narrative inquiry of a student-teacher's emotions and identities in teaching practicum', *Teachers and Teaching*, 22, pp. 1–23.

13 A stakeholder view of mentoring - reflections from those who mentor and have been mentored. What lessons can be learned?

Suzanne Lawson and Susan Wood-Griffiths

Introduction

This book has taken us through an exploration of mentoring from definition (Chapter 1), to beliefs and values (Chapter 2) and mentor knowledge and understanding (Chapter 3). We have focused on what the mentor does including developing an understanding of the fundamentals of the subject (Chapter 4) and supporting beginning teachers as subject specialists in food (Chapter 5) and design and technology (product design) (Chapter 6). The later sections have focused on the knowledge, skills and understanding mentors need to help beginning design and technology (D&T) teachers such as subject auditing (Chapter 7); planning, delivering and evaluating lessons (Chapter 8); teaching practical activities (Chapter 9); observing lessons (Chapter 10) and providing pre- and post-lesson discussions (Chapter 11). Finally, the focus moved to risk taking in the classroom (Chapter 12) moving mentees from pedestrian to innovative practice. The one voice that has not been absent but has not hit the spotlight is that of the beginning teacher and experienced mentors themselves. Finally, it is time to hear the views of those who have mentored and have been mentored. We are also offering our voice as teacher educators (working in teacher training) with over thirty (combined) years of experience in the sector. It includes the positives and things that could be 'even better' based on experience. It is time to sit back and listen. While the focus will largely be on best or good practice in mentoring there will be no hiding from where things do not go well and how mentors and mentees can learn from their less successful experiences. Finally, we will talk to experienced mentors and consider the benefits of mentoring as part of a professional process.

Objectives

At the end of this chapter you should be able to:

- Gain an insight into a range of perspectives on mentoring.
- Have a greater understanding of the impact of mentoring.

- Recognise that mentoring is not always a positive experience for mentors or mentees and how this can be addressed.
- Identify the benefits of mentoring as part of a process of continual professional development.

A range of perspectives on mentoring

In Chapter 1, it was noted that mentoring is a hugely rewarding but complex and demanding task. Looking at models such as Maynard and Furlong's (1995) categories of moving from an 'apprentice' to 'competent' and then 'reflective', Golder et al. in their chapter present a model for mentoring that is on a continuum, yet they critiqued that none of the models offered in their chapter are linear and reiterate the complexity of the role.

As teacher educators, we have seen the need to support mentors during this apprentice stage, as expectations are sometimes unrealistically high in the early phases. Schools and mentors often want 'the finished product' and you might feel impatient when progress at the start is slow or tentative. At a recent mentor training event a new mentor asked about beginning teachers' ability to monitor and review pupil progress in lessons. As noted in Chapter 1, using Katz's (1995) model, stage 1 is usually about 'survival' meaning that practice is self-focused and teacher centric. Delivering a lesson from start to end without a major behaviour or health and safety incident is an achievement. It is only as the beginning teacher moves to the consolidation phase that the focus moves to the pupil and individual learning needs. As mentors, you may not see the beginning teacher reach the renewal and maturity phases in the lifetime of the mentoring partnership.

When asked at the end of the training experience what their hopes had been at the start mentees told of the mismatch between the complexities of hope and reality as they operated in the apprentice role. '*I wanted a supportive mentor who is approachable and takes the time to discuss how progress can be made. I soon realised that teachers are busy though, so in reality this sometimes is not achievable*'. Many beginning teachers talk about the transition over time recognising that the early weeks were about survival

> I wished for a positive and supportive mentor, who was there for reassurance and encouragement when needed most. I thought it would be easy, I had so many ideas but when I tried to focus on lots of targets, I felt that I was not making any progress. I needed to go backwards before I went forwards so that I could get the basics right. That was hard as I wanted to be 'outstanding' from the outset.

This mismatch between hope and reality is a key feature of the early apprenticeship stage of the process when relationships are establishing. Wright (2018) notes that the mentoring relationship is rarely a bland or indifferent one. While the mentor is dealing with adult professional training, the beginning teacher is on an emotional rollercoaster and needs a friend or an ally to support. The relationship can be intense with the beginning teacher experiencing the relationship on a different level to the mentor. This intensity is demonstrated through these testimonials from successful mentoring partnerships. '*I have built positive relationships with my mentors and felt comfortable confiding in them when I felt worried or stressed and was able to get the support and help I needed*'. Another mentee confided '*I have gained a lifelong friend with Sharron!'* Time is a theme that we will return to throughout these re-flections and having sustained time to build relationships is valued by beginning teachers. *'In both my placement schools I feel the mentors have been very supportive, however during second placement I believe I have the time to build proper relationships with my mentor'*. On a similar theme a mentor noted

> It can sometimes take time to build the relationship. I have almost always made a fairly rapid connection. I think it's important to try to recall what it felt like to be starting this career-it can feel overwhelming when you begin.

For many, these relationships last beyond the placement due to the emotional investment and time put into the partnership between the mentor and mentee. *'A positive experience I have had as a mentee would be the daily chats I had with my mentor, even now after the placement is over'* (Task 13.1).

Task 13.1   Planning quality direct developmental time

Think about the direct developmental time you spend, or will spend, with your beginning teacher. Is there a dedicated time slot as well as ad hoc collegial conversations? What will be the expectations of the dedicated time slot? Have these been articulated beforehand so that you, and other colleagues, are aware of the importance of this time? For example, agreements such as booking or organising a quite space to meet, establishing a clear time frame (ideally one hour), having a 'meeting in progress, do not disturb' notice on the door, setting the agenda beforehand, providing clear guidance on the preparation required by yourself and the beginning teacher, agreements on procedures if the meeting has to be postponed. Will this dedicated time slot vary over the course of the year/term/placement?

Over time, discussions at weekly meetings will aid the transition for beginning D&T teachers to move from apprentice to competent mode. For some mentors and beginning teachers, this means moving to more autonomy yet there is sometimes a dichotomy between autonomy and direction. Mentees reflected *'I was very much left to my own devices. Some [beginning teachers] may not like this as I had total responsibility and very little guidance on lessons. I enjoyed this as it has helped me develop as a teacher'*. Others talked about *'being provided with feedback and being able to adapt lessons where I see fit'*. In contrast, some beginning teachers might feel that the expectations for autonomy and independence are too high and rather than flourishing, they flounder. Finding the balance is a mentoring skill that often comes with experience and depends on clarity, sensitivity and managing expectations. An experienced mentor notes *'let [beginning teachers] try out new ideas with groups ensuring they have a clear idea of what they want to achieve and ensuring that it fits with the subject assessment skills'*. Another supports this advice, suggesting,

> it's a balancing act, based on the personality of the [mentee], their subject knowledge, how realistic their expectations are and specific classes. I would always encourage [beginning teachers] to try new ideas but within a "high challenge, low threat" framework.

As a teacher educator asked for advice by mentors on the timeline for the transition from apprentice to competent mode that answer is always tentative. Every beginning teacher develops at different rates and sometimes the competent mentees in the early weeks plateau. Delivering one effective lesson per day is very different to managing a much heavier timetable.

Chapter 12 discusses the value of high challenge, low threat frameworks. Beginning teachers tell us that such frameworks make them feel valued and '*one of the team*'. For example, '*it was nice being involved in all aspects of the course and being asked to deliver an A level taster session with my thoughts and opinions wanted and valued*'. For mentors the art of making a beginning teacher feel valued is complex and for beginning teachers it is often time dependent. '*A not so positive experience would be from my first placement where I found that my mentor did not dedicate time to speak to me, apart from when she was in a rush*'. One strategy that makes mentees feel valued is if they are asked for advice. A mentor explained strategies for this

> a [beginning teacher] may be observing a lesson where a pupil struggles to understand the concept, one could ask for advice on ideas on how to try a different teaching style. Similarly how to make a not very exciting topic (food hygiene for example) more dynamic for the learner. Another example could be if a pupil presents challenging behaviour in the lesson-how could we manage this child better?

This inclusive collaborative practice is a useful training exercise – as a mentor you might even get some good ideas that you had not considered. '*Mentors need to be open to new ideas and accept that no matter how long they have been teaching we are all learning it is a continuous journey of gaining knowledge*'.

Freedom verses direction is one of the many attitudinal paradoxes in mentoring. Wright (2018) talks about others including the mentor/coach paradox. The mentor needs to be the assessor and judge but also to be human. Beginning teachers want a mentor '*to be supportive and encourage me but provide me with improvements*'. Wright (2018, p. 173) quotes a beginning teacher who says '*receiving feedback which is neither negative nor positive makes you feel like you are training yourself*'. Mentees reflect '*areas for improvement were provided without advice on how to meet them in some cases*'. Here the mentor had identified the 'what' without the guidance on 'how'. This links to the discussions in Chapter 11 on setting the beginning teacher targets. A mentor might identify that the beginning teacher needs to manage transitions in a practical lesson more efficiently. For this the 'what' might be to manage transition and the 'how' might be to write a script 'when I say I want you to...'. By being clear and unambiguous the beginning teacher does not feel undervalued but instead feels supported.

So, the mentoring relationship is a balance between making the beginning teacher feel valued and offering developmental critique. Having established a relationship based on friendship and trust there can be conflict when assessing and judging. Pragmatic beginning teachers might have a view similar to this beginning teacher, '*I did find school mentors more critical at times but I know it was because they were measuring my teaching against high standards*'. Others can find the challenge of meeting expectations too high as reflected in this comment.

> My school report, I was disappointed with this and the lack of progress it reflected. My mentors advised that in order to achieve outstanding I would have had to

showcase something special and very different so I could not argue with their assessment based on that logic.

Being the judge and jury in assessment also brings the challenges of equity and fairness, '*I am just not sure all mentors graded their mentees as toughly*'.

Understanding the impact of mentoring

Comparisons between one mentoring experience and another can impact on the perspectives of mentoring for the beginning teacher. One beginning teacher compared the experience of working with two different mentors '*there was quite a difference whereby one mentor was extremely busy and therefore sometimes struggled with time to discuss my progress and teaching*'. Another stated,

> Yes, one mentor was a little more chilled and always available when needed to ask advice or help but didn't provide me with as many resources. The other was more organised and gave me lots of information but was not around as much.
>
> First placement I found my mentor to always be rushing and therefore did not dedicate much time for me. She still helped me and I still made progress. However, second placement was the complete opposite. My mentor there gave me more time than I could have ever imagined and always helped me solve any problems that I had.

Comparisons of experiences shared in the staff room also need management '*Most of the other [beginning] teachers were given resources and lessons and told to adapt them*'. Invariably mentors also make comparisons between pairs of mentees working together or the experiences of having mentored several beginning teachers over time. For the beginning teacher and the mentor there is a need to press the 'reset' button to return to the start at any new placement and although comparisons are inevitable the need to focus on the 'now' is key (Task 13.2).

Task 13.2   Sharing good practice - mentor to mentor

Speak to other mentors in your school and other schools if possible. Share your mentoring experiences. Arrange to co-observe a lesson with another mentor and discuss the headlines for the feedback. Are there any areas of good practice that another employs that you could use in your role?

Another key role, and probable expectation, of any mentor is to support the development of subject knowledge. As examined in Chapter 7, the breadth and depth of the D&T curriculum can make subject knowledge development feel debilitating for beginning teachers. Experienced mentors offer advice on this, noting that

> it depends on their starting point, in the sense that most have very good subject knowledge from the start which has been supplemented through additional training... It is more of a case of teaching how to manage the teaching of the subject within the constraints of

a school timetable, as well as pupils' diminishing levels of experience of cooking and cleaning up afterwards in a home environment. In other words a trainee might be an expert on pastry making but managing the teaching of it by 24 children in a classroom designed for 20 in one hour will need additional skills in how the topic could be managed.

Another suggests *'ensure that they get a complete experience of all material areas either from teaching or through observing so they can understand and specialise in material areas'*. Task 13.2 below suggests that mentors can share good practice through collaboration while Task 13.3 focuses on collaboration between mentees as advised by this mentor *'allow trainee's to watch your lessons, observe out of department and direct them towards individual teachers who are noted for a particular strength e.g. computer aided design'*. As experienced teacher educators we would endorse this advice as our experience suggests that few beginning teachers have the breadth and depth of subject knowledge to teach their D&T specialism let alone that expected to teach across multiple disciplines. Subject knowledge develops from experience and collaborating with peers.

Task 13.3   Sharing good practice - mentee to mentee

What additional opportunities do you offer the beginning teacher to collaborate and learn from their peers? Sometimes being 'thrown in at the deep end' is the best way to develop subject knowledge but how can you manage the stress of doing by using collaboration with teaching and non-teaching colleagues?

Stress, workloads and time management

Arguably, any job with responsibility (and over a certain salary bracket) has its challenges and teaching is no exception. Teaching is stressful when you are an expert. Teaching as a novice is even more so. Recognising stress and empathising is a key characteristic of mentoring a beginning teacher desires. *'I wished for a positive and supportive mentor, who was there for reassurance and encouragement when needed most'*. *'I hoped for a supportive mentor that offered constructive advice and was positive and reassuring, at times when you felt a little low. I think I got this mostly'*. It is false to think that beginning teachers should not feel stress and, for many that keep positive, the stress is part of the excitement of the job. The beginning teacher wants empathy and understanding (Task 13.4).

> I hoped that my mentor would be supportive and there for me to guide me to become the best teacher I can be. Luckily the reality was even better than what I thought. This is because my mentor always checked in on me, assisted me in lessons, helped me build my confidence and became more than just a mentor.

A mentor offers the following advice:

> I think it is critical to not overwhelm the [mentees] who generally are hardworking and conscientious. I am open about the pressures of work but remind them it tends to come

in "waves." I liken it to being in a boat on the ocean. It is at times calm but it can get choppy, you can feel you're in a gale storm-but it does pass! I make it clear that it is a personal choice as to how much time one spends preparing for lessons once qualified. There are a lot of resources available, some colleagues like to prepare their own but many choose to spend time with family and friends to revitalise and re-energise. I make them aware that well-being is a current issue in teaching and work hard to maintain the well-being of my own [beginning teachers] through being a positive role model through trying to have a good work/life balance most of the time.

Task 13.4   Reducing workloads

In the document 'reducing workload: supporting teachers in the early stages of their career', the Department for Education (2018) note that excessive workload is the most common reason for 33% of beginning teachers leaving the profession in the first five years. What key advice/support do you provide to beginning teachers about workloads? How do you support mentees to use their additional non-teaching time effectively? How do you manage your mentees expectations of themselves and their teaching experience?

Qualities of a good mentor

There is a postcard that asks 'what is a teacher?' and listed as the answer is judge, social worker, friend, parent and so on. This came to mind when asking beginning teachers about qualities of a good mentor. Responses included '*Approachable. Knowledgeable. Understanding. Consistent. Efficient. Being supportive. Helpful. Understanding that we are only training and not yet fully qualified teachers. Creative. Friendly. Considerate. Patient. Kind. Funny. Supportive. Fair. Positive*'. No pressure then!

Of course, all mentors were once beginning teachers and this experience is bound to have an impact on the way that you work. One mentor reflected on providing feedback and regular meetings:

it makes me ensure the experience is as professional as possible in terms of not allowing interruptions to the session, ensuring it always takes place. Positive feedback is crucial, not to give negative feedback just before a holiday, for example where it can be dwelt on for longer than usual.

Our experience of working with mentors and mentees over many years concludes that being transparent and honest is always the best approach. Sometimes this means having difficult conversations. The root of most problems is poor communication, often a frank and honest conversation can clarify misconceptions and rebuild relationships. On rare occasions where relationships are irretrievable a fresh start or interruption might be needed. Sometimes, a new mentor with a different approach can be successful as can taking time out for the mentor and mentee to reflect and start again.

Mentors sometimes need to reflect on why they have agreed to take on the role when working under pressure with limited time. When asked this question mentors stated as reasons:

- Personal satisfaction in watching them progress and value your support
- Good for recruitment
- They offer excellent support to GCSE and A level groups
- Brilliant resources
- Keeps me up to date with recent initiatives in education
- A pleasure to work with
- New ideas
- Renewed pupil interest
- Reflect on own teaching/methods
- Good classroom support
- Further own professional development
- Good for rest of department to have new blood
- Sharing ideas
- Reminder to self of any areas which are a little 'tired'
- Extension of teaching skills
- Shared reports and marking
- Another colleague to talk to.

A mentor concluded,

> I have always found that the positives of working with a beginning teacher far our weigh any negatives. Mentoring raises my game and makes me re-evaluate my own teaching. If you suggest a mentee does something then you have to make sure that your own lessons showcase that expectation. The learning curve of a beginning teacher over a relatively short timeframe is significant and I gain a lot of job satisfaction from seeing someone moving from initially trembling calling the register to a competent colleague who is able to foster a love of learning. I also feel a moral obligation to nurture the next generation of teachers. I am the teacher that I am due to the support of my mentors and I want to give something back.

Summary

This chapter is based on the views and experiences of mentors, mentees and experienced teacher educators. It intended to stimulate, to counsel, to structure and to address problems. To gain an insight into a range of perspectives on mentoring we explored some of the attitudinal paradoxes including:

- Hope verse reality.
- Autonomy versus direction.
- Judge versus coach.
- The desire for empathy especially in relation to stress, workload and time management.
- Through discussions with those who mentor and have been mentored we have explored some of the impacts of mentoring including,

- Relationships and their importance – many of which last beyond the mentoring experience.
- The importance of beginning teachers feeling valued.
- Conflicts between assessing and judging someone who has become a colleague.
- Conflicts between comparisons with previous experiences whether it is beginning teachers comparing experiences in the staffroom or mentors comparing one mentee with another.

Finally, mentors told of the benefits of mentoring and how the experience is part of personal continuing professional development. We leave the final word to the beginning teachers who offer mentors the following advice:

> Be approachable. Be understanding. Provide strategies which can be trialled by the trainee.
>
> Ensure that you are approachable and make time for your mentee. Build a positive relationship from the start and if you don't have an answer to their questions - help them to find the answer don't just leave them to figure it out for themselves. Be honest.

References

Katz, L. (1995) The developmental stages of teaching. Available at: http://ecap.crc.uiuc.edu/pubs/katz-dev-stages/index.html (Accessed: 23 October 2018).

Maynard, T. and Furlong, J. (1995) 'Learning to teach and models of mentoring', in Kerry, T. and Shelton-Mayes, A. (eds.) *Issues in mentoring*, London: Routledge, pp. 10–14.

Wright, T. (2018) 'Dear mentor…', in Wright, T. (ed.) *How to be a brilliant mentor*. London: Routledge, pp. 162–175.

INDEX

Note: **Bold** page numbers refer to tables, *Italic* page numbers refer to figures and page numbers followed by "n" denote endnotes.

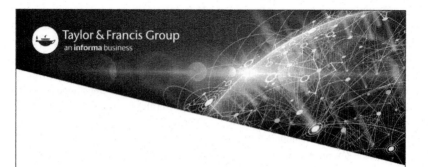